The October Crisis, 1970

THE October Crisis, 1970

AN INSIDER'S VIEW

William Tetley

OSBORNE

McGill-Queen's University Press
Montreal & Kingston · London · Ithaca

© McGill-Queen's University Press 2007
ISBN-13: 978-0-7735-3118-5   ISBN-10: 0-7735-3118-1

Legal deposit first quarter 2007
Bibliothèque nationale du Québec

Printed in Canada on acid-free paper.

McGill-Queen's University Press acknowledges the support of the
Canada Council for the Arts for our publishing program. We also
acknowledge the financial support of the Government of Canada
through the Book Publishing Industry Development Program
(BPIDP) for our publishing activities.

All translations are by the author unless otherwise indicated.

LIBRARY AND ARCHIVES CANADA
CATALOGUING IN PUBLICATION

Tetley, William
The October Crisis, 1970 : an insider's view / William Tetley.
Includes bibliographical references and index.
ISBN-13: 978-0-7735-3118-5   ISBN-10: 0-7735-3118-1
1. Québec (Province) – History – October Crisis, 1970.
2. FLQ.   3. Tetley, William, 1927–.   I. Title.
FC2925.9.O3T48 2006   971.4'04092   C2006-904944-0

Set in 11/14 Adobe Garamond Pro
Book design & typesetting by Garet Markvoort, zijn digital

To Rosslyn

Contents

Appendices on Tetley Website

C   "The Events Preliminary to the Crisis (in chronological order –
     1960 to 5 October 1970)" – English text – http://www.mcgill.ca/
     maritimelaw/crisis, Appendix C

D   "The Crisis *per se* (in chronological order – 5 October 1970 to
     29 December 1970)" – English text – http://www.mcgill.ca/
     maritimelaw/crisis, Appendix D

E   "The Aftermath to the Crisis (in chronological order – 1 January
     1971 to 2002)" – English text – http://www.mcgill.ca/maritimelaw/
     crisis, Appendix E

F   "General Contestation in Quebec Society (1960–1970)" – English
     text – http://www.mcgill.ca/maritimelaw/crisis, Appendix F

G   "Editorial of Jean-Paul Desbiens in *La Presse* (6 October 1970)";
     Jean-Paul Desbiens, Four Years Later – French text and English
     translation – http://www.mcgill.ca/maritimelaw/crisis, Appendix G

H   "The Manifesto of the FLQ (6 October 1970)" – French text and English translation – http://www.mcgill.ca/maritimelaw/crisis, Appendix H

I   "Newspaper Opinions (13–17 October 1970)" – http://www.mcgill.ca/maritimelaw/crisis, Appendix I

J   "The Petition of the Sixteen Eminent Personalities (14 October 1970)" – French text and English translation – http://www.mcgill.ca/maritimelaw/crisis, Appendix J

K   "Letters of Drapeau, Saulnier, Saint-Aubin and Bourassa (15/16 October 1970)" – French texts and English translations – http://www.mcgill.ca/maritimelaw/crisis, Appendix K

L   "Proclamation and Regulations of 16 October 1970, under the War Measures Act" and the War Measures Act – French and English texts – http://www.mcgill.ca/maritimelaw/crisis, Appendix L

M   "Actions of Students, Dropouts and Professors after the Proclamation of 16 October 1970 and Commentary" – English text – http://www.mcgill.ca/maritimelaw/crisis, Appendix M

N   "Legal Opinion to the Parti Québécois by lawyer Pothier Ferland" – French text and English translation – http://www.mcgill.ca/maritimelaw/crisis, Appendix N

O   "Minutes of the Parti Québécois National Council (18 October 1970)" – French text and English translation – http://www.mcgill.ca/maritimelaw/crisis, Appendix O

P   "Op-ed Article *Le Devoir* of William Tetley (4 November 1970)" – French and English texts. Letter of William Tetley of 18 October 2003, replying to article published 16 October 2003 in *Le Devoir* and the *Globe and Mail* by Guy Bouthillier and Robin Philpot (published in *Le Devoir*, 24 October 2003) – English text – http://www.mcgill.ca/maritimelaw/crisis, Appendix P

Acknowledgments

If I have seen further, it is because I have stood on the shoulders of giants.

Sir Isaac Newton (1642–1727)

A dwarf on giant's shoulders sees farther of the two.

George Herbert (1593–1633)

A dwarf standing on the shoulders of a giant may see further than a giant himself.

Robert Burton (1577–1640)

We are like dwarfs on the shoulders of giants, so that we can see more than they.

John of Salibury, 1159

We are like dwarfs standing upon the shoulders of giants and so able to see farther than the ancients.

Bernard of Chartres, circa 1130

Every researcher, like Sir Isaac Newton and his predecessors, benefits from the research, discoveries, and writings of all those who have gone before. Like Newton, I have stood on the shoulders of giants and hope that I have seen further in consequence. Like Newton, I owe a large debt to those who have already written on the October Crisis. Those persons and their works are given in the Bibliography and are also cited with appreciation and thanks throughout the text.

Additional material is available on my website at http://www.mcgill.ca/maritimelaw/crisis. Information about what is available there is found in the list following the table of contents.

I wish to thank the many students who assisted in researching sources, in particular Carl Dholandas and Victoria Netten. I especially wish to thank my associate Robert C. Wilkins for his suggestions, careful checking of citations, and his correction of the text, and Joan McGilvray of McGill-Queen's University Press for her incomparable editing.

The text is dedicated to my wife Rosslyn, my remarkable partner in everything for over fifty years.

William Tetley

Introduction

Do not go gentle into that good night, but rage, rage
against the dying of the light.

Dylan Thomas (1914–53)

On 5 October 1970 James Cross, the British trade commissioner, was kidnapped from his home in Montreal by a group of young French Canadian terrorists – the Front de Libération du Québec (FLQ) – intent on separating Quebec from Canada. Three days later Pierre Laporte, the minister of labour and the number-two man in the Quebec government, was kidnapped from the front lawn of his home in what appeared to have been a skilful commando operation on the part of another FLQ cell. Students and others demonstrated in favour of the FLQ throughout Quebec and called for the exchange of Cross and Laporte for twenty-three jailed FLQ terrorists who had been responsible for bombings, hold-ups, and six violent deaths. Some politicians, some labour union leaders, some members of the press, and some intellectuals also gave the FLQ support by not calling on them to release the hostages but instead publicly demanding the exchange of jailed terrorists (whom they termed "political prisoners") for the two hostages.

The Quebec government of Robert Bourassa and the federal government of Pierre Elliott Trudeau acted together, and firmly, refusing any prisoners-for-hostages exchange. At the request of Quebec, the federal government sent the army into the province on 15 October, and the following day, the two governments, acting together, brought the War Measures Act into effect and proclaimed a state of "apprehended insurrection." In all, 497 individuals were jailed without warrants, thus cutting off demonstrations that were threatening to turn to violence and bloodshed. When Pierre Laporte was found strangled on 17 October, public anger turned to revulsion. James Cross was released on 3 December, and his captors were flown to Cuba as part of an agreement reached with the authorities. Those responsible for kidnapping and murdering Laporte were captured on 28 December 1970.

Why Another Book on the Crisis?

Such, in brief, is the tale of what is now termed the October Crisis of 1970 but why does another book need to be written about it? The main reasons are: 1) to record new information; 2) to correct errors; 3) to fit the crisis into the larger context of French Canadian nationalism in Quebec and Canada; and 4) to deal with two taboo subjects, specifically, (a) the actions of the Parti Québécois (PQ) and intellectuals, as well as labour leaders, during the crisis and (b) the whole industry of revisionist history that has sprung up since 1970. These revisionist histories direct their comments on the crisis away from what happened, and the position that nationalists and intellectuals took at that time, towards a criticism of the application of the War Measures Act. No other work on the crisis, to my knowledge, even refers to these two aspects of the crisis, although their importance has always been evident.

The mere fact that federal and provincial cabinet minutes from the time are now available is also reason enough to write about the crisis again. New books have also become available in the last few years, not the least being Pierre Duchesne's biography of Jacques Parizeau and Carole de Vault's *The Informer*.[1] I draw upon these sources along with other books, newspaper articles, and documents (including ones that I have uncovered[2]). Further information is provided in several appendices available on my website (http://www.mcgill.ca/maritimelaw/crisis).

Errors of Fact and Misconceptions

The existing literature on the October Crisis is replete with small, but pertinent, errors of fact that recur persistently, because errors, once reported, are often repeated as true. For example, almost every author, and even Louis Fournier, an acknowledged authority on the FLQ, has declared that Pierre Laporte was vice-premier of Quebec.[3] This is not true: Robert Bourassa was very careful not to hand out the vice-premiership plum too early in his administration. Many such errors abound in the literature on the October Crisis, in part because the FLQ accused, at their various court proceedings, gave contradictory and misleading testimony. For instance, were Paul and Jacques Rose, their mother, Rosa, and Francis Simard in a car in either Texas or New York State, hoping to buy firearms, when they heard of the kidnapping of James Cross, and did they then head back to Montreal to kidnap Laporte four days later? The reports on this point are contradictory, even in testimony under oath in court.

Many other errors of fact are of greater significance. Here are four examples.

First, it is commonly thought that the Canadian army was brought into Quebec by the federal government at the same time as the War Measures Act was invoked. In fact, the federal government had called the army into

the Ottawa region on 12 October 1970, while Quebec called in the army
on 15 October 1970, as was the province's right, acting alone, under the
National Defence Act. The War Measures Act Regulations were enacted
the next day. They declared the FLQ and its activities to be illegal, and persons who aided and supported the FLQ to be in violation of the law, while
also outlining the rights, limits, and responsibilities of the authorities in
the light of the apprehended insurrection, which had been proclaimed at
the same time (see chapter 9).

Secondly, it is often said that it was Prime Minister Pierre Elliott Trudeau who was responsible for the imposition of the War Measures Act,
not Bourassa or the city of Montreal. This is wrong. Montreal called for
the application of the act on 15 October 1970 and the Quebec government
called for it on the following day (see chapter 8 and appendices K and L
on my website).

Thirdly, it is also generally believed that the War Measures Act Regulations of 16 October 1970 took away all civil rights. Again, this is quite wrong.
The Regulations permitted public meetings, demonstrations, and declarations against the governments and even against the War Measures Act itself.
Signs could be erected, posters posted, and pamphlets distributed but one
could not aid or support the FLQ.[4]

Lastly, opponents of the Quebec and Ottawa position during the October
Crisis have continually repeated that the application of the War Measures
Act Regulations reduced the authority of the Quebec government to little or
nothing. In reality, it was the chief of the Sûreté du Québec (SQ) who was
in charge of all police operations and security forces, including the municipal, provincial, and federal police forces and the army, while the Regulations
were in force. And the chief reported to the Quebec government. Quebec
and Ottawa shared responsibility during the crisis under the Constitution in
a most effective way (see chapter 19).

There are other misconceptions in the public mind today. In fact, each
of the chapters in this book corrects a fundamental misunderstanding of
fact. Thus, for example, chapter 8 contradicts the view that there never was
an apprehended insurrection; chapter 10 describes where the War Measures
Act was successful; chapter 11 examines where the Act went wrong; and
chapter 13 notes the actual extent of the *planning* for a possible provisional
government.

Of course, while a purpose of this book is to put the record straight on
many matters related to the October Crisis, I must add that my text probably

contains unintended, but regrettable, errors of my own. No doubt as well, the text may be seen to have a political bias. To keep the record straight, my political prejudices are encapsulated in an Appendix at the end of this Introduction.

The Roots of Misinformation

Why are there so many errors concerning the October Crisis, even today? How did they come about?

When one reviews the books written on the October Crisis, it is clear that those persons who oppose the actions of the Ottawa and Quebec governments have written extensively, while those who take a different view have not. Predictably, FLQ sympathizers have directed their attention to the War Measures Act, not to the fury and danger of the moment and the crimes of the FLQ. In particular, they avoid any analysis or discussion of the position the fledgling PQ took at the time. These persons, usually with a very political mission, often seem to be trying to revise history. They are actively at work with their publications, conferences, and websites.[5]

Since supporters of the Quebec and federal governments' actions in 1970 have been so silent, we ourselves are partly to blame for the slanted impression of the October Crisis that prevails thirty-six years later. We have perhaps assumed that we were right simply because the public overwhelmingly supported us (see chapter 12). For example, in 2002, Robert Demers, the Quebec government negotiator with the FLQ at the time of the crisis, spoke at a conference in honour of Robert Bourassa. Demers was a member of a panel on the October Crisis and noted that it was the first time he had ever spoken publicly on the subject in thirty-two years. In contrast, since 1970 his opposite number, Robert Lemieux, the negotiator for the FLQ, has spoken on the crisis repeatedly.

Government supporters are not the only ones who have been silent, however. So have most FLQ members themselves, and their silence too has contributed to misinformation about the October Crisis. The FLQ worked in cells and often did not know what other members were doing; nor did they keep notes or records. On the rare occasions when FLQ members have written or spoken publicly on the October Crisis, they have been reticent to reveal pertinent facts and to name names. For example, in *Pour en finir avec octobre*, the four kidnappers of Laporte – Francis Simard, Paul and Jacques Rose, and Bernard Lortie – collectively admit to having murdered

Laporte but refuse to say how or where, or which one of them actually did it. The book was published in 1982, when they were safely free from prosecution. It describes some of their actions but does not go into detail. Rather, the four philosophize and talk selectively of only certain events, as they remember them years later.

Silence has also been the approach of those FLQ sympathizers who occasionally participated in the group's activities. They were never arrested and most have never revealed the part they played. Some names of sympathizers and participants, however, have been mentioned in various accounts in the last thirty-six years. I myself have been able to identify 180 such persons.[6] No doubt there are many more, and no doubt they could tell us a great deal.

As Louis Fournier has said, "the history of an underground movement like the FLQ can never be fully told. It is by definition a secret history."[7] Thus Professor Robert Comeau of the Université du Québec à Montréal (UQAM), who was an FLQ member from at least 1970 until 1974 and no doubt has invaluable information on the crisis, has organized conferences and written extensively on the October Crisis but has never really disclosed his own role in the crisis or what detailed first-hand information he has. How much could he himself reveal about hard-core FLQ members and sympathizers?

Comeau's texts are excellent, but they disclose little that is not in the public domain. This is unfortunate, for there is a difference between refusing to disclose journalistic sources, on the one hand, and withholding secret personal knowledge, on the other. In particular, Comeau recruited Carole de Vault into the FLQ on 31 October 1970 and collaborated with her for a number of years, although, on occasion, he was suspicious of her.

Thirty-six years have now passed. Is it not time for those with personal knowledge to speak up?

Another reason for the misinformation that surrounds the October Crisis is that so many influential people have so much to forget or to hide. Who are these persons? They are, in particular, some members of the press, some labour leaders, and some politicians and intellectuals who, instead of remaining silent during the crisis, took a strong public position on how the governments of Quebec and Canada should act. I refer in particular to the sixteen "eminent personalities" who signed a petition on 14 October 1970 and held a press conference to urge the government of Quebec to release "political prisoners" – the term they applied to FLQ members who were being held in jail for over two hundred terrorist crimes. The sixteen opposed the violence and terror of the FLQ, but they themselves were anything but calm and discreet during the crisis. They also seem to have been opportunistic, supporting the FLQ request that terrorists be exchanged for Cross and Laporte, which would have irrevocably weakened, or perhaps even brought down, the democratically elected Bourassa government. It is now clear that the sixteen's petition, press conference, and newspaper articles, as well as radio and TV appearances (see chapter 6), served only to aid the FLQ.

Manon Leroux's *Les silences d'octobre*, published in 2002, is a useful work that describes the events and sets out what many persons involved in the crisis have since said. Leroux properly points out how some persons who could shed light on the crisis have not done so. On reading her book, one is struck by the approach of the revisionists: they provide, in their multiple publications, few facts that are not already available, but they are far from silent with respect to revising the actual roles of those who opposed the government. Like every committed author, Leroux has a point of view and, in describing the petition of 14 October 1970 of the sixteen "eminent personalities" and the possibility of a provisional government, she offers a single, brief paragraph,[8] even though far more can be said (see chapters 6 and 13). Yet Leroux, perhaps unintentionally, recognizes the silence of the sixteen "eminent personalities," because on the cover of her book, under the title *Les silences d'octobre*, is a photograph of five of the sixteen, taken at their press conference of 14 October 1970: Fernand Daoust, secretary general of the Fédération des travailleurs du Québec (FTQ); Louis Laberge, president of the FTQ; Marcel Pepin, president of the Confédération des syndicats nationaux (CSN); René Lévesque, leader of the Parti Québécois; and Matthias Rioux, president of the Alliance des professeurs de Montréal. Leroux has it right: the "eminent personalities" have been silent, refusing to discuss the press conference and petition after the October Crisis was over.

A striking example of revisionism also appears in Leroux's subtitle for the same photograph, which states that the petitioners "convened to make a plea for democracy during the October Crisis" (my translation). In fact, however, the petitioners had convened not to call on the terrorists to release the hostages but to call on the government to release imprisoned terrorists, whom they described as "political prisoners." Was this "a plea for democracy"?

Most commentators on the October Crisis do not seem eager to explain their own acts or those of persons on whose behalf they are writing. Thus, former FLQ members rarely talk of their crimes, Parti Québécois figures of October 1970 rarely mention the position that the party took, and reporters rarely write about the lack of calm exhibited by some members of the press. They, and their apologists, talk instead of injustices committed by the two governments, dwelling lightly, if at all, on the brutality of Laporte's murder or the bombings, robberies, and violent deaths for which the FLQ was responsible from its formation in 1963 until the October Crisis of 1970.

For example, at the day-long conference in 2000 at UQAM held on the 30th anniversary of the crisis participants and audience discussed the War Measures Act almost to the exclusion of all else. The conference pamphlet, posters, and documents bore a full-page photo of a helmeted soldier, who, on closer inspection, turned out to be a member of Chilean dictator Augusto Pinochet's special police. The organizers of the conference, who included former FLQ member Robert Comeau, said they could not find a photo of a helmeted Canadian soldier of October 1970. Incidentally, I was the only person invited to represent either the provincial or the federal government, while no Parti Québécois member, past or present, volunteered to speak at the conference. Similarly, in October 2000, Parti Québécois "old boys" refused to take part in the various radio and television panels on the crisis and the party itself refused to send representatives. On one hour-long television program in Montreal, where Claude Ryan, Marc Lalonde, and I appeared, Radio-Canada – faced with the PQ's continuing refusal to participate – brought former FLQ lawyer Robert Lemieux all the way from Sept-Îles.

On 21–23 March 2002, UQAM (with Concordia University) organized a conference on the political career of Robert Bourassa. The chief organizer, again Robert Comeau, did not invite any of Bourassa's cabinet to be part of the panel on the October Crisis. Nor could he persuade any PQ figure to attend. Instead, a Laval professor presented an outrageous and factually unsuppported theory that Bourassa was the murderer of Pierre Laporte and a UQAM graduate student read parts of his thesis on a collateral matter. Fortunately, Robert Demers was present, as was Jean-François

Duchaîne (named by the PQ to investigate the October Crisis) and Marc Laurendeau (author of the 1974 work *Les Québécois violents*), and they set much of the record straight.

Revisionists and Others

On the subject of the October Crisis, the roots of revisionism go all the way back to the days of the crisis itself. After Laporte's death, most FLQ sympathizers quickly came to the realization that they had been wrong and their efforts to recast their role began with a host of articles and books. In particular, the Parti Québécois, on 28 October 1970, printed 500,000 copies of an eight-page booklet entitled *C'est notre drame, à nous d'en sortir*, which ignored the position that the PQ and its leaders (René Lévesque, Camille Laurin, and Jacques Parizeau) had taken during the fateful days of 5 to 17 October 1970. The booklet ignored the PQ's lack of calm during the crisis and that it had failed, until 16 October 1970, to condemn the FLQ in unequivocal terms. Instead, the PQ booklet went on the attack, blaming the federal government for the loss of liberties under the War Measures Act and for intervening in a Quebec matter.

The long emergency debate on the October Crisis in the National Assembly, from 11 to 20 November 1970, demonstrated clearly how the Parti Québécois had already shifted its viewpoint. All seven PQ members spoke voluminously but did not mention the party's position on the reading of the manifesto, the calling in of the army, or the exchange of jailed terrorists for Cross and Laporte. Only Camille Laurin addressed the issue of whether terrorists should have been exchanged for hostages, and he did so almost as asides in what was a very long speech.[9]

René Lévesque, the leader of the Parti Québécois, wrote almost daily newspaper articles criticizing the Quebec and Ottawa governments during the October Crisis. Yet, after the brutal murder of Laporte, Lévesque soon turned to writing revisionist articles, and he continued to do so for years afterwards. This is what he says in *My Quebec*, the story of his political career to 1976:

Oct–Dec.: Mr. James Cross, head of the British commercial mission in Montreal, and subsequently, Pierre Laporte, Quebec Minister of Labour and Manpower, [were] kidnapped by the Quebec Liberation Front. October 17: "War Measures" are brought into force by P.E. Trudeau who imprisons all those opposing his federalist ideas. According to certain information received, the violence was remote controlled by the RCMP in the service of the politicians in power. Pierre Laporte is found, assassinated. Mr. James Cross is freed, safe and sound, on December 3. The FLQ is declared outlawed. René Lévesque declares: "Those who coldly executed Mr. Laporte, having seen him live and hope for so many days, are inhuman."[10]

Lévesque's revisionism continued in his *Memoirs*, although in that work there were occasional contradictions and refreshing flashes of frankness, which were his trademark. As an example of the book's contradictions, on the same page he states, and then denies, that leading Quebec figures considered the possibility of a provisional government.[11] As was his practice, he gave no details or sources.

To his credit, Claude Ryan, who was an influential figure during the crisis through his almost daily editorials in *Le Devoir*, never joined the revisionists. Instead, in interviews and speeches, he remained committed to the positions he had taken in October 1970. For example, he always adhered to the view that FLQ "political prisoners" should have been exchanged for Cross and Laporte, and he also remained convinced of the wisdom of the petition of the sixteen "eminent personalities," of whom he was one.

If Claude Ryan did not revise his views, he never admitted that he was wrong in any respect as regards the crisis. Nor did he satisfactorily explain a number of matters in which he was a key, if not *the* key, player – in particular, the discussions that took place on Sunday, 11 October 1970 with his four leading associates, whom he had convened at *Le Devoir*, concerning the possibility of forming a provisional government. Similarly, he never revealed what he and Montreal Executive Committee Chairman Lucien Saulnier discussed that afternoon in a conversation "purely private, consultative and confidential."[12] Nor did he explain what happened thereafter, notably, his participation in the petition and press conference of the sixteen "eminent personalities" on 14 October 1970.

Other political figures wisely remained silent during the crisis or even offered their support of the government – for example, Jean-Jacques Bertrand, the leader of the Union Nationale and of the Official Opposition, and Camille Samson, leader of the Crédit Social. These two political parties together had obtained 30.8 per cent of the vote in the previous election, as opposed to 23.1 per cent for the Parti Québécois. Yet Bertand and Samson acted wisely and discreetly. In consequence, neither was obliged to revise his position in later years.

One member of the press, Jean-Paul Desbiens, got it right from the very beginning. Desbiens was the famous Frère Untel, a figure who helped pave the way for the Quiet Revolution, known in particular for his 1960 book, *Les Insolences du Frère Untel*. In an extraordinarily prescient editorial published in *La Presse* on 6 October 1970, the day after Cross's kidnapping, Desbiens declared that the municipal, provincial, and federal governments should not give in to the blackmail of the FLQ. Calling for calm, which, unfortunately, much of the press and the Parti Québécois failed to display, he understood that the terrorists would not be willing to die for their cause. In 1974 Desbiens again offered his views on the crisis, and they had not changed in the intervening years.[13]

Huguette Roberge also made a far-sighted public statement in the midst of the crisis. On 7 October 1970, three days before Laporte's kidnapping, Roberge wrote in *La Patrie* that the terrorists had arrived at a point of no-return. She added: "If the government cedes to some of their demands, will not the FLQ proceed to another kidnapping? Who will be the next?"

Purpose and Approach

The present book is not a work of history: I leave that to professional historians. Rather, it is a commentary on a particular event, which took place thirty-six years ago, by a person who witnessed, and even participated in, parts of that event. As a minister in Bourassa's cabinet at the time of the October Crisis, I feel I have some claim to write on this subject, particularly because I kept a diary during those days (see appendix 1). Of course, my analysis is partisan, but at least it has the merit of presenting a point of view of which little has been heard. In the "unbiased" spirit of "often in error, but never in doubt" that I imbibed in the three great brotherhoods of self-assurance – practising lawyer (for eighteen years), politician (for eight years), and law professor (for thirty years) – I believe I should give my own views on the crisis.

Having decided to write, the non-historian must decide how to write. Does one give an analysis of cause and effect along with a description of events? George Kennan advised that, in any "historical drama," one should describe not only the *what* – the events – but also the *how* – that is, how actors perceived the facts and how they related to them "as a matter of critical analysis." I go further. It seems to me that one writing on the past must fulfil three major requirements. The first is, in Kennan's terms, to set out the *what* – the facts – of the drama as best one can. The second is, again following Kennan, to explore the *why* of the drama: the motives of the parties to the event and why they acted in the way they did. And I add a third requirement of my own – to describe the *place* of the drama, by which I mean the broad general historical context.

And so this book attempts to answer several basic questions concerning the October Crisis. These questions are:

- What was the social, economic, and political background of the crisis?
- What was the FLQ?
- How many members did the FLQ have?
- Should the FLQ manifesto have been published?
- Should imprisoned terrorists have been exchanged for Cross and Laporte?
- What was the rationale behind the petition of 14 October 1970, and what was the petition's effect on the FLQ?
- Should the army have been called in?
- Was there an "apprehended insurrection"?
- What were the alternatives to the War Measures Act?
- What went right with the application of the War Measures Act?
- What went wrong with the application of the War Measures Act?
- What was the reaction to the War Measures Act?
- Was there a plan to form a provisional government?
- Was there panic, and, if there was, who lost their heads?
- Who killed Pierre Laporte? And how did he die?
- What caused the end of the violence, and of FLQ terrorism, in the short and long run?
- Should the National Assembly have been convened?
- Was the crisis principally a Quebec matter?
- Was there intentional polarization of the crisis on federal/provincial lines?
- Did federalism work successfully during the crisis?

- What did the Duchaîne Report say about the crisis?
- What conclusions can we draw?

The text, although supported by references, presents a particular point of view. I make no apologies. This is neither a novel nor a narrative. I have tried to keep to the facts, while my opinion on any question usually appears at the end of each chapter and especially at the end of the volume. Because almost all works on the crisis have been written from the point of view of the FLQ or its apologists, I have incorporated many quotations, details, sources, documents, and references into the text to support my conclusions, when they differ from the conventional literature.

May I also suggest that the present book makes available an abundance of source material, which, I hope, will assist others in the ongoing study of this important period in Quebec and Canadian history.

I welcome comments from the reader.

William Tetley
WilliamTetley@mcgill.ca
McGill Law Faculty
3644 Peel Street
Montreal H3A 1W9
Website: http://www.mcgill.ca/maritimelaw/crisis

Appendix: My views on the Quebec/Canada political confrontation

I believe that Canadian federalism is the best form of government for Quebec and Canada, providing amongst other things a system of checks and balances. Nevertheless I also believe that Quebec (or any other province such as Alberta or B.C.) has the right to separate from Canada, provided there is an unambiguous referendum question, a clear majority vote, and the terms of the separation are negotiated fairly with good will.

Although I find the French/English, federalism/separatism confrontation to be tiresome, I do not find it entirely sterile or debilitating. Rather, I believe that the debate has been beneficial in the long run, because it has forced us to ask ourselves who we are, what Quebec wants, and what the Rest of Canada ("ROC") wants. The Bloc Québécois presence in Ottawa may be an anomaly in a federal state, but it is a useful pressure valve showing that Quebec nationalism can be heard in the Canadian Parliament. Nor has the federalism/separatism polemic always hindered the development of Quebec and Canadian society. In fact, the economic, social, and cultural achievements of both jurisdictions since 1960 have been astounding.

The constitutional and language confrontation in Canada is much like the debate over Protestantism and Catholicism in sixteenth-century Elizabethan England, which, despite being a period of great upheaval, and even war, is now seen as a Golden Age, an era of unprecedented cultural and political flowering. This was the time of Shakespeare and his literary contemporaries, of Sir Walter Raleigh, of England's laying claim to America, and of the defeat of the Spanish Armada. Similarly, Quebec and Canada have made extraordinary advances – cultural, scientific, industrial, and commercial – in the last fifty years of constitutional debate.

In other words, the real challenge facing Quebec and Canada is not our economic and cultural development; rather it is our ability to *respect* both the French and English languages and cultures, as well as the rights of majorities and minorities. We Canadians and Quebecers must also be *generous* to all levels of our society, and to the masses of people in Third World countries and elsewhere who are far less fortunate than we. And, lastly, there must be *integrity* in our government, our corporations, our labour unions, our universities, colleges and schools, our workplaces, and our homes and private lives. Our problems will be solved not by Quebec independence or by Canadian federalism but by the triumph of respect, generosity, and integrity.

And, whatever the outcome of the Quebec/Canada confrontation, neither Quebec nor Canada can ever have genuine independent, sovereign status, in the light of modern commitments to the United Nations, NATO, NAFTA, a host of international agreements and conventions such as the Convention on the Elimination of All Forms of Discrimination against Women (1979), the UN Convention on the Law of the Sea (1982), the Convention on the Rights of the Child (1989), the Comprehensive Nuclear Test-Ban Treaty (1996), the Kyoto Protocol (1997), and participation in such international bodies as the UN and its many agencies (e.g. ICAO, ILO, IMO, UNCITRAL, UNCTAD, UNESCO, UNICEF, and WHO), the G8 countries, the International Monetary Fund (IMF), the World Bank, the Organization of American States (OAS), the Commonwealth, la Francophonie, and the World Trade Organization (WTO).

Nor can Quebec or Canada ever again be as economically sovereign as we were even in 1970 because of today's massive world trade and foreign investment, which know no national borders, and because of today's giant multinational companies, which move capital, manpower, assets, expenses, and profits across frontiers to suit their own interests.

Finally neither Quebec nor Canada, in the light of our huge territories, our great natural resources, our relatively democratic political systems, our safe, rich society replete with public health and educational systems, can expect, in the next ten or twenty years, to hold back waves of legal and illegal immigrants from crossing our thousands of miles of unprotected borders and our even longer unguarded coastlines. We occupy a large part of the world's lush temperate zone, with our enormous unused available fresh water, which will suffer relatively less from climate change than other parts of the world. Will we not be the subject of irrepressible movements of humanity who, legally or otherwise, will enter our territory and irrevocably change our linguistic balance and social systems? The United States is estimated to have between eleven and twenty million illegal immigrants. How many do Quebec and Canada now have? How many will we have in the near future? The immigrants must, however, conform to our mores, languages, and laws.

In other words, I do not believe that either Quebec or Canada can be sovereign and independent today or in the future in the same way as was thought possible in 1970.

Chronology, 1963–2001

February 1963: The FLQ (Front de Libération du Québec) is founded by Georges Schoeters (age thirty-three), Gabriel Hudon (age twenty-one), and Raymond Villeneuve (age nineteen, who gave the FLQ its name). From 1963 to 1970 various precursor and parallel groups, such as the RR (the Réseau révolutionnaire), the ALQ (l'Armée de libération du Québec), and the ARQ (l'Armée révolutionnaire du Québec), are absorbed into the FLQ.

7–8 March 1963: The first FLQ bombings take place when three Canadian Army barracks are bombed. Two hundred more bombings occur between 1963 and October 1970.

16 April 1963: The first FLQ manifesto is written.

21 April 1963: An FLQ bomb kills night watchman Wilfred (Wilfrid) O'Neill (O'Neil), age sixty-five.

29 August 1964: Leslie MacWilliams (age fifty-six) and Alfred Pinisch (age thirty-seven), employees of a firearms company, are killed during an FLQ robbery.

1965: Charles Gagnon and Pierre Vallières secretly join the FLQ. The number and size of the bombs and the labour unrest increase markedly.

5 May 1966: A parcel bomb sent by the FLQ kills Thérèse Morin (age sixty-four), during a CSN strike at La Grenade shoe factory.

14 July 1966: FLQ member Jean Corbo (age sixteen) is killed by a bomb he was depositing at a strike scene.

24 July 1967: General DeGaulle declares "Vive le Québec! Vive le Québec libre!"

29 April 1970: The Liberals win the general election with 72 seats and 45.4 per cent of the vote; the Union Nationale: 17 seats and 19.6 per cent of the vote; the Crédit Social: 12 seats and 11.2 per cent of the vote; the PQ: 7 seats and 23.1 per cent of the vote; others: no seats and 0.7 per cent of the vote.

June 1970: Robert Comeau writes the second FLQ manifesto.

24 June 1970: An FLQ bomb kills employee Jeanne d'Arc Saint-Germain (age fifty) at National Defence Headquarters in Ottawa.

Mon., 5 Oct. 1970: James Richard Cross (age forty-nine) is kidnapped.

Wed., 7 Oct. 1970: The FLQ 1970 manifesto is read on CKAC by Louis Fournier.

Wed., 7 Oct. 1970: Specialist doctors begin their strike to oppose Medicare.

Thurs., 8 Oct. 1970: The FLQ 1970 manifesto is read on Radio-Canada television.

Sat., 10 Oct. 1970: The Chénier cell kidnaps Pierre Laporte (age forty-nine).

Sun., 11 Oct. 1970: Claude Ryan discusses the possibility of a "provisional government" with four senior *Le Devoir* editors and then with Lucien Saulnier, chairmain of the Montreal Executive Committee.

Mon., 12 Oct. 1970: The Canadian Army begins patrol of the Ottawa region.

Mon., 12 Oct. 1970: The Parti Québécois Executive Council publicly supports "the liberation of political prisoners."

Tues., 13 Oct. 1970: The Bourassa cabinet agrees not to exchange hostages for imprisoned FLQ terrorists.

Wed., 14 Oct. 1970: Robert Bourrassa declares Quebec's willingness to recommend parole for five eligible prisoners and states that the kidnappers will be given safe conduct to Cuba or elsewhere in exchange for the release of Cross and Laporte.

Wed., 14 Oct. 1970, 9 p.m.: Sixteen "eminent personalities" hold a press conference and sign a petition calling for the exchange of "political prisoners" for hostages.

Thurs., 15 Oct. 1970, 11 a.m.: The Quebec government calls the army into Quebec.

Thurs., 15 Oct. 1970, 9 p.m.: The Quebec government issues a six-hour ultimatum to the FLQ.

Thurs.–Fri., 15–16 Oct. 1970: *"Le Grand Soir"* – three thousand supporters chant "FLQ, FLQ, FLQ!" and listen to the incitements of Pierre Vallières, Charles Gagnon, Robert Lemieux, Michel Chartrand, and others at the Paul Sauvé Arena.

Fri., 16 Oct. 1970, midnight: The National Assembly unanimously adopts three Medicare bills.

Fri., 16 Oct. 1970, 4 a.m.: The War Measures Act and Regulations are put into effect by the Trudeau cabinet after receipt of Bourassa's letter of request.

Sat., 17 Oct. 1970: Pierre Laporte is murdered.

18 Oct. 1970: The Federal government creates the Committee to Aid Persons Arrested under the War Measures Act, chaired by Jacques Hébert.

19 Oct. 1970: The House of Commons approves the government's action in invoking the War Measures Act by a vote of 190 to 16.

25 Oct. 1970: Jean Drapeau overwhelmingly wins the Montreal municipal election.

5 Nov. 1970: The Public Order (Temporary Measures) Act, 1970 is adopted in second reading in the House of Commons, with only one Member of Parliament voting "nay" (David MacDonald, MP for Egmont, PEI). The Act came into force on 3 December 1970.

6 Nov. 1970: Carole de Vault, PQ and FLQ member, goes to the Montreal police and the next day becomes an informer at the suggestion of Alice Parizeau and with the subsequent concurrence of her husband, Jacques Parizeau.

6 Nov. 1970: Bernard Lortie is captured. The three other Laporte kidnappers hide behind a wall in a cupboard and escape twenty-four hours later.

3 Dec. 1970: Cross and his kidnappers are discovered. Cross is released. Jacques Lanctôt (with his wife and child), Marc Carbonneau, Yves Langlois, and Jacques Cossette-Trudel (and his wife) are flown to Cuba.

19 Dec. 1970: In Quebec, a statute abolishing the eighteen "protected counties" in the Eastern townships and another granting a pension to the widow of Pierre Laporte are assented to and come into force.

28 Dec. 1970: Paul Rose, Jacques Rose, and Francis Simard are found in a twenty-foot tunnel in Saint-Luc, near Saint-Jean, Quebec.

4 Jan. 1971: The Canadian Army leaves Quebec at the request of the Quebec government. Sporadic bombings continue. Ten years later it is learned that, because of informants (e.g., Carole de Vault, François Séguin, and, apparently, Claude Champagne), from November 1970 onwards, the police were usually aware of bombings in advance.

4 Jan. 1971: Francis Simard declares that, in his presence and that of Paul and Jacques Rose, Laporte was strangled.

3 February 1971: Federal Justice Minister John Turner reports that, of the 497 persons arrested under the War Measures Act, 435 had been released and 62 had been charged, of whom 32 were being held without bail.

12 March 1971: The Bourassa government declares that Quebec will provide compensation of up to $30,000 for each person unjustly arrested under the War Measures Act. The Quebec ombudsman is to decide if compensation is justified and, if so, in what amount.

30 April 1971: The War Measures Act Regulations are repealed.

6 July 1971: Louis Marceau, Quebec's ombudsman, reports that 103 of the 238 complaints arising from the application of the War Measures Act are justified and will receive compensation.

3 Sept. 1971: Charles Gagnon announces that he has left the FLQ to found a Marxist-Leninist party.

24 Sept. 1971: FLQ member Pierre-Louis Bourret (age twenty) is killed during a robbery.

13 Dec. 1971: Pierre Vallières leaves the FLQ, renounces terrorism, and joins the Parti Québécois. He is praised by René Lévesque and castigated by Charles Gagnon.

8–9 Jan. 1973: The RCMP breaks into PQ offices and steals the party's membership list.

29 Oct. 1973: Bourrassa's Quebec Liberal Party wins 102 seats with 54.7 per cent of the vote; the Parti Québécois wins only 6 seats, although receiving 30.2 per cent of the vote; the Crédit Social obtains 2 seats with 9.9 per cent of the vote; and the Union Nationale, with 4.9 per cent of the vote, fails to win a single seat.

26 July 1974: RCMP officer Robert Samson places a bomb at the residence of Mel Dobrin, president of Steinberg's. In 1976 Samson is condemned to seven years imprisonment.

17 Dec. 1974: The CECO commission (Commission d'enquête sur le crime organisé) finds no evidence linking Pierre Laporte to organized crime.

29 Sept. 1975: Claude Ryan notes that he does not subscribe to the thesis that the federal government had used the October Crisis to crush separatism.

15 November 1976: The PQ wins the general election with 71 seats and 41.4 per cent of the vote; Liberals: 26 seats and 33.8 per cent of the vote; Union Nationale: 11 seats and 18.2 per cent of the vote; Crédit Social: 1 seat and 4.6 per cent of the vote; and Parti National Populaire: 1 seat and 0.8 per cent of the vote.

16 March 1977: Charles Gagnon denounces the Parti Québécois for its "reactionary nationalism."

16 June 1977: Three senior police officers, one each from the RCMP, the Sûreté du Quebec, and the Montreal police, plead guilty to a break-in at l'Agence de Presse Libre du Québec on the night of 6–7 October 1972.

28 and 31 Oct. 1977: The solicitor general of Canada, Francis Fox, admits that the RCMP had stolen PQ membership lists in 1973 and had also illegally burned a barn and stolen dynamite in the Montreal area.

16 Dec. 1977 and 21 March 1978: Francis Fox is unsuccessful, again, at getting the courts to stop the Keable Commission (Commission d'enquête sur les opérations policières en territoire québécois).

23 March 1978: Charles Gagnon declares that Quebec workers should unite with workers from the rest of Canada to build a socialist country.

20 May 1980: The Quebec referendum vote on separation is "Yes," 40.4 per cent; "No," 59.6 per cent.

9 July 1980: McGill University electrical engineering graduate Nigel Barry Hamer is arrested and on 17 November 1980 pleads guilty to kidnapping James Cross. On January 1981 Hamer denounces FLQ terrorism and his part in it.

27 Jan. 1981: The Duchaîne Report of the PQ government finds no evidence that the October Crisis was provoked by politicians to discredit the independence movement.

13 April 1981: Election of the Parti Québécois with 80 seats and 49.2 per cent of the vote. The Liberals win 42 seats and 46.1 per cent of the vote.

7 Dec. 1981: René Lévesque is astounded and upset when ex-FLQ member Jacques Rose receives a standing ovation at a PQ convention.

1982: Francis Simard declares in his book *Pour en finir avec octobre* – "co-signed" by Bernard Lortie and Paul and Jacques Rose – that Pierre Laporte was killed. His death "was not accidental."

1 Nov. 1984: Raymond Villeneuve, one of the three founders of the FLQ in 1963, is the last member to return from exile and spends eight months in prison.

29 Oct. 1995: The second Quebec referendum is narrowly defeated: "No," 50.6 per cent; "Yes," 49.4 per cent.

Oct. 2001: FLQ member Rhéal Mathieu, who had been sentenced in 1967 to nine years in jail for two bombing deaths, is arrested for fire-bombing three Second Cup coffee shops in Montreal.

Jan. 2002: Raymond Villeneuve pleads guilty to criminal harassment and to counselling others to commit criminal offences against Brent Tyler, lawyer of Alliance Quebec, journalists Don Macpherson, Josh Freed, and Tommy Schnurmacher, and Jacques Dupuis, a Liberal MNA.

The October Crisis, 1970

Chapter 1	# The Setting

It is an age frequented by violence as desperate men
seek ill-defined goals.

> Speech from the Throne, Canada,
> *Hansard*, 8 October 1970

The time is out of joint.

> William Shakespeare (1564–1616), *Hamlet*

It is a capital mistake to theorize before one has data.

> Sherlock Holmes, as quoted by his creator,
> Sir Arthur Conan Doyle (1859–1939)

To understand the October Crisis, one must take into account the larger context, both international and domestic, in which it occurred. Unrest and even violence were then common in many countries of the world, and governments frequently fell not just by democratic means but by undemocratic ones as well. The Front de Libération du Québec (FLQ) operated within this context and was encouraged by it, just as it gained support as a result of a variety of social, economic, and political factors within Canada itself.

Before the October Crisis, kidnappings for the release of political prisoners and other forms of terrorist blackmail were a common occurrence. While governments almost always ceded to the terrorists, the exchange of prisoners for hostages saved the lives of only some hostages, while the kidnapping and terror continued. Central and South America provide many examples.

The kidnappings of the October Crisis, of course, took place in a democratic country – Canada – and this fact alone made all the difference. Democratic countries have much to lose in giving in to blackmail by kidnapping. Even if the hostages are released, the terrorism will not cease, because the kidnappers, once successful in one kidnapping, will realize that they have a potent weapon to defeat the democratic process. Not only will the government be obliged to face another kidnapping and the same dilemma but it will have failed to carry out one of the main duties for which it was elected – the preservation of the democratic system. In other words, a democratically elected government is a trustee charged with the task of preserving the rights and freedoms of the society that chose to elect it and, accordingly, it has no mandate to cede its authority and responsibilities to terrorists. Such was the attitude of the governments of Canada, and Quebec, during the October Crisis. And it was, I believe, the correct response to the criminal behaviour of the FLQ, who challenged the very basis of Canadian democracy.

Turmoil in the Health-Care System

It is often forgotten that the October Crisis coincided with a strike by specialist doctors in Quebec that had been called in response to the imposition of Medicare. The government of Canada had adopted Medicare under the Medical Care Act, which was passed on 21 December 1966 and came into effect on 1 July 1968. The act left to each province the adoption of its own Medicare system within certain guidelines: the federal government would provide the financing and each provincial government was free to put the universal system in place, if it wished. Saskatchewan had had a provincial plan in force since 1 April 1962 (despite a long strike by the province's doctors) and entered into the federal plan on its first day, 1 July 1968, as did British Columbia. Manitoba, Nova Scotia, and Newfoundland followed suit on 1 April 1969, Alberta on 1 July 1969, and Ontario on 1 October 1969. The three remaining provinces put Medicare into force in the next two years: Quebec, on 1 November 1970; Prince Edward Island, on 1 December 1970; and New Brunswick, on 1 December 1971.

In Quebec's case, the adoption of Medicare was the work of the Liberal government led by Robert Bourassa. By the time of the provincial election on 29 April 1970, Bourassa, as the new Liberal leader, had convinced Claude Castonguay to present himself as a Liberal candidate with the promise that, if Liberals were elected and Castonguay won his seat, he would be given a cabinet post in order to put Medicare into effect. Both the Liberal Party and Castonguay himself were victorious, and, as minister of social affairs, Castonguay prepared Bill 8, the Medical Insurance Act, which passed first reading on 21 June 1970. The bill passed second reading on 2 July 1970 with the support of all eighty-five members present and all four political parties. Subsequently, on 10 July 1970, it passed third reading even though the opposition parties voted against it, more on questions of form than of principle.

Negotiation on the details continued into July and August 1970. Agreement was reached with dentists, ophthalmologists, and all doctors except the specialists by 1 October 1970. By not putting the plan fully into effect, Quebec was losing $12 million in federal transfer payments per month, and the public and the vast majority of the medical profession were losing out.

Quebec doctors, like those in other provinces, were concerned about their incomes, their professional liberties, and the quality of medical services under the new system. They were also spurred on by the American Medical Association, which by 1970 had already staged a giant rally in the Montreal Forum to oppose Medicare in Quebec and Canada. On 7 October 1970, two days after the Cross kidnapping, the specialist doctors of Quebec went on strike and continued to strike when Laporte was kidnapped. By 8 October 1970, the hospital and health-care system in Quebec was in disarray. The strike was described in the press as a kidnapping by the specialists; in effect, the Bourassa government was negotiating simultaneously with the specialists and the FLQ. The Ligue des femmes du Québec (Women's League of Quebec) declared:

The kidnapping of a people by the specialists is no less serious than the kidnapping of two people for large sums of money. The LIGUE DES FEMMES DU QUÉBEC encourages the government to take urgent measures to save the lives of thousands of people who are in danger because of the attitude of the specialist doctors who are on strike ... We deplore this sad situation of two honourable people [Cross and Laporte] whose lives are threatened by their kidnapping. Nevertheless, we believe that if the government does not act very promptly concerning the specialist doctors of Quebec, we will witness the kidnapping of a people, abandoned into the hands of a minority whose weapons are no less dangerous than guns.[1]

In the afternoon and evening of Thursday, 15 October, the National Assembly debated three Medicare bills: one offered amendments to Bill 8 that were requested by the general practitioners and opting-out provisions that were requested by the specialists; another put Medicare in force on 1 November 1970; and the third ordered the specialists back to work. The final votes on all three bills were taken by midnight on 16 October and they passed easily without a recorded vote. The House then adjourned, and shortly afterwards Premier Bourassa had a letter delivered to the federal government calling for the application of the War Measures Act Regulations, which came into effect at 4:00 a.m. on 16 October 1970.

While there was no direct connection between the specialists' strike and the October Crisis, the turmoil that prevailed in the health-care system in October 1970 added to the climate of tension in which the crisis unfolded. It also added to the pressures bearing down on the newly elected Bourassa government.

A personal aside is in order here. During the early days of the bitter negotiations with the doctors, I, as minister of revenue, asked my deputy minister to advise me of the average income declared by active doctors for purposes of their income tax. The Quebec Revenue Department had the most advanced computer system for taxation in Canada at the time and my deputy soon advised me that full-time doctors, on average, declared $23,000 before expenses. We were offering $35,000 and so I relayed this information to Bourassa, believing that it could be a useful piece of information if necessary during the negotiations. To his credit, he refused to use it.

The Parti Québécois and the October Crisis

During the October Crisis, the Parti Québécois took positions both inside and outside the National Assembly that did much to exacerbate the crisis by giving comfort, if not encouragement, to the FLQ. For example, the PQ opposed the public reading of the FLQ manifesto and the calling in of the army and openly advocated the exchange of hostages for "political prisoners." One might well ask how the October Crisis would have unfolded if, on the day Cross was kidnapped, the PQ executive, its National Council, and René Lévesque had unequivocally opposed the kidnapping and appealed to the FLQ to release Cross. It was not until the evening of 16 October 1970 that the National Council took a firm position and, without qualification, called on the FLQ to release Cross and Laporte.

At this time, many French Quebecers felt that they were not adequately represented politically because the Parti Québécois had only seven seats in the National Assembly even though it had won 23.1 per cent of the vote in the election of 29 April 1970. (The Liberals, with 45.4 per cent of the vote, had won 72 seats; the Union Nationale, with 19.6 per cent of the vote, had won 17 seats; and the Crédit Social had won 12 seats with only 11.2 per cent of the vote.) Jean-Jacques Bertrand of the Union Nationale was the leader of the Opposition.

Bourassa, to his credit, gave the Parti Québécois and the Crédit Social "party status" in the National Assembly, which meant a budget, staff, and so on, much like the Official Opposition. Further, the PQ did not effectively suffer from its small representation in the National Assembly. House business in opposition can be easily done by seven members, particularly when there are two other opposition parties with a combined popular vote of 30.8 per cent. The PQ members basked in their lack of numbers, conducted filibusters, and took up the time of the Assembly as though there were twenty-five of them, not seven, while the Liberal backbenchers (like government backbenchers in any parliament) were obliged to sit in virtual silence. The fact that there were only seven PQ members in the House garnered considerable sympathy for the party and its views.

As well, on 16 December 1970, within eight months of his election, Bourassa introduced Bill 65, An Act respecting Electoral Districts, which abolished thirteen constituencies protected under section 80 of the British North America Act of 1867 (since renamed the Constitution Act, 1867). There were actually eighteen such constituencies by 1970, and, though they had few voters, their boundaries could not be enlarged without constitutional change. They had seriously distorted Quebec elections for fifty years but no premier had dared to face the problem. Bill 65, which was adopted on 19 December 1970, went a long way to solving the problem of Parti Québécois representation in the National Assembly.[2]

The Parti Québécois had been formed, in large part, through the personal vision, energy, conviction, and prestige of one person – René Lévesque. The party leadership in October 1970, however, was divided between the charismatic Lévesque, then living in Montreal, who was leader of the party but who had not been elected to the National Assembly, and the seven elected PQ members in the National Assembly under their parliamentary leader Dr Camille Laurin. Lévesque spoke directly to the press and to the public through his daily writings in *Le Journal de Montréal*. Laurin, a far less public but more deliberate person, spoke in the National Assembly and to the press in Quebec City.

The division in the new and inexperienced Parti Québécois was magnified because Lévesque rarely consulted his party executive but instead spoke publicly and passionately, almost without reflection, on all matters concerning the October Crisis. Typical of the behaviour of the PQ's divided leadership at the time was its reversal of the party's position on calling in the army. On 15 October 1970, Laurin agreed in the House to the calling in of the army and then reversed himself a few hours later, apparently after a conversation with Lévesque and pressure from Parti Québécois riding associations. Such problems are endemic throughout the world whenever the leader of a political party is unelected and does not sit in parliament.

Not all Parti Québécois positions during the October Crisis could be attributed to internal divisions, however. On 12 October 1970 the Executive Council of the Parti Québécois made a public declaration in favour of "the liberation of political prisoners." The Council took this step despite its admitted ignorance of all the facts: "even though we do not possess any more information than does the citizenry in general, we believe that it is our duty to make this statement."[3] Almost daily, as well, Lévesque, in his articles in *Le Journal de Montréal*, advised the governments of Quebec and Canada on how to act, in particular urging them to negotiate the freeing of some terrorists in exchange for Cross and Laporte. Lévesque also signed, with Jacques Parizeau (president of the Parti Québécois Executive Committee), Camille Laurin, and thirteen other "eminent personalities," the petition of 14 October 1970. Finally, the activities of various party constituency committees also significantly added to the unrest, particularly during the week of 12 to 17 October 1970.

The Three PQ Dilemmas

The Parti Québécois should not be confused with the FLQ, but the PQ appeared unable to realize that its support for the FLQ's aims, despite its opposition to the group's methods, directly encouraged the terrorists. Why did it take the positions that it did? The Parti Québécois was, and is, principally interested in separating Quebec from Canada, but by peaceful means. The October Crisis, however, posed at least three major dilemmas for the Parti Québécois leadership.

First, the PQ leadership wanted a solution to the crisis, but one decided on by Quebec. It objected to the federal government's intervention and even to Ontario premier John Robarts's strong declaration against the FLQ's strategy of trying to achieve separation through terrorism. To Lévesque, the problem was not only one of terrorism but also of federal and outside interference in a Quebec matter. Of course, this position ignored the fact that, under the Constitution, both the federal and Quebec governments had a role in questions involving the justice system, the release of convicted prisoners, the calling in of the army, and the invoking of the War Measures Act. Furthermore, by criticizing the federal government, the PQ turned the October Crisis into another clash between Ottawa and Quebec, which is exactly what the FLQ wanted.

Secondly, the Parti Québécois, although opposing violence, was reluctant to criticize the FLQ, because it shared the latter's goal of Quebec separation. In consequence, Lévesque and the PQ did not unequivocally advise the FLQ to release Cross and Laporte until the evening of 16 October 1970, eleven days after Cross's kidnapping and six days after Laporte's. Pierre Bourgault voiced the PQ dilemma regarding the FLQ violence when he said: "Violence perhaps never excuses itself, but it explains itself oddly."[4]

Thirdly, the Parti Québécois sought the youth vote and was reluctant to curb or even criticize the students who were demonstrating in favour of the FLQ. Those students were, for the most part, PQ members or supporters, and their support of the FLQ was never criticized by the PQ leadership.

The Union Nationale and the Crédit Social

The other opposition parties were more discreet in their response to the October Crisis. On Sunday, 12 October 1970, in the Queen Elizabeth Hotel, Premier Bourassa briefed Rémi Paul, representing the Union Nationale, Camille Laurin, representing the Parti Québécois (René Lévesque could not be reached), and Camille (Camil) Samson, leader of the Crédit Social (officially the Ralliement des Créditistes). As a result, Jean-Jacques Bertrand, leader of the Opposition, and Samson took calm, rational, and wise positions – they remained silent and did not second-guess the government. As Bertrand declared in the emergency debate in the National Assembly on 11 November 1970:

The official Opposition was, in certain places, criticized and sharply so, not to have, during all this drama, all this crisis which has lasted since the beginning of October, given an opinion or raised the problem before the public. This is an attitude which we voluntarily and deliberately took. We believed that in circumstances such as these, to speak too much would have not only harmed those who were speaking, but even more the cause of public interest and public safety in Quebec.

Our reasons are elementary. In this domain, Mr. President, we have avoided verbal sparring, because, inevitably, verbal sparring leads to chaos. At any given moment, there were so many rumours in the public that to add comments would have created a greater climate of confusion. We tried to understand this crisis rather than condemning right and left. We wanted to try to be witnesses, undoubtedly quiet, but on the other hand perhaps more impartial. We did not want to throw oil on the fire.[5]

Jean-Noël Tremblay of the Union Nationale, himself a strong nationalist, explained that the confusion of the FLQ with the Parti Québécois was due to the imprudence of the separatists and "indépendantistes" them-selves: "It is not my duty here to divide up certain responsibilities, to clear up ambiguities and to prevent the confusion of FLQ action with that of separatists or indépendantistes. This confusion was born of the careless-ness of those who played with fire, and who, for electoral reasons, did not want, at the appropriate time, to draw the line of demarcation which would have made it clear that the ends and the means were not the same depending on the group."[6]

The Role of the Press

In October 1990 former FLQ member Robert Comeau explained on the Radio-Canada program *Le Point* that the press was important, if not essen-tial, to the FLQ's hopes for success in the October Crisis.[7] Certainly, once the first kidnapping had taken place, radio – the dominant medium at the time – played an important role. It was on radio that the crisis was reported and, through messages received directly from the FLQ, radio itself became part of the news. The whole population followed the crisis on radio, which reported on developments and held panel discussions and call-in programs around the clock, almost without a break. It was said at the time that radio journalists contributed to the crisis by their constant reporting and, in particular, through incessant and often inflammatory commentary. The police also found that the constant reporting, commentary, and conjecture on every tidbit of news harmed their work. As *Le Devoir* reported:

In publicizing all sorts of rumours without verifying their authenticity and exhausting headquarters with questions, the journalists "considerably harm the work of the police," a spokesperson for the Montreal Police declared yesterday to Le Devoir.

While understanding the journalists' responsibility to inform the population, the superior officer of the Montreal Police wished that they would demonstrate a greater concern for accuracy in accomplishing their work and take into consider-ation the difficulties encountered by the police force charged with protecting the population.

In response to questions put in the House of Commons, the Prime Minister declared in substance that the media are wrong to give so much publicity to the FLQ and one cannot call political prisoners those who are only prisoners under common law.[8]

In retrospect, I believe that it was essential to keep the public informed and radio provided this service. Still, it is undeniable that the public acted with much more calm and wisdom than some of the radio announcers.

It also needs to be said that much of the press, both written and electronic, French and English, considered itself as a counterweight to Quebec's governing Liberal Party. Reporting, at times, seemed slanted towards the Parti Québécois and, on occasion, reporters said privately that they had a role not merely to report the events as they occurred but to criticize the government because of the Liberal Party's disproportionate number of seats in the National Assembly. When Claude Ryan, editor of *Le Devoir*, was asked about the PQ's treatment by the media, he replied that the party "'received more publicity than its actual support would seem to justify,'" but he added "'that it was the duty of the press to view the PQ in terms of its potential impact.'"[9]

In my view, the general sympathy of the press for the Parti Québécois caused some of its members to support PQ positions during the crisis, even when those positions were wrong or debatable. Thus, for example, many members of the press initially supported the Lévesque/Parti Québécois view that convicted terrorists should be released in exchange for Cross and Laporte. The press also failed to note that the activities of the PQ constituency associations were aiding and abetting the FLQ and passed lightly over the activities of René Lévesque, Camille Laurin, and Jacques Parizeau during the crisis and the effect of the petition of the sixteen "eminent personalities" on those supporting the FLQ. That the Parti Québécois declarations on the crisis inadvertently aided the FLQ, or that the Parti Québécois might have acted opportunistically, was never raised by the press at the time.

Mutual Antipathies

It must be remembered, too, that some Quebecers in 1970 considered the federal government to be too favourable to the English-speaking population of Quebec and to the Rest of Canada. This added to the feelings of frustration of separatists in particular, who, eventually in 1990, would form the Bloc Québécois in order to represent the cause of an independent Quebec in Ottawa. In my view, the Bloc Québécois is a useful institution. It acts as a pressure valve for separatist frustrations, while also reminding

Quebec federalists that their constituency in Quebec is limited. In addition, it serves notice to the ROC of the beliefs of a large number of Quebecers and, at the same time, provides evidence to separatists that they can be represented in a federal state.

Of course, many persons in the ROC, both in 1970 and today, believe that Quebec is too independent and is treated too generously by Ottawa. Such is one of the dilemmas of federalism.

The Montreal Municipal Election – FRAP

Another often forgotten element of the background to the October Crisis, but one of considerable importance, was the Montreal municipal election that was held at that time. By then, the Front d'Action Politique (FRAP), a left-wing municipal movement, had been formed as a political party opposed to Mayor Jean Drapeau of Montreal and his Civic Party administration. The election was to take place on 25 October 1970 and the campaigning coincided with the October Crisis.

Many FRAP members supported the FLQ, without always distinguishing the FLQ's aims from its methods. Paul Cliche, the head of FRAP, was reported to have said on 12 October 1970 that FRAP's "principal objective was the taking of political and economic power by the workers of Quebec and, in that sense, they are in agreement with the FLQ."[10] Later, Cliche backtracked slightly, announcing that he was opposed to FLQ methods although supporting its objectives.

Michel Chartrand, chairman of the CSN Central Council in Montreal, addressed a FRAP rally at the Saint-Louis-de-France church hall and another, larger rally at the Paul Sauvé Arena, where the crowd chanted incessantly "FLQ, FLQ, FLQ!" On 25 October 1970, however, Drapeau was re-elected mayor, with 92 per cent of the vote, and his Civic Party won all the seats on the city council.[11]

The Intellectuals

A phenomenon that is particular to Quebec and no other province is the use of the term "intellectual." Many Anglo-Canadians would be aghast (or, at the very least, would smile) if they were to be called "intellectuals," while the public would laugh at the presumption of anyone applying the name to himself or herself in English. The term is used with more reverence in Quebec, and Latin countries, although Premier Maurice Duplessis disparagingly defined "intellectuels" as "artists."

English and French dictionary definitions of "intellectual" are telling. The Webster Universal [English] Dictionary defines "intellectual" as follows: adjective – "of high mental capacity; having the power of understanding; or of appealing to the intellect"; noun – "one well endowed with intellect (used disparagingly, in political circles for one better equipped on the theoretical side than on the practical)." *Le Petit Larousse*, on the other hand, defines "intellectuel/intellectuelle" as follows: *adjectif* – "qui est du ressort de l'intelligence: *la vie intellectuelle; un travail intellectuel* – qui concerne, qui définit l'intelligence – *quotient intellectuel*"; *nom* – "personne qui s'occupe par goût ou par profession, des choses de l'esprit." Intellectuals played an important part in the October Crisis while it was unfolding, and also in the revisionist interpretation of it in the years that followed. Intellectuals rarely dare to hold elected public office but often gravitate to academe, to the civil service, to non-governmental organizations (NGOs), or to government, as advisers to politicians. Nor do they often hold office in competitive industrial or commercial corporations or businesses.[12] They are nevertheless a necessary part of our culture, but of late, despite their privileges, they do not seem to be any more objective than any other segment of society.

Corporatism

A concept that is central to Quebec political life, but is not usually found in the other provinces, is that of corporatism, meaning the supposed right of institutions to have a say in government. Thus, on 16 October 1970, the Société Saint-Jean-Baptiste de Montréal (SSJBM) stated that, "before the Crisis, the governments should have consulted with moderate groups."[13] The SSJBM seemed to believe that it had a right to be consulted on the October Crisis, and, accordingly, it called for the convocation of "a constituent assembly" to address the matter. As reported in *La Presse* on 31 October: "the Société Saint-Jean-Baptiste de Montréal ... called on the government of Quebec to convene in a truly democratic spirit, a constituent assembly in order to give to the people of Quebec the opportunity to endow themselves with the policies and constitution they desire."[14] Evidently, the recent election of 29 April 1970 was to be ignored. The petition of the sixteen "eminent personalities" on 14 October 1970 was another example of corporatism at work in Quebec.

The Construction Unions, Front Commun

It should also be remembered that the October Crisis took place in the midst of the confrontation between the government and the trade-union movement in the construction industry. Organized labour had formed a "Front Commun," whose seven major leaders (all of whom signed the petition of the sixteen "eminent personalities") were preparing for tough public-sector contract negotiations. The Front Commun had also aligned itself with the Parti Québécois during the past election and continued to do so during the events of October 1970. On 29 October 1970, Bourassa took the extraordinary and courageous step of appointing Jean Cournoyer, who had been labour minister in the former Union Nationale government, to replace Pierre Laporte, his deceased labour minister. Bourassa had a large Liberal caucus, all of whose members wanted to get into the cabinet and believed they had a stronger claim to the portfolio than Cournoyer. Cournoyer had never been a Liberal and indeed had been a defeated Union Nationale candidate in the 29 April 1970 election.

At the time, I questioned the wisdom of Bourassa's decision to take Cournoyer into the cabinet, but I now believe it was necessary and wise. That Bourassa could appoint Jean Cournoyer, as minister of labour, in the middle of the October Crisis, showed courage and foresight, since there was no one then sitting in cabinet or the caucus who could match Cournoyer's political skills or knowledge of the trade-union movement – qualities that were essential to meeting the challenge posed by the Front Commun.

Summary

The October Crisis was an extraordinary event that occurred in extraordinary times in Quebec, Canada, and the world. It was a period of converging forces, including international and national revolutionary movements, that used violence and kidnapping against democratic and undemocratic regimes. Medicare was being implemented in Canada and the Quebec specialist doctors chose to strike at the height of the crisis. The press, too, unwittingly took a new and important role and contributed to the lack of calm, while the Parti Québécois leadership was split between the elected caucus in the National Assembly in Quebec City and René Lévesque in Montreal. There was a construction industry confrontation and finally, FRAP, a highly vocal, left-wing municipal party, was mounting the first challenge to Montreal Mayor Jean Drapeau's leadership in years.

Chapter 2

The FLQ Defined

Freedom means the right to do as we ought to do, it does not mean the right to do as we wish to.

> Pope John Paul II (1920–2005)

O liberté! O liberté! Que de crimes on commet en ton nom!

> Mme Roland (1754–93), when on her way to the guillotine.

A violently active, dominating, intrepid, brutal youth – that is what I am after.

> Adolf Hitler (1889–1945)

À vaincre sans péril, on triomphe sans gloire.

> Pierre Corneille (1606–84)

In the minds of the public then and since, the Front de Libération du Québec (the FLQ) consisted of a handful of young French Canadians who, in order to separate Quebec from Canada, caused a political crisis from 5 October to 28 December 1970. The truth is much different.

The October Crisis was not merely a series of events that took place from October to December 1970. It was rather one episode in an accumulation of revolutionary, clandestine, and terrorist activities from 1963 to 1973 by at least 150 FLQ members or sympathizers, whose declared aim was to form a workers' state in Quebec and to separate Quebec from Canada. These people were aided, wittingly or unwittingly, by what is probably an equal number of persons who could be counted on to appear during a public demonstration or to assist secretly in some clandestine act. Many others lent their voices in support of FLQ aims and methods, particularly during the period of the October Crisis.

The FLQ was not a monolithic whole but was composed of related and often discordant groups. At any given moment, some participants were arriving as others were leaving, some were being jailed as others were being released. All sought a separate Quebec. All shared strong views about social ills in Quebec, but only some believed enthusiastically in the formation of a workers' state, despite public declarations to that effect. The preservation of the French language and culture was only a very secondary consideration for many members of the FLQ.

FLQ Aims and Ideas

The FLQ began at the end of February 1963 as a separatist, revolutionary movement without socialist or Marxist aspirations or ties. On 16 April 1963 the fledgling organization, which then styled itself the Front de Libération Québécois, issued a "Notice to the population of Quebec" that declared, among other things, that "no FLQ member is a member of the OAS[1] or of the Communist Party. We regret that people have tried to discredit us in the eyes of the public by appealing to these old myths and bogeymen." This notice appeared alongside the first FLQ manifesto, entitled "FLQ Message to the Nation," also dated 16 April 1963.[2]

The FLQ manifestos of 1963 and 1970 demanded a separate Quebec, but the 1970 manifesto[3] called as well for a workers' state, which was one of the major contributions of Pierre Vallières and Charles Gagnon, two political activists who joined the organization in 1964. Which was more important, the Marxist program or separation? Were the two aims compatible? The dichotomy was never resolved by the membership as a whole.[4]

The FLQ publications read like 1940s broadsides of Algerian and Cuban revolutionaries. The 1970 manifesto accepted as a sine qua non that all but a few workers were exploited in Quebec, and it called for a government of workers to end the exploitation. Yet only one of the seven demands made by the FLQ kidnappers of James Cross on 5 October 1970 concerned "workers and social ills": dealing with the Lapalme postal workers, it was soon dropped. The six other requests concerned the FLQ kidnappers themselves: the publication of the manifesto, the name of an informer (to whom they no doubt intended to apply their own version of social justice), $500,000 in gold, the release of jailed terrorists, and the transport of themselves and jailed terrorists to Algeria or Cuba.

College and university students were particularly active at demonstrations in favour of the FLQ. "Schools, CEGEPS, and faculties were regularly occupied by the students supporting the Union générale des étudiants du Québec (Quebec Student Union), an independentist and moderately socialist group, just as they also supported the other leftist groups, the FLP, the Mouvement syndical politique (MSP) and also the FLQ."[5]

The large number of dropouts from universities and CEGEPS in the 1970s further swelled the student ranks. With plenty of time on their hands, they were ready to demonstrate, and, like many students, they acted impulsively rather than rationally. Jean-François Cardin describes the students and dropouts in these terms: "Often politicized, for the most part viscerally opposed to the society in place, they wanted to be close to the workers and desired to concretely support their cause."[6] I generally agree with Cardin, though I am not sure that many students really wanted to be "close to the workers." Instead, they seemed to want white-collar jobs, often with the government. After the imposition of the War Measures Act Regulations and Laporte's death, student demonstrations melted away, except for a few leaders and hardened rank-and-file activists.

Two of the leading figures in the early FLQ were Pierre Vallières and Charles Gagnon. Vallières and Gagnon joined the FLQ informally in 1964 and by 1965 had been able to redirect its activity towards the instigation of labour unrest. In their view, an intensified bombing campaign (more and bigger bombs) would lead industrial and rural workers to rise up. This, of course, did not happen. The FLQ targets were not just the English but business and political establishments generally.

Vallières and Gagnon were also key players during the October Crisis. It was they who, with Michel Chartrand and Robert Lemieux, persuaded the students in universities and colleges to strike, protest, and hold meetings during the crisis, culminating in a giant rally of 3,000 students, dropouts, FLQ sympathizers, and young Parti Québécois members on the evening of 15 October 1970 at the Paul Sauvé Arena.

Most FLQ "worker members" were interested in action, not ideology, while the students were more inclined to theory than practice. As François Schirm, who led the robbery at International Firearms in Montreal in August 1964, where two employees were killed, was to declare: "All the members who had voluntarily accepted to be part of the commandos were manual workers, who were very instinctively drawn to action rather than reflection, while the other members of the ARQ, generally born of the student movement, felt themselves to be more at ease in theories than in their practical application."[7]

The "worker members" were generally not members of labour unions. Nevertheless they were more militant than the student activists as can be seen from the fact that only one student member seems to have taken part in the kidnappings of Cross and Laporte, Nigel Hamer, a McGill engineering student.

Although the protection of the French language was, and is, a cause that preoccupies much of the population of Quebec and Canada, and all Quebec political parties, it was not something that particularly concerned the FLQ. In fact, the 1970 manifesto, like many other FLQ messages and pronouncements, was written, at least in part, in colloquial French, with occasional phrases in slang and "franglais." In this way, the FLQ intentionally distanced itself from the intellectuals of Quebec and the bourgeoisie. The second paragraph of the FLQ's 1970 manifesto, for example, read: "Le Front de Libération du Québec veut l'indépendance totale des Québécois, réunis dans une société libre et purgée à jamais de sa clique de requins voraces, les 'big-boss' patronneux et leurs valets qui ont fait du Québec leur chasse gardée du cheap labor et de l'exploitation sans scrupules."

The FLQ members' view of Quebec and Canadian society was not only dated but very shallow. The various manifestos and pronouncements in *La Cognée*, the principal FLQ journal, and other publications went into no detail and proposed few solutions to social injustices. As sociologist Fernand Dumont said: "Generally speaking, terrorists are not much concerned about making a profound or subtle analysis of the problems of a given society. If the Quebec terrorists thought they were giving Canada freedom by the acts they committed, I can only say: They don't understand a thing."[8]

In 1964 one FLQ member, Pierre Schneider, wrote from prison: "In Canada, democracy never existed."[9] The FLQ's rudimentary knowledge of history was evident in its members' comparison of themselves to the *patriotes* of 1837–38. Schneider wrote: "The only man of the Quebec state who was truly honest and patriotic was L.-J. Papineau, who dared to use violence when faced with anti-democratic English forces."[10] In fact, Papineau opposed the use of force by his followers and left Quebec before the fighting began in 1837, only returning years later. Robert Nelson was probably the real *patriote* of 1837–38 and virtually the only rebel leader who did not return to Canada. It was he who wrote the 1838 Declaration of Independence, which made much more sense than the FLQ 1970 manifesto.[11]

FLQ Strategies, Methods, and Organization

In 1968 a secret eight-page document entitled "Revolutionary Strategy and the Role of the Avant-Garde," understood to have been written by Pierre Vallières, outlined the FLQ's long-term strategy of successive waves of robberies, violence, bombings, kidnappings, and selective assassinations, culminating in insurrection and revolution. (The document was not made public until 31 October 1970.)

In the same year *La Cognée* described the four stages of the revolution: 1) organization; 2) training, agitation, and propaganda; 3) a show of force; 4) the coming to power of a provisional government of Quebec.[12] By 1970, the FLQ believed that only violence, terror, kidnapping, and assassination would bring about the changes it hoped for.

No detailed organizational diagram or plan by the FLQ at that time has ever been found and it was unlikely that one was ever drawn up – or, in fact, could have been. Rather, there were common methods of action and, above all, guarded communication, with a few secret meetings.

The organization, like its philosophy, depended on the views of the members at any given time. The FLQ's cells were constantly breaking up and reforming because of police raids, arrests, and convictions in court, and also because of differences among the members. The group's membership was drawn from a number of precursor organizations, such as the Comité de libération nationale (CLN), le Réseau de résistance (RR), l'Armée de libération du Québec (ALQ), and l'Armée révolutionnaire du Québec (ARQ).[13]

Revolutionary Fervour and Its Limits

How dedicated were the FLQ members? Their often-used slogan was "*l'indépendance ou la mort*," and the FLQ kidnappers' communiqué of 8 October 1970 declared that they would never be captured: "When we decided to kidnap the diplomat Cross, we weighed all the possibilities, including the sacrifice of our own lives for a cause we believed to be just. If the repressive police forces should discover us and attempt to intervene before the release of the British diplomat Cross, be sure that we will sell our lives dearly and that Mr. Cross would immediately be liquidated. We have enough dynamite in our possession to feel perfectly 'secure.'"[14]

Yet, when the kidnappers of Cross were finally discovered in their safe house on 3 December 1970, they chose exile rather than martyrdom. They did not ask for social changes to benefit the society they were presumably fighting for; nor did they insist on the original demands of their first communiqué of 5 October 1970. Later, they returned to Canada, preferring the Canadian justice system to the "social justice" and Marxism of Algeria and Cuba.

The four kidnappers of Laporte, rather than escaping to the United States or Cuba, hid first in a Montreal apartment and later in a tunnel under a house near the city. And when captured, they also chose trial under the Canadian justice system. After their convictions, and when their modest prison terms had expired, they wrote a book,[15] admitting to the murder of Laporte, but without expressing real remorse and without commenting on how they had managed to save their own skins.

No FLQ member, when captured, ever chose to defend himself "unto the death," not even those who killed four innocent persons by bombs and caused the deaths of two innocent bystanders during an armed robbery.

In retrospect, it is clear that, as Jean-Paul Desbiens noted, the dedication of FLQ terrorists did not extend as far as putting their own lives at risk. Instead, they were tried under our system of justice, which they had denigrated, and took every advantage of it. Had they been in Cuba or

Algeria, they would have been shot. Desbiens also rightly predicted that they would serve short jail sentences and then would work for the government or continue their studies in France.[16]

Marginalized Men and Their Audience

The hard-core FLQ terrorists were in many ways socially marginalized. They usually had considerable education but most were not the dedicated blue-collar workers whose cause they espoused. Marc Carbonneau of the Libération cell, who drove the car used to kidnap Cross, was an exception. At his trial following his return from exile in 1981, the judge was sympathetic because Carbonneau was the only member of the cell who was "*un véritable travailleur*."[17]

Nor were the hard-core FLQ terrorists at home anywhere in Quebec, a point made perceptively by John Gellner: "the FLQ candidate is at home neither at St. Catherine and Peel nor in the east-side slums. He is not at home anywhere in the Montreal of our day. It is the city from which he is estranged, and from the city dwellers. The strange exodus of some FLQ stalwarts to the rocky seashore of the Gaspé before the great crisis was perhaps a reaction of escape from the perceived oppressiveness and inhumanity of the megalopolis. That they were hounded there, by unsympathetic local inhabitants – French like themselves – must have confirmed in them their sense of utter isolation."[18]

In conclusion, the FLQ was not a single association of enthusiastic, card-carrying members but a movement of generally like-minded persons with different degrees of dedication and often quite different aims and means. Even at the time of the FLQ's formation in 1963, its ideology and agenda were very dated, modelled as they were on the Marxist ideology of Che Guevara and the anarchist concepts of Algerian revolutionaries, while also completely ignoring the social and political reality of Quebec and Canada. Nevertheless, if the FLQ was an anachronism, it stirred the hopes of many separatists at the time of the October Crisis. Parts of the FLQ message – written in the language of the "little guy" – touched a genuine nerve in individuals at all strata of Quebec society. Some of these people supported, or at least sympathized with, many of the aims of the FLQ. Some even sympathized with their methods.

Chapter 3

FLQ Membership

There are three kinds of lies: lies, damned lies and statistics.

Benjamin Disraeli (1804–81)

Statistics are to a politician, what a lamp post is to a drunk. They are more for support than for casting any light.

Andrew Lang (1844–1912)

A few honest men are better than numbers.

Oliver Cromwell (1599–1658)

As a secret movement, the FLQ kept no membership lists. Even today, the names of its members, supporters, and workers have not been divulged by those with that information. For instance, in 1963, Claude Savoie explained that, despite the title of his book, *La véritable histoire du FLQ*, he had not told the full truth: "Obviously, I will not name my informants; my purpose is to inform the public about the real intentions of the FLQ, their goals and the means by which they hoped to accomplish them, and not to act as the police. This is why, in the first part of this book, the names of the suicide commandos are fictitious and their actions purposely mixed up, in a way that makes it impossible to identify one or the other. Nevertheless, all the facts are true, and confirmed by at least two witnesses. The conversations which I created between my characters are not all real, but always have verisimilitude and are always done along their lines of thought."[1]

Assessing the Problem

To be fully accepted as an FLQ member, one had to have committed a crime for the cause. Claude Savoie writes: "One of the principles of the FLQ was to involve all their members, so that no one felt his responsibility less than that of the others. The members who had not set off bombs would thereafter be put to the test."[2]

There were also active and occasional participants, supporters, collaborators, and sympathizers of the FLQ, all of whom were not, strictly speaking, members. Their number is still unknown. Writings by FLQ members, sympathizers, and apologists often speak of persons who took part in meetings, bombings, the delivering of communiqués, and the hiding of FLQ members but do not always give their names. Were the sympathizers who hid Jacques Rose not aiding and abetting terror? How does one classify them? And how does one classify the persons who obviously knew of Nigel Hamer's part in the Cross kidnapping but never denounced him? From 1963 to October 1970, the FLQ would not have been able to commit a large number of crimes without the assistance of many supporters and sympathizers. Which category do these people fit into?

And in listing FLQ supporters, should one not number those who withheld information on the organization? Even small bits of information could have been pieced together to assist the police in finding Laporte or Cross, or in convicting FLQ members for their crimes during the years from 1963 to October 1970. Should not a member of a democratic society who happens to know of illegal activities, particularly by terrorists intent on overthrowing the government of that society, inform the police of the names of those terrorists and the nature of their acts? Is there not a duty to do so? What side was Claude Savoie on when he declared without compunction in 1963 that he would not name the persons who gave him information on the FLQ for his book?[3] Was he on the side of the terrorists or of society? Would his information not have been helpful in October 1970?

And what of members of the public in general? Did they, too, not have a duty to inform? It may have seemed odious to do so, but was it not more odious to remain silent? On what side were these non-informers? And why the denigration of informers, such as Carole de Vault? If a person describes someone who gave the police valuable information about criminals as a *délateur*, or an informer, is not that person on the side of the criminals?

And how do we classify members of the Comité d'aide au groupe Vallières-Gagnon and of the Mouvement pour la défense des prisonniers politiques québécois (MDPPQ)? Louis Fournier writes that the latter "took up the work" of the former.[4] Both groups demonstrated violently against the imprisoning of convicted FLQ members, whom they classified as "political prisoners," although these terrorists were responsible for six violent deaths. Were not these persons, who supported the violence of the FLQ, accomplices of the FLQ? Was it not wise to put such people in jail during the height of the October Crisis?[5]

On 17 October 1970, Serge Mongeau, a member of the executive of the MDPPQ, declared from jail that he had been kidnapped by the police: "I am a 'prisoner of war,' of this war which no one declared, but whose proclamation permits authorities to carry out more thoroughly the repression which has already been going on for a long time."[6] Mongeau concluded by accusing Bourassa of subjecting the people to an *écrasement* (crushing oppression), and he predicted that the consequences might be drastic.[7] How benign was this group or how innocent was its involvement? How do we count these persons – as members of the FLQ? as sympathizers? or as something else? Did they not aid the FLQ cause, directly or indirectly?

Writing with authority on the October Crisis and the activities of the Mouvement de libération populaire (MLP), and its successor, the Front de libération populaire (FLP), Jean-François Cardin described the close connections between these groups and the FLQ: "Among the groups which had the most influence, we must mention the Mouvement de libération populaire, born in June 1969, and whose only permanent member was none other than Pierre Vallières, who joined the FLQ at the same time."[8] Cardin then went on to recount the birth of the separatist and socialist FLP, which inspired groups of confrontational workers: "It was these organizations, such as the MLP and of course, the FLP, which acted side by side with the members of the FLQ and the leftist unions."[9] How do we classify the members of the MLP and FLP and the leaders of the "leftist unions"?

Many people are unable, philosophically or morally, to understand that in a democratic society one must not support terrorists, even indirectly. As an example, consider an article written by Lina Gagnon on behalf of ten theology students from the Université de Montréal that was published in *Le Devoir* at the height of the October Crisis. Gagnon criticized the Catholic Church for its silence during the crisis and particularly for its failure to support socialism, which was supposedly one of the aims of the FLQ. She called on the people to act more courageously and even refused to disavow FLQ violence, writing: "It is up to the people at the grassroots of society to express their socialist vision for Quebec. And they must act in order that this political view can be made possible. Certain people have chosen to act in a violent way; I respect their choice."[10]

The same simplistic, and dangerous, position was taken by those who condemned government action and yet did not condemn the FLQ terrorists or call upon them to release Cross and Laporte, whom they called "political prisoners." These people cannot be numbered as FLQ members but, in their own way, they nevertheless indirectly aided and abetted the terrorists at a critical moment.

Conflicting Numbers

Those who wish to play down the number of FLQ members usually do so in order to cast doubt on whether there was an apprehended insurrection and whether it was necessary to invoke the War Measures Act. Conversely, those who support the application of the War Measures Act usually exaggerate the size of the FLQ's membership.

In May 1965 the FLQ journal *La Cognée* reported: "Recruiting continues ... and it can be said that at the present moment the FLQ has almost a thousand members. Selection is still very strict and, contrary to what happened in the past, the divisions between the various levels of the organization are still water-tight so that the movement can never be destroyed in its entirety."[11] Five years later, in October 1970, as a result of the proclamation of the War Measures Act Regulations, according to the records of the federal Department of Justice, 497 persons were arrested. However, Louis Fournier, in his history of the movement, was able to list the names of only 355, despite assistance from La Fondation Octobre 1970, "which campaigned so that the Governments of Canada and of Quebec would grant compensation to the prisoners of war."[12] The remaining 142 no doubt include persons who still do not want their connection to the FLQ to be disclosed publicly.

Jean Marchand, then federal minister of regional economic expansion, undoubtedly exaggerated when he declared in Parliament on 16 October 1970: "Anybody who properly understands the organization of the FLQ at this precise time cannot help but perceive that Quebec and the federal state are really in danger in Canada. The most pessimistic say that there are nearly 3000 members of the FLQ. I don't know if that number is exact, but I do know that there are some. And I also know something else: they have infiltrated all the vital strategic locations within the Province of Quebec, all the jobs where important decisions are made."[13] Marchand was a hardnosed labour organizer who had paid his dues at strikes, the most famous being the Asbestos strike of 1949, where he was one of the real heroes. He knew the labour movement inside out and had no illusions about the degree of violence a few radical leaders could engender; he no doubt exaggerated the numbers of FLQ militants, but not the threat that they posed. Marchand, unlike some of the people who challenged his claims about the FLQ, was no intellectual, but he was well aware of the violent, radical slant of some of his fellow labour activists. I knew Marchand and would rather follow him than most of his critics.

On 26 November 1970, Jérôme Choquette, then Quebec justice minister, declared that the FLQ had about 100 to 125 men, a number large enough to justify the government's concern that an insurrection was possible.[14] At the end of the year, Gérard Pelletier, the federal secretary of state, gave the following general description of the FLQ: "Just as I subscribe to the belief that the FLQ – or at least what we know of it at present – represented only a limited threat to our democratic institutions, I am equally convinced that there existed, and still exists in Quebec, as in most large North American cities, two or three thousand people who, without having direct organic links with the FLQ terrorists, can easily be drawn into violent action (spontaneous or organized demonstrations which turn into rioting, more or less serious crimes, looting, etc.)."[15] Pelletier further stated: "I think it would be wiser not to speak of the FLQ membership at this particular moment. All that can be said perhaps is that the FLQ has enough sympathizers and active members to be a real threat to the people who are in office at the moment."[16] He gave the following breakdown of FLQ members: 40 to 50 extremists (perhaps 100) ready to plant bombs, kidnap, and even murder; a permanent information cell; 200 to 300 active sympathizers ready to assist financially or by concealment; and 2,000 to 3,000 armchair, passive sympathizers.[17]

On the other side of the debate, Marcel Rioux, one of the sixteen "eminent personalities," wrote in 1971 that "the FLQ never consisted of more than a few cells, a few dozen people at most." But Rioux did not cite any authority for this assertion[18] and in fact there is reason to doubt its accuracy. The historian Jacques Lacoursière stated in 1971 that there were nine FLQ cells in all. Two were the Chénier and Libération cells, which conducted the kidnappings of Cross and Laporte. The other seven were the Cellule Wolfred Nelson, the Cellule André Ouimet, the Cellule Édouard-Étienne Rodier, the Cellule François-Xavier Hamelin, the Cellule François Nicolas, the Cellule Viger, and the Cellule Peuple Saint-Denis.[19] These seven cells (except for the Cellule Viger) were never heard from publicly but no doubt existed and probably assisted in the activities of the FLQ.

In 1974 Marc Laurendeau, in his well-documented *Les Québécois violents*, listed the names of 100 "suspected terrorists."[20] The following decade, in 1981, Jean-François Duchaîne, appointed by the PQ government to investigate the October Crisis, claimed that the FLQ had only thirty-five members by October 1970.[21] Yet, with the slightest research, and particularly with all the powers vested in him, Duchaîne should have at least found the names of the one hundred "suspected terrorists" whom Marc Laurendeau publicly named. In my own case, realizing that the issue of how many members, participants, sympathizers, and occasional supporters the FLQ had is central to understanding the threat that the organization posed, I began to collect the names of persons referred to by other authors. After consulting only five such authors – Louis Fournier, Marc Laurendeau, Serge Mongeau, Carole de Vault, and Manon Leroux – I identified more than 180 people.[22] All were FLQ members, participants, and sympathizers or were involved in related movements or related events that turned violent. I suspect there are at least an equal number of persons who, from time to time, were also involved in the FLQ in some way but whose names have never been revealed.

Conclusion

It seems clear that we will never know the exact number of hard-core FLQ activists, the number of non-members who assisted them, or the number of FLQ sympathizers who had already aided the organization by the time of the October Crisis. Nor will we ever know the number of persons who, from 1963 to 1970 and during the crisis itself, had personal knowledge of the FLQ and its activities but never gave that information to the police. Most of these people could be counted on to demonstrate in support of the FLQ or to assist it in various ways, including by their silence and their refusal to inform.

Chapter 4   The F L Q Manifesto

Publish or be damned.

Duke of Wellington (1769–1852)

I'll publish right or wrong: Fools are my theme, let satire be my song.

Lord Byron (1788–1824)

There were three FLQ manifestos. The first, dated 16 April 1963, was distributed to the press but only small parts were published. It was finally published in full on 15 October 1965 in *La Cognée*, the official, but secret, organ of the FLQ. It was written in an academic (*petit bourgeois*) style and called more for the separation of Quebec from Canada than for social justice. The second manifesto, written by Robert Comeau of the Université du Québec à Montréal, was shorter, avoided talk of violence, and was sent to the press in June 1970 but never published. The third manifesto was received by the press and the authorities on Tuesday, 6 October 1970, the day after the kidnapping of James Cross.[1]

Publication of the 1970 manifesto was the first of seven demands from Cross's kidnappers. Radio-Canada decided to read the 1970 manifesto (which was written only in French) on its television network. The decision, in my view, was the correct one. Our critics, however, took the opposite view.

The Text of the 1970 Manifesto

The 1970 manifesto was written in rapid-fire, moving, and provocative language, with imaginative, cadenced epithets following one after another. It was intended to shock, and parts of it touched a sympathetic nerve when it mentioned evident inequalities in Quebec society.[2]

Small parts of the manifesto were written in "franglais," no doubt to distance the FLQ from the intelligentsia and the bourgeoisie and to link it with what it perceived to be the working classes. In particular, the language of the 1970 manifesto made it clear that the FLQ did not really stand for the protection of the French language and culture but was more committed to fomenting social revolution. Thus the 1970 manifesto, probably written by André Roy and edited, when the October Crisis began, by Jacques Lanctôt, distinguished itself from the more academic-sounding manifesto of 1963, which had likely been written by Denis Lamoureux.[3]

Whereas the 1963 manifesto spoke mainly of separation, the 1970 manifesto emphasized the need for a workers' revolution – a change that was due to two Marxists – Pierre Vallières and Charles Gagnon – who had secretly joined the FLQ in 1965. Balancing separatism with a workers' revolution, or even with social justice, was a dilemma that the FLQ never resolved.

The 1970 manifesto also contained the standard diatribes against the Liberal governments of Bourassa in Quebec and Trudeau in Ottawa, as well as against the "*big boss patronneux et leurs valets*": "We live in a society of terrorized slaves, terrorized by the big bosses like Steinberg, Clark, Bronfman, Smith, Neapole, Timmins, Geoffrion, J.L. Levesque, Hershorn, Thompson, Nesbitt, Desmarais, Kierans. (Compared to them, Rémi Popol [Rémi Paul, parliamentary leader of the Union Nationale], the lousy good-for-nothing, Drapeau the Dog, Bourassa the lackey of the Simards, and Trudeau the fairy, are peanuts.)"

The 1970 manifesto contained two brief derogatory references to the Roman Catholic Church, which until that time had usually been antagonistic to liberalizing forces in Quebec. In contrast, the 1963 manifesto had not criticized the church at all. This was in keeping with the FLQ's stance at the time – on 6 June 1963 it had ended one of its communiqués declaring responsibility for recent bombings with an expression of regret on the death of Pope John XXIII.[4] And on 15 January 1965 *La Cognée* implied that Quebec's Catholic clergy were really on the FLQ's side when it stated: "Our clergy are now dynamic and nationalist."

Despite the appeal that the 1970 manifesto had for some people (particularly students), it was a long, rambling document that said little about how the proposed workers' state would deal democratically and fairly with the whole of Quebec society, let alone workers. It read, in part:

Workers of Québec, start today to take back what belongs to you; take for yourselves what is yours. Only you know your factories, your machines, your hotels, your universities, your unions, do not wait for some organization to perform miracles.

Make your own revolution in your neighbourhoods, in your workplaces. And if you don't do it yourselves, technocrat usurpers or others will replace the handful of cigar-smokers we now know, and everything will have to be done over again. Only you are capable of building a free society ...

In the four corners of Québec, let those who have been contemptuously called "lousy French" and alcoholics vigorously undertake the fight against the bludgeoners of liberty and justice and render harmless all the professional robbers and swindlers: the bankers, the businessmen, the judges, and the sold-out politicians.

We are the workers of Québec and we will struggle on to the bitter end. Together with all the people, we want to replace this slave society with a free society, functioning by itself and for itself; a society open to the world.

Our struggle can only lead to victory. An awakening people cannot long be kept in misery and contempt.

Long live free Québec!

Long live our political prisoner comrades!

Long live the Québec revolution!

Long live the Front de Libération du Québec!

The manifesto not only ignored the lack of freedom enjoyed by populations under Marxist dictatorships such as those in the Soviet Union and East Bloc countries, it seemed to be addressed to the needs of some undemocratic Third World country rather than Quebec and Canada. As Louis Fournier wrote: "This document is a mixture of indépendantisme and utopian socialism and proposes a vague, spontaneous liberation strategy. ('Make your own revolution.')."[5]

Of course, the 1970 manifesto should be assessed in the context not of today but of 1970, which was a time of great unrest in Quebec. There was considerable turmoil in the rest of the world, too, not only in countries that had just made the transition from colonialism to independence but also in France, Germany, and Italy. The manifesto gained sympathy, if not support, from many young people, who were intoxicated with the possibility of setting the world right by a single act. On the other hand, Bourassa had been in office only five months when the October Crisis broke out. He had not yet had time to carry out any of the reforms and projects he had in mind, and was eventually to implement by the time he left office in 1976, including changes to the electoral system, protection of the French language, improvements to the province's schools, consumer safeguards, controls on foreign investment, the first environmental laws, a bill of rights, and a better business and labour atmosphere. The 1970 manifesto did not mention any of these projected reforms, all of which were to be found in Bourassa's 1970 election platform. Nor did it touch upon the issue of Bourassa's energy policy, which promoted hydro-electric power – the James Bay project – rather than atomic power, which the Parti Québécois preferred.

In summary, the FLQ manifesto of 1970 was intended to shock. Some of its language was appealing – its cadence, its popular language, and its brisk tempo throughout – but the document as a whole did not stand up to scrutiny or reflection. Those persons who were sympathetic to the FLQ's point of view came out in support of the manifesto while, at the same time, usually distancing themselves from the FLQ's violence and conveniently ignoring the lack of information on how the proposed workers' state would be organized and who would be in charge. In effect, they approved the FLQ's criticisms of Quebec and Canadian society without giving thought to how to achieve the solutions the manifesto proposed.

The Reading of the 1970 Manifesto

The 1970 manifesto was first read on 7 October 1970 on radio station CKAC by journalist Louis Fournier, without government permission or opposition. On the evening of 8 October 1970, it was read on Radio-Canada TV by Gaëtan Montreuil. When he had finished, Montreuil said, according to Laurent Picard, executive vice-president of Radio-Canada, "It was such a bad commercial."

Radio-Canada's decision to read the manifesto on the air was taken on its authority alone. In Ottawa, cabinet ministers Mitchell Sharp and Gérard Pelletier wanted it published, while Trudeau was opposed. According to Picard, Trudeau had his principal secretary, Marc Lalonde, telephone Picard to oppose the reading. Picard refused and then Trudeau came on the phone and Picard refused again. Trudeau replied that he admired Picard's independence but that he reserved the right to call Picard a damn fool in Parliament. Montreuil then proceeded. This is one of the rare cases where René Lévesque, the intellectuals, and Trudeau agreed on some matter concerning the October Crisis. Years later, Trudeau, in his *Memoirs*, recognized that Mitchell Sharp had been right and he had been wrong.[6]

As to why the intellectuals, FLQ supporters, union leaders, the Parti Québécois leadership (including René Lévesque[7]), and, in particular, the sixteen "eminent personalities," with the exception of Claude Ryan, opposed the reading of the manifesto on television, it seems to me that these people hoped, consciously or unconsciously, despite their protestations to the contrary, that the provincial and federal governments would ignore their advice and agree to the reading, since it seemed a small price to pay if it succeeded in getting the hostages released.

At the time, the effect on the public of publishing the manifesto seemed minimal. As Gérard Pelletier was to say, "Did the FLQ really suppose that as a result of the publication of its manifesto the population of Quebec would go into the streets, or at least join in a mass protest movement against the Government? A general strike, for instance ... If such was the case, their strategic error was considerable."[8] There was no labour uprising or strike, let alone a general strike. Students held meetings in their colleges and universities, but there were no demonstrations or marches in the streets, no riotous confrontations with police, no breaking of windows, no looting, no property damage, and no personal injury or arrests. The students debated, drafted resolutions, and made declarations. It was only during the week following the kidnapping of Laporte that the meetings, demonstrations, and college and university closings started in earnest.

On 15 October, eight days after the first reading of the manifesto, and after Université de Montréal authorities had refused an application to hold a large meeting on the campus, 3,000 people gathered in the Paul Sauvé Arena. The rally's organizers intended "to explain the FLQ Manifesto,"[9] but, as it turned out, it was the petition of the sixteen "eminent personalities" that was distributed to the gathering. Adoption of the War Measures Act Regulations at 4:00 a.m. the following morning put an end to the demonstrations that were planned for that day.

Outside the ranks of the FLQ and its supporters and apologists, unequivocal support for the manifesto was rare. One who expressed such a view was, as we have seen, Paul Cliche, president of the Front d'Action Politique, the political party opposed to Montreal Mayor Jean Drapeau in the municipal election scheduled for 25 October 1970, who declared on the 12th of that month that FRAP supported the FLQ's position as expressed in its manifesto,[10] though he later qualified his statement. Further, support for the manifesto was voiced by groups, as opposed to individuals, only when radical leaders were in charge. For example, the Executive Committee of the Confederation of National Trade Unions (CNTU) in Montreal, of which Michel Chartrand was president, declared: "The Executive Committee of the Montreal Central Council of the CNTU has expressed its unequivocal support of the manifesto issued by the FLQ after the kidnapping of British Trade Commissioner Richard Cross."[11]

Fernand Dumont, a distinguished professor of sociology at Université Laval and one of the sixteen "eminent personalities" who signed the petition of 14 October 1970, believed that the manifesto had a great effect:

"This was not the first time the FLQ had weighed in, and its manifesto contained nothing that amounted to a revelation on Quebec's problems. Why then did it so abruptly arouse the sensitivities of so many of our fellow citizens?"[12] Dumont does not give any evidence for his statement that the manifesto had, in fact, "aroused" people. In fact, for three days after the reading of the manifesto until Laporte's kidnapping, the situation was relatively calm; the manifesto was too long, too ambiguous, and too illogical a document, capable of bearing neither scrutiny nor serious reflection, to set imaginations alight, except among FLQ members and their supporters. Dumont later made what seems, given his participation in the petition of 14 October 1970, to be a self-serving statement concerning the reasons for the manifesto's alleged effect: "I see no other explanation than that this was the sudden eruption, expressed by a symbol that could have been quite different, of the bitterness and hopes accumulated over the years, already revealed furtively in various lights by so many other crises."[13] No doubt Dumont and his fellow intellectuals saw an "eruption," and perhaps they themselves felt "bitterness and hopes accumulated over the years," but did the manifesto propose a solution that was acceptable to them? And why did Dumont and the other sixteen "eminent personalities," in their petition of 14 October 1970, not denounce the manifesto and the FLQ? Did they believe in the aims advocated by the manifesto in whole or in part? Why did they not see that agreeing to exchange Cross and Laporte for imprisoned terrorists, whom they called political prisoners, would weaken the Quebec and federal governments, which was also the aim of the FLQ?

Looking back now, I believe that the decision to read the 1970 manifesto on television was a wise one, because the document was not convincing. There was some sympathy with the complaints listed, but the vast majority of the population was unimpressed with the solutions it proposed. The positive impression the manifesto may have made was quickly displaced by popular revulsion at the FLQ's methods.

In any event, a refusal to read the manifesto on television would only have given it publicity. The document was already in the hands of the press, it had already been read on CKAC and printed in at least one paper, and it was being distributed by student leaders. In short, it was no longer secret. Keeping the manifesto from the public at this point would have only elicited interest in it and provoked criticism.

Chapter 5

Terrorists for Hostages

There is only one thing viler than being a blackmailer
and that is giving in to blackmail.

Jean-Paul Desbiens, 1970

Blackmail, in early English law, was a rent paid in
grain, base money or cattle by farmers in Northern
England to Scottish chieftains in exchange for
protection from being robbed. Whitemail was a
normal rent paid in silver.

Ransom: The purchase of that which neither belongs
to the seller, nor can belong to the buyer; the most
unprofitable of investments.

Ambrose Bierce (1842–1914)

And that is what's called paying the Dane-geld;
But we've proved it again and again,
That if once you have paid him the Dane-geld
You never get rid of the Dane.

Rudyard Kipling (1865–1936)

Whether or not to exchange convicted terrorists for innocent hostages is one of the most difficult and heart-rending decisions that any government can face. The Bourassa government was obliged to make the decision, not merely because of its premier role under the Canadian Constitution as to the administration of justice in the province, and not merely because the FLQ addressed its messages to it, but because of the legal status of the twenty-three terrorist prisoners whose freedom the FLQ demanded. Five of these prisoners were eligible for parole and six others, who had been charged but had not been convicted, could have been released by the minister of justice of Quebec under the simple procedure of *nolle prosequi*, which means that there would be no further proceedings.

The alternatives facing the government were to attempt to save the lives of two human beings by releasing convicted criminals, inviting further kidnappings and violence when the FLQ prisoners were released, or to hold firm and refuse to negotiate, risking the lives of the hostages. The first option meant permitting terrorist activity to replace the courts and legislature of a democratic society, where social and political reform can come about by democratic means.

Kidnappings and the Government's Response

Having been responsible for bombings, hold-ups, and six violent deaths over the previous seven years, the FLQ then turned to kidnapping as the next step in its plan to stage an insurrection and overthrow the government. In effect, the kidnappings of James Cross and Pierre Laporte had three purposes. The first purpose was to obtain the release of the twenty-three FLQ members jailed for bombings, robberies, and violent deaths or awaiting trial for those crimes. As Louis Fournier pointed out: "for examples of profitable kidnapping don't forget that very recently, June 11 in Brazil, the kidnappers of the West German ambassador to Rio de Janeiro, M. Ehrenfried Von Holleben, at the end of 6 days, succeeded in getting 40 political prisoners released – a new record – plus a plane to Algeria. Why, the militants of the FLQ asked themselves, cannot we obtain the liberation of twenty or so of our incarcerated comrades in exchange for an American Consul to Montreal."[1] The second purpose was to cause confusion, fear, and turmoil in the minds of the public and to gain publicity and even sympathy for FLQ aims, while the third was to trigger both an insurrection and capitulation by the government. From the beginning, Pierre Bourgault (one of the three founders of the Rassemblement pour l'indépendance nationale (RIN) and its president from 1964 to 1968, when it became part of the PQ) recognized this reality. A clear thinker and frank speaker, Bourgault said three days after Cross's kidnapping: "The government must accept *the parallel power* which the FLQ was given by kidnapping the British diplomat. The government must, among other things, stop the action of their police apparatus, they must offer impunity to the planners of the kidnapping, they must find a way to enter into contact, without danger, with this faction of the FLQ, and they must immediately commit themselves to accept the most important proposition of the FLQ."[2]

On 5 October 1970, the day of Cross's kidnapping, many people decided that Quebec had no choice but to release convicted terrorists in exchange for Cross's life. The next morning, *Le Devoir* took this position, as did other newspapers, including the Toronto *Star*.

Jérôme Choquette, Quebec's minister of justice, disagreed. In a communiqué of 10 October 1970, he declared unambiguously: "No society can consent to have the decisions of its judicial and governmental institutions challenged or set aside by the blackmail of a minority, for that signifies the end of all social order." Choquette explained that the decision made, in the name of the two governments, to offer safe passage to Cross's kidnappers – without any further concessions – had been aimed at "safeguarding the essentials of a democratic society." He gave six reasons to support this decision, noting in particular that "to permit odious blackmail without safeguarding the principle of order, which is fundamental to the exercise of freedom, would be to introduce an alteration of this system for the future." It would also mean "accepting the practice of kidnapping or of abduction to checkmate a system of justice which is among the most impartial in the world, despite everything one might say about it."

After the kidnapping of Laporte, the whole Bourassa cabinet met over a three-day period, from 11 to 13 October 1970, and took the painful but necessary decision not to exchange convicted terrorists. Even then, the government tried to continue negotiations, in the hope that, in the interim, Cross and Laporte would be found. We would make only minor concessions: to recommend the parole of the five FLQ prisoners currently eligible for parole and to fly the kidnappers to Cuba or Algeria or any other safe haven in exchange for Cross and Laporte, but not to release all the twenty-three jailed terrorists. The reading of the 1970 manifesto on Radio Canada television, on 8 October 1970, had also seemed reasonable. The government was not prepared to go any further.

The press and the Parti Québécois suggested that were differences of opinion in the cabinet, especially during the period when Pierre Laporte was in the hands of the FLQ. Certainly, different views were expressed when we met together on Sunday, 11 October, Laporte having been kidnapped the evening before. I, for example, at first wanted to release the prisoners in the hope of saving the lives of Laporte and Cross (see appendix). But we discussed the matter openly and at length and eventually achieved a consensus. That there was a debate, as well as strong differences of views and even a brief withdrawal from the cabinet room by Jérôme Choquette, before we reached a unanimous decision, was a sign not of a weak cabinet but of a strong one. A cabinet that cannot discuss a question at length, even heatedly, does not have genuine solidarity and will not reach proper decisions.

The atmosphere around the cabinet table at the time was captured in my diary for Tuesday, 13 October 1970:

We meet in Hydro again in the P.M.'s office. The big raid of last night was a flop. Our negotiator, Robert Demers, is continuing to stall and will not comply with all the FLQ demands. We only offer: a) safe conduct to the kidnappers; b) recommend parole, but we do not want to do even this.

The papers are howling and the French press is calling us down. Lemieux is having press conferences every few hours and is the darling of the noisy press.

(Medicare, which was for yesterday in the House, was put off).

Bourassa is wavering still. I am hawkish and want to call in the troops, impose martial law, etc. I have completely changed in two days. Bourassa kindly reminds me that two days before I was for releasing all 23 prisoners. Bourassa is calm, fair and human. He is remarkable for his composure and handling of the matter. Choquette threatens to resign. As the discussion continues, he walks out of the room. I go after him and bring him back or at least get him to stop in one of the outer offices, where we talk. Later he comes back.

Jean-Claude Leclerc of *Le Devoir* (who, in every other way, was critical of the government and who even took a couple of good shots at me) stated with respect to the threats of resignation in the Bourassa cabinet: "This would indeed be the first time in political history that a minister, in the heat of discussion, would not at least pretend to withdraw or that such and such an opinion would not have bold proponents. All of that is normal elsewhere, especially in time of crisis: why should the Bourassa Cabinet have escaped a similar experience?"[3] As it turned out, there were no resignations from the Bourassa cabinet in 1970.

The government's reasons for not releasing the FLQ terrorists were set out by Justice Minister Choquette in the debate on the subject in the National Assembly on 13 November.[4] They may be summarized as follows:

1) the twenty-three FLQ prisoners were not "political prisoners" but rather were either convicted criminals or were awaiting trial for their crimes;

2) to have given in to the FLQ's demands would have been to accept its system of kidnapping and to defeat our impartial system of justice;

3) a democratic society cannot accept violence as an argument for the course a government should follow;

4) violence begets violence, with the result that anarchy replaces the rule of law;

5) cowering in the face of blackmail would have led to its repetition; and

6) giving in to terrorist kidnappers would have made it difficult, if not impossible, to prosecute other terrorists in subsequent cases.

The FLQ Reaction

The FLQ was stunned by the hard line taken by the Canadian and Quebec governments. When the kidnappers of Cross left for Cuba early in the morning of 3 December 1970, they left behind tapes of conversations which revealed their misunderstanding of democracy and the responsibility of democratically elected governments. One tape contained the following statement: "We really thought that the government was ready ... that the government was going to agree. When we did the kidnapping we said: 'Maybe in four or five days, a week at the outside, the government will agree to negotiate.' What can you make of that, the all-out refusal, the final No of Trudeau ... Bourassa ... and then, what has our action achieved so far?"[5] This long tape ended with the standard "Long Live the Front de

Libération du Québec" but without the often used slogan "indépendance ou la mort" (independence or death).

The FLQ may have been surprised, but the country's political class was not. The vast majority of representatives of political parties agreed with the sentiment expressed in the House of Commons by R.N. Thompson, the member of Parliament for Red Deer: "For the past nine days we have seen the subjugation of democratic values to terrorism, the subjugation of human life to political expediency, the subjugation of justice by law to oppression by anarchy." He then added that "to bargain with those who would equate reason and reform with abduction and murder is to bargain with no less than the stability of society itself."[6]

Press Reaction

From the outset, there was wide support in the press for the government's decision not to exchange terrorists for the hostages. The Winnipeg *Tribune* editorialized: "Ottawa should follow the example established by Great Britain during the recent hijackings by the Palestinian guerillas. The British government resisted all sorts of pressure, calling on it to surrender to the demands of those who detained innocent hostages in Jordan. It is this firmness, adopted from the start, more than anything else, which defused a dangerous situation and led to necessary compromises with the authors of the blackmail."[7] Similarly, the Winnipeg *Free Press* stated: "The dilemma in which the terrorists have placed the governments of Quebec and Canada is an agonizing one. Yet, when the scales are balanced – and the lives of two men are in one – it is difficult to see how a government can give in to blackmail and hope that good can emerge. If the terrorists were to be given what they demand, it would serve only to whet their appetite, to make them more daring, to continue on the course on which they are set. Who would be the next victim? Where would it end?"[8]

Le Devoir was an exception. Its editor, Claude Ryan, took the position that we must negotiate and he held fast to this view throughout the October Crisis – and afterwards. His editorial in *Le Devoir* on 6 October 1970 reviewed examples of recent terrorist kidnappings in Brazil, Guatemala, and Paraguay, where in most cases the exchange of terrorists had resulted in more kidnappings and more terror, but, despite this evidence, he stuck to his position, maintaining that "these examples prove nothing." In particular, Ryan failed to distinguish between kidnappings in democratic regimes, where concessions will destroy the democratic fabric of government and where social reform can come about by democratic means, and in undemocratic regimes, where democratic reform is impossible and where there is no democratic order to destroy. Nor did Ryan ever explain how a democratic regime, which has once released terrorists, should then face the next acts of terrorism and kidnapping by those same terrorists and others, who are emboldened by the success of their previous actions. Does not one capitulation only encourage further acts of terror?

To the end of his life, Ryan believed that he had been right about exchanging prisoners and the whole matter preyed on his mind, along with his antipathy to Trudeau, which came to include Marc Lalonde. In October 2000, on the thirtieth anniversary of the October Crisis, I was invited to an hour-long television panel, with Ryan, Lalonde, and Robert Lemieux, on the programme *Maisonneuve à l'écoute*. At first I refused, because I expected the discussion to be unnecessarily bitter, but Lalonde, who did not wish to be the only one deflecting Ryan's occasional acerbic debating style, convinced me to attend. It was tense – it was always difficult to have a real discussion with Ryan – but we all survived. Afterwards, Ryan offered to drive me home. Instead of parking in the distant guests' parking lot, far behind Radio-Canada, he had parked exactly in the centre of the front door, where taxis and everyone else could only discharge passengers. When we got into his ancient, low-slung, yellowed vehicle, he was saluted and greeted with "Bonsoir, Monsieur Ryan." We glided off majestically and he chuckled, saying: "You know, at my age, I understand civil servants and they understand me."

Claude Ryan was an anomaly. It is impossible to overestimate the great reputation he enjoyed on matters concerning Quebec and Canada or the great respect that ordinary French Canadians held for him. Intellectuals and people active in politics, however, were intensely divided in their assessment of him.

Jean-Claude Leclerc of *Le Devoir* went even further than Ryan. He seems to have supported every aspect of the FLQ program, including violence and kidnapping as a means of blackmail for political gain. Leclerc believed that the twenty-three prisoners who had been found guilty of two hundred bombings, many robberies, and six violent deaths were not criminals but "political prisoners": "For as long as there are 'political prisoners,' whether this expression pleases or not, and as long as states treat them like common criminals, one risks having other kidnappings or other similar dramas."[9] He put dictatorial regimes in Brazil, Guatemala, and Argentina on the same footing as the democratically elected government of Canada and believed that we should have released FLQ criminals in the same way as those regimes released captured terrorists. Nor did Leclerc distinguish between the place of dissent in democratic regimes such as Quebec and Canada and that of dissent in totalitarian regimes such as the Soviet Union, Hungary, and Czechoslovakia of 1970. "How many Soviets, Hungarians, or Czechoslovaks no longer pay allegiance to their country?" He concluded that the FLQ were not "bandits and assassins" but were conducting a "political struggle." "In Canada, the government takes the FLQ for a group of bandits and assassins. These dissidents, on the contrary, proclaim a political struggle. From this perspective, the liberation of James Cross, even without governmental compensation, would not be an international precedent, but would nevertheless have great local and international reverberations."[10]

Such thinking found no favour with Jean-Paul Desbiens, the famous "Frère Untel." On 6 October 1970 Desbiens declared in a signed editorial in *La Presse*:

neither the municipal government, the provincial government, nor the federal government should at any time give in to this blackmail. *I don't mind if they appear to be giving in*, on condition that they are sure of catching the malefactors. But they must simply not give in to the basic demands behind the blackmail. I have already discussed this in connection with the bombs which exploded in the night of 30 and 31 May last, and I repeat: there is nothing more disgusting than blackmail, except giving in to blackmail.

If one objects that there is a man's life at stake, it must be answered that terrorist philosophy does not burden itself with the lives of men, and that to give up now, would to be to commit oneself to pay the absolute price later on: thousands of lives and even the existence of the society, in which we live.[11]

Parti Québécois Reaction

When James Cross was kidnapped, René Lévesque argued in *Le Journal de Montréal* that an exchange of Cross for imprisoned terrorists should be arranged.[12] He continued to hold this view even after Laporte was kidnapped. However, in his *Memoirs*, years later, he did not discuss either this subject or the more general issue of what the effect of the release of convicted criminals would have had on future terrorist activity, let alone on democratic government. Lévesque's position was conceived on the spur of the moment, like many of his decisions throughout his public and private life, and apparently he had not consulted either the PQ leadership or the party's caucus in the National Assembly beforehand. On 12 October 1970, the Parti Québécois Executive Council issued a statement endorsing the release of "political prisoners" in return for guarantees as to the fate of Cross and Laporte.[13]

On 14 October, Lévesque was among the sixteen "eminent personalities" who signed a petition calling for the exchange of "political prisoners" for Cross and Laporte.[14] In the future, none of these individuals would comment on the effect of the petition on the FLQ kidnappers, or why released terrorists and others would not be encouraged to continue their kidnappings, which had been so successful up to that point; nor did any of them ever explain their motivation. Even on 18 October 1970, after the death of Laporte, the Parti Québécois, Claude Ryan, and the three main leaders of the Front Commun made another appeal for negotiations, again without explaining the potential consequence of such an exchange.[15]

As far as the Parti Québécois is concerned, the question needs to be asked: How did the party's leadership come to a decision different from that taken by the Quebec and federal governments and by the other opposition parties in the National Assembly? A partial answer to this question is that the leadership was not – nor could it have been – fully informed. It did not meet often or for long sessions together, as did the Bourassa cabinet, and it was divided geographically, as we have seen, between Lévesque in Montreal and the PQ caucus in the National Assembly in Quebec City. Further, the PQ leadership was inhibited, if not bound, by the positions that Lévesque took publicly not only on the exchange of prisoners but on every other question relating to the October Crisis.

On the evening of Friday, 16 October, the Executive Council of the Parti Québécois called for the unconditional release of Cross and Laporte, thus contradicting Lévesque and the other "eminent personalities."[16] However, the question of exchanging prisoners and the purpose of the petition were hardly addressed by the Parti Québécois in its 28 October eight-page, special edition of *Pouvoir*, the PQ magazine (500,000 copies of this issue were

printed). Here, the PQ focused on criticizing the use of the War Measures Act and asserting that Quebec alone was entitled to resolve a crisis
involving Quebec separation. Lévesque's and the party's position on the
exchange of prisoners was passed over lightly, while the consequences of
such a course of action were not mentioned at all.

The long debate on the October Crisis in the National Assembly on the
PQ's "motion d'urgence" continued from 11 November to 20 November.
In that whole time, only one person – Camille Laurin – proposed that the
government should have released prisoners, and he, as already noted, did
so in a single sentence in what was a very long speech.[17] Laurin declared:
"[The government] should have agreed to exchange the life of two hostages for the exile of the Front de Libération du Québec prisoners and then
track down, without mercy and by every means, terrorist organizations."[18]
He did not explain how, after releasing twenty-three convicted terrorists,
one could "track down without mercy and by every means" the remaining
FLQ members, let alone the twenty-three, who would not necessarily lead
exemplary lives after their release. No other PQ member of the National
Assembly even mentioned Laurin's argument.[19] Instead, they dwelt on the
War Measures Act and the effect of the October Crisis on the economy.

All in all, the Parti Québécois leadership, like the "eminent personalities" and most intellectuals, were nationalists who were sympathetic to
the aims of the FLQ and therefore had difficulty in criticizing the group's
methods, and, at the same time, they did not want to support the government. They therefore equivocated until it was too late.

The Duchaîne Report of 1981, commissioned by the Parti Québécois,
criticized the FLQ for its naive expectation that governments would have
no choice but to accept its demands.[20] Perhaps those who wanted us to
exchange prisoners for hostages were naive too.

The October Crisis Kidnappings in the International Context

Before the October Crisis, kidnappings for the release of political prisoners, and capitulation by governments in the face of this strategy, were not
uncommon. For example, in the Western Hemisphere alone, during the
first nine months of 1970, there were more than twelve kidnappings of
foreign diplomats and officials in Central and South America.[21] Yet the
release of "political prisoners" in exchange for hostages never stopped fur-

ther kidnappings or terror; on the contrary, it resulted in more kidnappings and more violence. In the case of Brazil, the West German ambassador to that country was kidnapped by terrorists in June 1969 and traded for forty political prisoners. In September of the same year, the U.S. ambassador to Brazil was kidnapped; later he was traded for fifteen prisoners.

Following the October Crisis, the vast majority of commentators, authorities, and newspapers throughout the world agreed with the Canadian and Quebec governments' position on the exchange of convicted terrorists for hostages. And, increasingly, other democratic regimes – and even despotic ones – refused to yield to terrorism. For instance, when the Swiss ambassador to Brazil was kidnapped in December 1970, "the Brazilian government followed the Canadian model ... [It] decided to modify its policy ... in order to end extortion of this type and despite its recognition of all the consequences of its decision. This was the opinion expressed in governmental and military circles, where for the first time, it was openly stated that the policy to accept terrorists' conditions was finished."[22]

One notable exception is Munich, Germany, in 1972. The Fedayeen ("men of sacrifice") were members of the Arab terrorist group Black September, a name used by Fatah (which, in turn, is an acronym, spelled backwards, for "Palestinian Liberation Movement"). At 4 a.m. on 5 September 1972, Black September, which was collaborating closely with the German Baader-Meinhof Gang, broke into the rooms of several Israeli athletes in the Olympic village apartments. After a struggle, they captured nine athletes; others were able to escape, while two athletes died defending themselves. The terrorists demanded the release of 234 prisoners held in both Israel and West Germany, including Ulrike Meinhof and Andreas Baader, the co-founders of the Baader-Meinhof Gang.

The Israeli prime minister, Golda Meir, held discussions with German Chancellor Willy Brandt, during which she declared her intention to not negotiate with the terrorists. The West Germans, after repeatedly negotiating the extension of the deadlines imposed by the terrorists, organized a rescue attempt at Fuhrstenfeldbruck Airport. The Israelis wanted to use their own agents for this operation, but their request was denied. The German police were not as well-trained as the Israeli Special Forces, and their rescue attempt failed when all nine prisoners were killed during the confrontation between the police and the terrorists. The police did manage to capture three of the terrorists, the others having died in the gunfire.

But even that small victory was short-lived: on 29 October the German government released these three terrorists when a plane was hijacked, thus demonstrating that, unlike Israel, it had been willing all along to negotiate with and grant major concessions to terrorists. Eventually, the West German government was to realize the folly of this strategy, since it led only to more kidnappings and more terrorism, and thereafter it refused to make deals with terrorists. The same was true of Italy.

Today, politically motivated kidnappings are rare in democratic countries but not in non-democratic ones (where there is often public sympathy for the kidnappers, because the governments themselves have been guilty of terrorism). In such countries, governments sometimes capitulate to terrorist demands, by exchanging prisoners for hostages or in other ways (such as paying ransom), only to find that the terrorism does not stop.

Conclusion

The decision not to exchange convicted terrorists for Cross and Laporte was the most difficult one I have ever been involved in. It was taken with great trepidation and yet seemed correct at the time and still seems correct today.

This is not to downplay the tragedy of Pierre Laporte's death. His murder was a brutal, senseless act that devastated his family and all of us who were closely involved in the events of October 1970, as well as many members of the public. It is hoped that later generations will understand that he still had much to contribute as a proven leader and an accomplished author and historian, one who was a witness to so many important events in Quebec and Canadian history.

Chapter 6

The Petition of 14 October 1970

The sublime and the ridiculous are so often so nearly related, that it is difficult to class them separately. One step above the sublime makes the ridiculous, and one step above the ridiculous makes the sublime again.

Thomas Paine (1737–1820)

On Wednesday, 14 October 1970, at 9:00 p.m., an astonishing petition, signed by sixteen persons, was distributed to the public at a press conference convened at the Holiday Inn on Sherbrooke St. West, Montreal. The conference was chaired by Claude Ryan and the petition was read by René Lévesque, in the presence of six other signatories.[1]

The signatories (known generally as "the sixteen eminent personalities" – a name probably given them by Marcel Pepin) – were René Lévesque, leader of the Parti Québécois; Alfred Rouleau, president of Assurance-vie Desjardins; Marcel Pepin, president of the Confédération des Syndicats Nationaux; Louis Laberge, president of the Fédération des Travailleurs du Québec; Jean-Marc Kirouac, president of the Union Catholique des Cultivateurs (UCC); Claude Ryan, editor and publisher of *Le Devoir*; Jacques Parizeau, president of the Executive Council of the Parti Québécois; Fernand Daoust, secretary general of the Fédération des Travailleurs du Québec; Yvon Charbonneau, president of the Corporation des Enseignants du Quebec (CEQ); Matthias Rioux, president of the Alliance des Professeurs de Montréal; Camille Laurin, leader of the Parti Québécois caucus in the National Assembly; Guy Rocher, professor of sociology at the Université de Montréal; Fernand Dumont, director of the Institut supérieur des sciences humaines at the Université Laval; Paul Bélanger, professor of political science at the Université Laval; Raymond Laliberté, past president of the Corporation des Enseignants du Quebec; and Marcel Rioux, professor of anthropology at the Université de Montréal.

The petition was published the next morning in *Le Devoir* with approximately 150 names attached. Apparently, it had been signed by 1,000 persons by the end of the next day, but those names were never revealed. Nor is it known how the signatures were obtained.

As to the petition's authorship, Jacques Parizeau suggested that it was Ryan who drafted the petition, while he (Parizeau) only organized the contacting of the signatories, using the telephones at the Parti Québécois headquarters. As Pierre Duchesne notes: "In the preparation of this petition, Jacques Parizeau played a secondary role. In fact, he was only the telephone operator (*standardiste*). 'The telephoning did not let up at all. I was at Party headquarters and it was as the President of the Executive, that I put everything together. The only thing I knew was that there was incredible telephone traffic during the day or two before they completed their plan.' Jacques Parizeau had the impression that it was Claude Ryan who directed the operation."[2]

The Petition's Text

There are several features of the petition that are worthy of comment. First, in calling for the release of Laporte and Cross in exchange for "political prisoners" – "we wish to give our most urgent support to negotiating an exchange of the two hostages for the political prisoners"[3] – the petition favoured the FLQ position that the two governments should act in compliance with terrorist demands. (Significantly, the next day, the petition was circulated by such FLQ members and supporters as Pierre Vallières, Charles Gagnon, Michel Chartrand, and Robert Lemieux.) Also striking is the petition's statement that the October Crisis was primarily a matter for Quebec to resolve: "The Cross-Laporte affair is above all a Quebec drama." This ignored the British North America Act of 1867, now renamed the Constitution Act, 1867. Sections 92(6), (14), (15), (16), and even (13) of that document give the provinces jurisdiction over the administration of justice within their boundaries, including the constitution and organization of provincial courts of both civil and criminal jurisdiction; the enforcement of provincial laws by fines; penalties and imprisonment; and the maintenance and management of provincial prisons. The federal government, however, under sections 91(27), (28), (29) and 96, has authority over criminal law and procedure; the appointment of superior, district, and county court judges; and federal penitentiaries (see chapter 19). In short, even the most cursory study of the law makes it evident that the immediate solution to the crisis fell within the jurisdiction, authority, and responsibility of both the federal and provincial governments.

The petition's argument was flawed in other respects as well. Its references to Ontario Premier John Robarts and to Ottawa's rigidity – "some outside commentaries, the last and most incredible of which is that of Premier Robarts of Ontario, adding to the virtual military atmosphere of rigidity that can be detected in Ottawa" – added nothing to the point being made. Indeed, one must ask whether the petitioners were really trying to save the lives of Cross and Laporte, as they declared, or attempting to promote Quebec sovereignty while taking a passing swing at Ontario and Ottawa. Further, far from encouraging calm, the petition itself was written in polemical and disputatious language. Finally, the signatories were not really representative of all of Quebec society, despite their declaration to that effect. They were all openly members of the Parti Québécois or had supported it in the last election, with the exception of Claude Ryan. There were no women and there were no businessmen, apart from Alfred Rouleau. Six were leaders of the Front Commun and a seventh, Raymond Laliberté, had also been a labour leader in the past, as head of the CEQ. Four signatories were academics. There were no lawyers or persons with legal training. The only lawyer listed among the 150 signatories the next day in *Le Devoir* was Richard B. Holden.

The Issue of Motivation

There are several unanswered questions regarding the petitioners' motivations. Why did the petitioners not approach the Quebec government before going public? Were they really trying to help the government when they addressed themselves to the people and the media at a press conference and then distributed the petition immediately for signatures and published it in *Le Devoir* the next morning? It is noteworthy that Lévesque began the press conference with the words "Quebec no longer has a government."[4] Did some of the petitioners perhaps hope to form a coalition government and expect that they would be part of it? Did they not realize, or did they subconsciously hope, that their petition would not help the Bourassa government but would rather make matters worse and thus would help the cause of a coalition government?

Jacques Parizeau offered this explanation for the petition: "'I think that it became evident in the minds of a number of people: if the government falls, we would take up the slack. But, I was not a party to these discussions. I spent a weekend putting them in contact with one another.'"[5] Marcel Rioux, another signatory, offered a different rationale: "A group of Quebec personalities, aware of a slight breach between the position of the Ottawa government and that of Quebec, decided to come to the aid of their government and to make a determined effort to save the lives of the two hostages."[6] This tidy explanation does not explain, of course, why the sixteen signatories, in calling for the exchange of hostages, referred to the FLQ as "political prisoners" and not as persons responsible for six violent deaths and over two hundred bombings. Nor does it shed any light on why the signatories did not unequivocally ask the FLQ to release Laporte and Cross but instead asked the government to negotiate with the terrorists.

The motivation of the labour leaders who signed the petition seems clear. The Front Commun, formed of the three large *centrales syndicales* (the FTQ, the CEQ, and the CSN), intended to bring the government down, or at least to force the Quebec and federal governments to recognize organized labour as an important player on the Quebec political scene. The union leaders thought that the petition would serve this larger purpose, but they were wrong. Instead of publicizing a political position, the petition put organized labour on the side not just of the Parti Québécois but of the terrorists as well and gave labour's support to the idea that a democratically elected government should recognize the legitimacy of terrorist kidnapping as a solution to political problems. As Marcel Pepin would write later: "I, like others, lived through the Crisis and played an active role. The FLQ, in my opinion, very much helped the 'right'; it very much slowed the rise of union power. We were at our peak and had, up to then, taken part in one of our toughest social battles, where our national goal was a more equal and more socially just society. Though we were progressives and, one could say, part of the 'left,' we were often assimilated to the FLQ."[7] In addition, the petition aligned labour with the middle class. Jean-François Cardin wrote: "This October 14th press conference will constitute the major event in the alliance of the central unions with the PQ and other representatives of the nationalist bourgeoisie."[8]

In retrospect, participating in the petition and embracing the position it espoused was a grave error by the leaders of the labour union movement. It aligned them with the intellectuals, the bourgeoisie, the Parti Québécois, and even with the FLQ. Today, the labour movement would dearly like to forget this episode. Thus many commentaries on the October Crisis that are written by persons sympathetic to organized labour speak little, or not at all, of the petition or its consequences for labour, for society, or for Cross and Laporte, concentrating instead on the War Measures Act.

As for the academics who signed the petition, on 20 October 1970 Fernand Dumont said: "For a reason which amounts with me to a principle (and which is the first criterion I apply to all these phenomena of violence), the means already determine the end. If you wish to liberate a people, you must use means that put liberty to work."[9] But, if "liberty" was a such an important "principle," a "first criterion," why did Dumont sign a petition which did not condemn the "violence" of the FLQ or ask unequivocally for the release of Cross and Laporte but instead condemned the action of the governments of Quebec, Ontario, and Canada, thereby giving comfort to terrorists whose cause was the weakening, if not the overthrow, of the Quebec government?

Marcel Rioux is a scholar who normally writes in measured terms. Yet, one year after the October Crisis he declared: "On Saturday, October 10, Quebec's Minister of Justice, Jérôme Choquette, *a lantern-jawed heavy-weight*, read a declaration, with the blessing of the government of Canada, to the effect that there would be no deals."[10] Why would Rioux resort to an ad hominen in respect of such an important matter? Was it because Choquette got it right and refused to submit to terrorist blackmail, while Rioux was one of those who publicly supported exchanging terrorists for Cross and Laporte?

The Petition's Critics

Claude Castonguay, the social affairs minister of the Bourassa government at the time of the October Crisis, said in a letter to the editor of *La Presse* on 4 May 2001:

The Federal Cabinet minutes of October 1970 also noted the petition of about fifteen personalities who had requested that 23 prisoners, said to be political, be liberated with the goal of saving Pierre Laporte and James Cross, who were being detained as hostages. This request was interpreted in Ottawa as an attempt to form a parallel provisional government. It seemed completely inadmissible to us in Quebec. Although it appeared necessary for us to negotiate with the kidnappers in order to save the two lives in question, it was clear that we could not yield to blackmail. This would have clearly been the case if we had yielded to the request to free the prisoners, who, for the most part, had committed crimes.

Far from worrying us, the gesture of the group of fifteen [sic] appeared to us as not being something deserving lengthy consideration. Besides, one needed a good dose of imagination to believe that Ottawa saw the petition as being an attempt to form a provisional government. At no time, in spite of the seriousness of the events, did I feel that our government felt itself threatened by the petition.[11]

The historian J.L. Granatstein, who at first opposed the imposition of the War Measures Act, wrote in 1998, after years of reflection, that the petition "called, in inflammatory language, on the Quebec government to negotiate 'an exchange between hostages and political prisoners.' The group and the document it produced were the inspirations of René Lévesque, the Parti Québécois leader who, while strongly condemning terrorism, had his own game to play in destabilizing Quebec and attacking Ottawa." Granatstein added that the "political prisoners" were in fact FLQ activists and hoodlums who had been jailed for their part in bombings in the 1960s.[12]

The Petition's Supporters

It is clear that both Robert Lemieux, negotiator for the FLQ, and the FLQ itself regarded the petition of the sixteen "eminent personalities" as a source of great support for their cause. The petition was distributed to the students who were striking and assembling in the CEGEPS and universities, and in fact it offered the main, if not the sole, support that the FLQ received from anyone in society other than the students, professors, intellectuals, and labour leaders who assembled on the night of 15–16 October 1970 in the Paul Sauvé Arena.

On Thursday evening, 15 October 1970, Robert Lemieux learned of the government's ultimatum giving the FLQ six hours to release Cross and Laporte in exchange for exile in Cuba or Algeria. *Le Soleil* reported Lemieux's reaction: "Such an attitude will only result in more deaths." The article continued:

Mr Lemieux expressed the opinion that "the government totally ignores the ten [sic] leaders of society (chefs de file) representing the quasi-totality of the workers of Quebec, who called for the liberation of the 23 political prisoners in order to save the life of Messrs. Cross and Laporte." The negotiator for the kidnappers was referring to the declaration of Messrs. Marcel Pepin, président of the CSN; Louis Laberge et Fernand Daoust, respectively president and secretary general of the FTQ; Yvon Charbonneau, president of the Corporation des enseignants du Québec; Jean-Marc Kirouac, president of the UCC; Claude Ryan, director of *Le Devoir*; Matthias Rioux, president of the Alliance des professeurs de Montréal; Alfred Rouleau, president of the Caisses populaires Desjardins; René Lévesque,

Camille Laurin, and Jacques Parizeau, respectively president, parliamentary leader, and treasurer of the Parti Québécois.

Mr Lemieux said he was astounded "that the government thus mocked these persons who represented 95% of those who provided the riches of production, of business and essential services in Quebec."[13]

In a similar vein, the Montreal *Gazette* declared on 16 October: "Front de Liberation du Quebec negotiator Robert Lemieux last night rejected Premier Bourassa's 'final offer' of parole for five 'political prisoners' in exchange for the lives of James R. Cross and Pierre Laporte."

"I urge the government to meet, not in the next few hours, but in minutes, and reconsider," he shouted.

At a hastily called press conference in Old Montreal shortly after the premier's offer was announced, Mr. Lemieux said the offer was "an incredible mockery."

"My mandate has ended," he said. "I have nothing more to say."

... In what he described as his last word on negotiations with the kidnappers "in response to a deteriorating situation," Premier Bourassa had issued a statement shortly after 9 p.m. in which he turned a deaf ear to most of the terrorists' demands.

Before making his withdrawal announcement, FLQ spokesman Lemieux named 10 [sic] leading Quebecers, who a day earlier, had appealed to the government to allow all 23 prisoners sought by the terrorists to go free, and said the Bourassa offer mocks their position and, through them, that of all Quebecers.[14]

Conclusions

In retrospect, I have reached two conclusions about the petition of 14 October 1970. First, it seems clear to me that the sixteen "eminent personalities" who signed the petition should have realized that if the Quebec government had exchanged terrorists for the hostages, as they suggested, the whole basis of government and justice in the province would have been imperiled and replaced by terrorist blackmail. In such a case, a provisional government might well have been necessary. Was that the subconscious rationale behind the petition? It could have been. Or, alternatively, perhaps the petitioners wanted only to weaken the government. Whatever the case, they were naive to believe that the terrorists would stop after two successful kidnappings.

The sixteen have been misleading, or silent, about the purpose of their petition, and they have not discussed fully why they did not unequivocally call on the FLQ to release Cross and Laporte, why they described the jailed FLQ members as "political prisoners," and what the consequences would have been if the government had complied with the terrorists' demands. Since October 1970, the sixteen have instead directed their comments towards the application of the War Measures Act, only rarely referring to the petition and never in any detail.

My second conclusion is that even if the sixteen were not hoping to serve in a provisional government, their petition nevertheless provided the principal intellectual support that the FLQ received. Much the same point is made by Léon Dion: "Words are weapons and, when used without precaution, they are even more dangerous perhaps than physical weapons because they corrupt men's minds which, once corrupted, prompt ever more unconsidered actions."[15] The words of the petition were indeed "weapons" and, having been "used without caution," were "even more dangerous perhaps than physical weapons, because they" corrupted the minds of the FLQ and their supporters, "which, once corrupted," could only "prompt ever more unconsidered actions."

We are left asking ourselves: what would have been the answer to Bourassa's final offer if the sixteen petitioners had called on the FLQ to release the hostages and accept exile outside Canada? What would have been the outcome if they had used their names and their prestige to support the democratically elected governments' refusal to exchange the two hostages for jailed terrorists? It is impossible to say for certain, but the questions are worth asking.

Chapter 7

Calling in the Army

It is necessary only for the good man to do nothing, for evil to triumph.

> Edmund Burke (1729–97)

L'armée est une nation dans la nation; c'est un vice de notre temps.

> Auguste Barthélemy (1796–1867)

While the Canadian public regards the use of the War Measures Act as central to the October Crisis of 1970, most of those living in Quebec at the time associate the crisis more with the presence of Canadian troops in the streets. Regardless of which event one chooses to emphasize, there needs to be a clear distinction drawn between the calling in of the Canadian army and the invoking of the War Measures Act. They were completely different measures, taken under different laws, at different times, in different manners, at the behest of different persons, and under different circumstances.

Decision and Reaction

When the federal government sent the army into the Ottawa region on 12 October 1970, the only person who seemed to have doubts was John Diefenbaker. The former prime minister's attitude was recorded in the minutes of the federal cabinet meeting held on 15 October, prepared by the secretary to the cabinet, Gordon Robertson, and is an example of Trudeau's wit, despite the tension of the moment. The minutes note that the prime minister had met the Conservative leader, Robert Stanfield, the NDP leader, Tommy Douglas, and Réal Caouette, leader of the Social Credit Party, to discuss special legislation under the War Measures Act and all had agreed. "As to Mr. Diefenbaker," whom Trudeau had also met, Robertson recorded: "It appeared that he was mainly objecting to the army wearing helmets in the federal capital and the Prime Minister suggested that perhaps they wear something else, at least in the sight of Mr. Diefenbaker."[1]

The Quebec government, for its part, called the army into Montreal on 15 October and "the movement of troops from Valcartier to St Hubert had started at 12:00 noon." The troops were sent at the request of Quebec in aid of the "civil power," as was the province's right under the National Defence Act.[2] Kendal Windeyer of the Montreal *Gazette* wrote: "Premier Robert Bourassa's call [to Ottawa] came in at exactly 2:00 p.m. and by 2:30 a 200-truck convoy was speeding down the Trans-Canada highway for Montreal carrying officers and men from the Royal 22nd Regiment."[3] About 1,000 troops in all were moved to Montreal. Windeyer reported: "'We aren't saying we usually move that fast,' an officer said last night in Montreal. 'We were ready for a few days.' 'Guard duty is now completely in the hands of the army,' a senior Quebec Provincial Police officer said wearily, but with relief. 'At least that gives us a few more men to work with.' The soldiers themselves seemed almost embarrassed about their new task. The few officers who could be reached continually emphasized that 'we are not here to take over. We are simply here to assist the civilian authorities – not give orders. We take our orders from the police.'"[4]

On 15 October 1970, at 3:07 p.m., the National Assembly convened and Bourassa announced that the Quebec government had called in the army. All three leaders of the opposition parties – the Union Nationale, the Crédit Social, and the Parti Québécois – rose in turn in the National Assembly and agreed with the decision. Camille Laurin, parliamentary leader of the Parti Québécois, stated:

Mr. President, the call that came from the premier was perfectly comprehensible and justified in the circumstance. I take this occasion to tell him that at this point the members of my group deplore the unhappy fate which befell one of our colleagues [Pierre Laporte] today, and the blow which it strikes to the institutions of Quebec.

I would also like to tell him that we share in the tribulation which has struck the Cabinet, as well as the Liberal Party. I would finally like to tell him that we hope that this crisis will know, in the briefest delay possible, a happy ending for our colleague, for the government and for all of Quebec.

This is the reason why we bow to the government's call and for our part, we will do everything to adopt the procedures which seem the most expedient in the circumstances.[5]

At that point Bourassa thanked the three parties and the members of the National Assembly for having supported the government in its decision to call in the army:

Mr. President, I would like to sincerely thank the three party leaders who have responded positively to my call. I believe that this in itself is already a significant gesture which will permit us to reconcile and to realize the two objectives of which I talked earlier, that is to say, to not open the way to anarchy and to safeguard two human lives, one of whom is particularly precious to us, in a special way, a colleague, a parliamentary leader and for whom I believe, all members, without exception, have an unquestionable and real regard.

The horrible trial which has come to him, and which could come to anyone of us, certainly shows in itself the deterioration of the state in Quebec. That is why we must take legitimate measures, in the circumstances, to end this deterioration.

Once again, my thanks to the three party leaders and to all the members for their collaboration, in the circumstances.[6]

Two hours later, however, Camille Laurin, clearly under pressure from Parti Québécois riding associations and René Lévesque, declared that he had been misunderstood and that he opposed bringing in the army. *Le Devoir* reported: "On listening to the various radio stations, it is clear that militant Péquistes have rapidly made known their displeasure with the first declaration made by their representative in the National Assembly. Presidents of approximately twenty PQ associations in the Montreal area have, at once, begun circulating a petition requesting a meeting with the National Council for Sunday, in order to force the parliamentary leader to explain himself."[7] The Montreal *Gazette*'s Richard Cléroux reported from the National Assembly: "A spokesman for Dr. Laurin's office said later that Dr. Laurin had been commenting in the National Assembly on the government's three amendments to the Medicare legislation, not on calling on the army ... However, the spokesman's explanation didn't cut much ice with veteran observers here ... The spokesman denied Parti Québécois leader René Lévesque, who is in Montreal, had ordered Dr. Laurin to reverse his stand."[8] On 30 October, René Lévesque reversed himself and again undercut Laurin, declaring that calling in the army had been the right decision. "The army occupies Quebec. It is disagreeable but without a doubt necessary in moments of crisis."[9]

Neither Laurin nor any other Parti Québécois member raised the question of calling in the army during the debate on the October Crisis held from 11 to 20 November 1970 in the National Assembly. The seven PQ members spoke at length on the *motion d'urgence* but dealt only with the state of the economy and the War Measures Act.

Except for the PQ, the decision to call in the army met with general approval. Claude Ryan wrote in *Le Devoir*:

The police forces, on alert for nearly two weeks, are on the edge of exhaustion. The new problems caused by the recent tactics of the FLQ have multiplied the work, lengthened the days, and obliged the forces of law and order to stay continually on alert.

Before the call to go to the streets sent out by Mr. Robert Lemieux and his friends, the Quebec government, remembering the experiences of the last few years, considered that they had to call upon the assistance of the armed forces. It was right to do so. They would have failed in their duty by acting otherwise.[10]

Similarly, Gilles Boyer of *Le Soleil* stated in an editorial written on 15 October 1970: "The decision of the Bourassa government to call in the army, to Quebec and to Montreal, is justified in the circumstances. It is less a question of repressing a real insurrection (but one which could be apprehended) than of lending a strong hand, with federal assistance, to the police forces in the province. The armed forces, especially since the kidnapping of both Mr. Cross and Mr. Laporte, have become a continuation of the police forces, which are faced with an emergency situation, or a situation which could become one."[11]

On 14 October 1970 Trudeau described the army personnel as additional peace officers: "We have not taken action against the FLQ, as though it was a question of war. We have used certain elements of the army as peace officers so that the police forces would be free to accomplish their real duties and would not be obliged to spend their time protecting your friends from another kidnapping. I believe that it is more important to rid ourselves of those who seek to impose their will on the government through a parallel power which resorts to kidnapping and extortion. I consider that it is our duty as a government to protect members of the government and important members of our society from those who make use of such forms of extortion."[12]

Jean-François Duchaîne wrote in his 1981 report on the October Crisis:

In the meantime, the Quebec Cabinet had declared the situation critical and all the forces of law and order in the province of Quebec were placed under the direction of Mr. Maurice Saint-Pierre, director general of the Sûreté du Québec. When the War Measures Act was invoked by the federal government on October 16th in response to the letters of the provincial government and Montreal municipal authorities, the powers of Mr. Saint-Pierre were increased again, since in accordance with the application of the Act, he could order any man under his command to detain anyone or to search anywhere without a warrant, when it was judged necessary.

The Armed Forces that were used in Quebec, although receiving their orders down through the normal military hierarchical chain, were in fact directed by the civil authorities, through intermediaries of the director general of the Sûreté du Québec, acting in the name of the Minister of Justice. All the tasks assigned to the soldiers were only granted at the request of Mr. Saint-Pierre. And when the Armed Forces were called to support a police operation (a clean-up or a raid), only Mr. Saint-Pierre was authorized to officially make the request to the Armed Forces. To avoid delays, he delegated his powers to two high-ranking officials in the force, Assistant Director General Descent and Division Inspector Benoît. The Armed Forces, then, did not act on orders from their own chief; throughout the crisis, they remained under the control of the public authorities. In the circumstances, a close connection had to be maintained between the army and the police forces, particularly the Sûreté du Québec ...

On 4 January 1971, Operation 'Essai' was officially ended and the army withdrew, the Minister of Justice of Quebec having requested Ottawa to put an end to the intervention of the Armed Forces in its territory.[13]

The Army's Conduct

During the October Crisis, the Canadian troops effectively fulfilled the modern role of peacekeepers – in this case, in their own country. There were no incidents whatsoever as the result of their presence: the soldiers acted with circumspection, calm, and dignity during their whole period of duty, which ran from 15 October 1970 to 4 January 1971. Claude Ryan summed it up thus: "The presence of the armed forces in Quebec is all the more acceptable in that, on the whole, the military who for many weeks assured the protection of political leaders, buildings, and public places, have generally conducted themselves in an honorable manner. In addition to our personal observations, we have received the views on this subject from a number of other witnesses. All agree that the soldiers who are presently in service in Quebec have exhibited an exemplary conduct, discipline, and genuine cordiality which has won them the sympathy of the citizenry."[14] In fact, the population at large welcomed the army warmly when it arrived and commended it when it left.

Claude Ryan noted another remarkable fact about the Canadian army's presence – no public declarations were made by the army officers or troops: "We equally remarked that during this long crisis, no military leader has let slip the slightest statement which might have aggravated matters. Those in charge of the armed forces have, on the contrary, observed an exemplary discretion, such that we have almost forgotten that they must be somewhere on hand. We take, from this extraordinary sojourn of soldiers amongst us, that a delicate and explosive task has been accomplished with tact and efficiency and that their leaders were surely not strangers to this performance."[15]

Conclusion and Postscript

Although the Quebec government called in the army on 15 October 1970, the application of the War Measures Act was not requested by the city of Montreal until that same day, or by the Quebec government until the following day. Many commentators miss this point. For example, Hugh Segal, usually a most level-headed person, does not realize that the army had already been called in when the War Measures Act was invoked. He wrote in 1996: "The War Measures Act was not the only vehicle available to authorities. Marshal [sic] law could have been imposed. The army could have been invited in, as it was in Oka when the police were clearly overwhelmed."[16] And in his memoirs, published in 1986, René Lévesque confused the calling in of the army, which took place on 15 October 1970 at the request of Bourassa alone, with the request by Drapeau and Bourassa for the application of the War Measures Act on 16 October 1970. "That's the only excuse [general unrest in Quebec], if it is one, that can be found, for Jean Drapeau and Robert Bourassa reaching the point of calling for the military occupation of Quebec."[17]

One may conclude that calling in the Canadian army was the proper course to take and its effect was beneficial. The presence of the army reassured the public and freed up the police to do police work, while the officers and men of the military acted in an exemplary fashion. There were no cases of the armed forces acting badly towards the public or of the public acting badly towards them.

Everyone living in Montreal during the October Crisis has an army story. In my own home, we had two soldiers living with us. They were polite and cheerful. They sat on our large front porch and, for exercise or in order to relieve the boredom, would march endlessly around the house. Eventually, their boots wore a deeply packed groove in the lawn which encircled the house, like one of those ancient Indian trails which are still visible hundreds of years after their use has ended and which have been now declared national heritage sites. I once thought of trying to preserve the path for posterity, but unfortunately, in a year or so, it had been wiped out by my erratic gardening.

Chapter 8

Apprehended Insurrection

Liberty, too, must be limited in order to be possessed.

Edmund Burke (1729–97)

Le bonheur de l'homme n'est pas dans la liberté, mais dans l'acceptation d'un devoir.

André Gide (1869–1951)

Liberty means responsibility. That is why most men dread it.

George Bernard Shaw (1856–1950)

W hat caused the city of Montreal and the government of Quebec to call upon the government of Canada to declare a state of appre-hended insurrection under the War Measures Act on 16 October 1970? Of course, it must be understood that the War Measures Act *at that time* could be used in only three circumstances: war, insurrection, or *appre-hended insurrection*. The act has since been repealed (see chapter 9).

Was there an *apprehended* insurrection? I believe that there was and in consequence the application of the act on 16 October 1970 was the proper course, that its effect was beneficial, and that we acted just in time.

The Background

Gérard Pelletier has graphically described the social and political temper of Quebec from 1963 to 1970, a period of leftist demonstrations leading to confrontations and violence.[1] Similarly, Louis Fournier, in his detailed chronology of the October Crisis from 1962 to 1970, gives example after example of violent demonstrations in Montreal.[2] Here are a few:

- In 1966, 2,000 people marched against the jailing of Pierre Vallières for the murder of Thérèse Morin. The march ended in violence and vandalism.
- In 1968 the Mouvement de libération du taxi (MLT) organized a demonstration against the Murray Hill Limousine Company's monopoly on taxi service from Dorval Airport. The result again was violence and vandalism.
- On Saint-Jean-Baptiste Day (24 June), 1968, a demonstration against the prime minister of Canada, Pierre Trudeau, turned into a riot (known as the *Lundi de la Matraque*). The result was 250 injured and 292 arrests.
- On 7 October 1969, when the Montreal police were on an illegal strike, the MLT again demonstrated violently in front of the head office of the Murray Hill Limousine Company. Security guards of the company fired into the crowd, killing a plainclothes police-man, Corporal Robert Dumas of the Sûreté du Québec. There were dozens of injuries. The army was dispatched to Montreal.
- In October 1969 there were province-wide demonstrations against Bill 63, the Union Nationale government's language law, orga-

nized by the Front du Québec français. On 31 October 1969 in Montreal, the last demonstration took place. The result was about forty wounded and seventy arrests.

- On 7 November 1969 a demonstration called *Opération Libération*, in favour of releasing Vallières and Gagnon from jail, resulted in "fire bombs at City Hall, at the headquarters of the Montreal police and against the banks."[3]

After the Kidnappings

After the kidnapping of Cross, and especially after the kidnapping of Laporte, the *débrayages* (walkouts) of students, *décrocheurs* (student dropouts), teachers, professors, young PQ members, and other FLQ sympathizers were increasingly disruptive and played into the hands of the FLQ. The closing of CEGEPS and UQAM and some Université de Montréal faculties on 15 October left students and others free to take the next step – marches, riots, and confrontations with the police and the Canadian Armed Forces.[4]

On 14 October, at 10:30 a.m., Lemieux, Vallières, and Gagnon read the 1970 manifesto to social-science students at UQAM. As reported in *La Presse*:

Lemieux encourages the students to support the FLQ; a committee wants to organize a walkout. It is not impossible that demonstrations in the street – like those which took place during the presentation of Bill 63 – and gigantic assemblies will be organized by the end of the weekend. It will be a way for everyone who sympathizes with the FLQ to take part. It will not, however, be before the end of the morning that one will definitely know what the students intend to do during the coming hours.

Charles Gagnon endorsed Lemieux's suggestion in requesting that they organize effectively, so that the government finally sees the real parallel power, that of the Quebec people.[5]

Even Eric Bédard, who downplays the "apprehended insurrection," notes that on the morning of 15 October, UQAM students adopted resolutions supportive of the FLQ and occupied two university buildings.[6]

By evening (15 October 1970), matters had so progressed that 3,000 people in the Paul Sauvé Arena endlessly shouted "FLQ, FLQ, FLQ!" As reported by Lysiane Gagnon in *La Presse*: "Last night, at Paul Sauvé Arena, an assembly of some 3,000 people overtly demonstrated their support for the FLQ, shouting the name of the movement and vigorously applauding Pierre Vallières, Charles Gagnon, Robert Lemieux, and Michel Chartrand. It was as if for this crowd, mostly made up of students and youth but where one also found a rather large number of older people, the word 'FLQ' had suddenly ceased being taboo."[7]

After the crisis was over, some critics of the use of the War Measures Act spoke lightly of the violence that had been building before October 1970. For example, George Bain, in December 1970, referred to "scattered other acts of violence which the Front de Liberation du Québec has been known to have committed during the past seven or eight years."[8] Bain seemed to have forgotten the campaign of terror that the FLQ had waged since its founding in 1963.

I take a different view from Bain. Given the climate of unrest at the time – as well as the fact that, although the FLQ's strength and resources were unknown to the police or to governments, there was considerable evidence of a build-up that, it was thought, could lead only to even greater violence than had already occurred – I believe that there was sufficient reason for the federal government to invoke the War Measures Act. Authors George Radwanski and Kendal Windeyer agree:

On the evidence available ... it appears that recourse to the Act was not only justifiable, but wise in the circumstances. The federal government is empowered by the terms of the Act to invoke it not only in time of war, but also in the face of "a state of insurrection, whether real or apprehended." In the days following Pierre Laporte's kidnapping, there was every reason to apprehend an uprising against the constitutional governments of Quebec and Canada. In addition to the sheer audacity of the blow against a top-ranking minister, there were other signs of a deteriorating situation – support for the FLQ among students and radical labor groups was growing to the point where it might spill over into the streets, the terrorists had threatened to begin a program of selective assassinations, and the general confusion was so advanced that some of Quebec's most prominent citizens were at least theorizing about the creation of a provisional government.[9]

Anthony Westell is of the same opinion: "By the middle of the second week, it was a reasonable judgement, although not by any means certain beyond doubt, that riots could explode in the streets, leading to more violence and a further decay in democratic authority. The War Measures Act was a rough but effective way to cool the situation by taking possible agitators and FLQ sympathizers out of circulation and by assuring the populace that the Governments had firm control."[10] A third witness, Gérard Pelletier, a liberal, rational man who was secretary of state in Trudeau's cabinet at the time of the October Crisis, also believed that there was an apprehended insurrection. "As to the seriousness of the threat that hung over Montreal between the 12th and the 15th of October, one would have had to blind oneself deliberately not to perceive it."[11]

The Case for Using the War Measures Act

When Bourassa announced that his government had decided to ask the federal government to invoke the War Measures Act, *La Presse* carried this story:

The premier of Quebec, Mr. Robert Bourassa, declared yesterday that his government had asked Ottawa for the application of the War Measures Act because he believed that the members of the FLQ were at the point of putting into operation the fourth step of their terrorism plan, namely selective assassination.

Mr. Bourassa added that the police authorities had convinced the Council of Ministers that their struggle with the Front de libération du Québec would be ineffective if they did not obtain extraordinary powers of arrest and search.

"It is with enormous reluctance that the government decided to resort to the measures of the last few hours (calling in the army and the application of the War Measures Act)," said the premier. He well understands the implications of these decisions, but the successive actions taken by the FLQ – violent demonstrations, bombings, kidnappings – left him only one choice, if he did not wish to forsake his mandate as leader of a democratically elected government.

Mr. Bourassa said he is morally convinced that the escalation observed for the last three years will be pursued until the complete execution of the terrorism plan disclosed in the document given by the FLQ to the authorities on the occasion of Mr. James Cross's kidnapping, nearly two weeks ago.

The fourth and final phase of this plan consists of selective assassination. According to reliable information, Mr. Pierre Elliott Trudeau, Mr. Jean Drapeau and Mr. Robert Bourassa figure at the top of the list of eventual FLQ targets.

The Quebec premier "believes and hopes that the emergency measures will only be applied for a restricted period."

"Everything will depend on the results of police action," said Mr. Bourassa. "It is a matter of dismantling a small group of several hundred people or more. The population accepted these exceptional measures with an exemplary calm and there is every reason to be optimistic."

Asked about the possibility that more severe measures could be implemented, the premier responded that "the extraordinary powers given to the police are actually considerable and that he does not believe it necessary that one day they will have to be increased."

Mr. Bourassa refused to give any details concerning either the information that the Sûreté du Québec furnished him to help him decide whether to ask for the emergency measures; or on the effectiveness of the police action.

... It was at about 2:55 yesterday morning that Mr. Bourassa sent a written request to the Canadian Government that "emergency powers" should be granted to the police forces of Quebec.

The Quebec cabinet, at the same time, adopted an order-in-council to put into application the emergency powers provided for in the Provincial Police Act and to confer on the director general of the Sûreté du Québec the command of all the police forces in Quebec.

The soldiers of the Canadian army posted in Montreal and Quebec are equally dependent upon the direction of the director general of the SQ.

Questioned as to whether it was at the request of the federal government that the Quebec government made its request for emergency powers, Mr. Bourassa retorted that he had done it in an "absolutely, totally and completely free" manner.

"The Quebec government," affirmed Mr. Bourassa, "has until now kept complete control of all operations and we started to do so on Thursday afternoon (with the call for the support of the army). We then asked for certain emergency powers to increase the effectiveness of police action and we waited until last night before acting. And it is we who adopted this position. It is not a question of the Quebec government losing control of operations."

Yet, the Minister of Finance, Mr. Raymond Garneau, who also met with the parliamentary journalists yesterday at Parliament, was a little more talkative and let it be understood that the number of the terrorists ready and able to move into action could be more than one hundred, but without a doubt less than 200. Mr. Garneau did not indicate however, how many cells of FLQ members were prepared to act.[12]

Subsequently, on Thursday, 12 November 1970, during an emergency debate in the National Assembly, Robert Bourassa again set out the reasons for the invoking of the War Measures Act. After citing the mounting demonstrations and the risk of anarchy, he continued:

The third reason, Mr. President, for our decision on Thursday night and on Wednesday evening, were the previous four days of negotiations and daytime demonstrations. How long should the police forces be required to work with one hand behind their back? For days they had been preparing to exercise the powers necessary in order to face a force of terrorism without precedent in North America. And it was the Government of Quebec which restrained the police by all possible means, to avoid all signs of provocation.

These reasons, Mr. President, added to the others which are already known, being the four-step plan which was made public by Mr. Saulnier: violent demonstrations, bombs, kidnapping and selective assassinations. It is true that some people were sceptical; Mr. Saulnier himself admitted that several Quebecers could not believe that such a plan could be conceived in Quebec, by Quebecers, with the freedom of expression that we know. We are the only country in the world, in the history of the world, which permits complete freedom of expression to a party which wishes to destroy the regime. It is a fact that we are one of the only countries which freely allows a party, with all the means it possesses, to destroy the regime. We could not conceive that persons in our society would resort to violent means, to terrorist methods.

But Mr. President, the three steps had been taken. We had had violent demonstrations. We had had bombs. We had had kidnappings.

What could have been the Quebec government's position? What could have been the rational position, the responsible position of the Quebec government in the circumstances? To cross our arms? To wait for more kidnappings? To wait for selective assassinations? What was our essential responsibility, our first responsibility? It would have been unpardonable not to have acted in the circumstances.

And as for the timing, Mr. President, set out above are the reasons which justify, in my view, the government's action.[13]

In the same debate, Justice Minister Jérôme Choquette offered this defence of the imposition of the War Measures Act:

The regulations, which went into force on October 16, 1970 and which concerned public order and the detention of many noisy FLQ sympathizers, had many results:

Firstly, the breaking up of a partially improvised plan or strategy, if one may so describe it, of propaganda, of demonstrations, and of cries of alarm, intended to disorganize society and the state.

Secondly, the forcing of terrorists into clandestinity.

Thirdly, the calming, temporarily at least, of the students and other movements sympathetic with the manifesto, because the FLQ had now become illegal.

Fourthly, the seizing of large quantities of firearms and dynamite.

Fifthly, the finding of proof of acts of insurrection and terrorism, as well as information on terrorist activities.

We learned, Saturday evening, October 17th, of the murder of Pierre Laporte. Communiqué number 6 of the Chénier cell announced that the execution had been done by the Dieppe cell. Following that, further communications announced the arrival on the scene of other FLQ cells.

Nearly all the newspapers of the world supported the position adopted by the Government. Even a paper such as Rudé Právo of Prague disapproved of terrorist action in Quebec. The only exceptions were one newspaper in Algeria and Le Devoir. Even Lord Hume, Minster of British Government Affairs, expressed – I saw it in a November 13 paper – his approval of the attitude of the Canadian and Québécois Governments and, yet, James Cross is a British Diplomat.[14]

Such was the government's case, and, in my view, it was a strong one. I accept all of its elements, particularly the claim that the police needed help. By the night of 15–16 October, the police were exhausted trying to maintain order and did not have sufficient forces to continue their search for Cross and Laporte. A city of Montreal letter to Prime Minister Trudeau, dated 15 October and signed by Mayor Jean Drapeau and Executive Committee Chairman Lucien Saulnier, spoke of "apprehended insurrection" and included a letter of the same date from Marcel Saint-Aubin, director of the Montreal Police Department.[15] The latter read:

The threat to our society of this seditious conspiracy and the incredible amount of checking and searching imposed upon us have taxed and are taxing to the utmost the resources available to our police department.

The extreme urgency of obtaining concrete results in uncovering all the ramifications of this organization and its seditious activities, the volume and complexity of evidence to be gathered and filed and finally the enormous task we must carry out without resorting to unhealthy and undesirable repression make it essential for higher levels of government to come to our assistance if we are to succeed.

The arrival of Canadian soldiers, the day before, eased the police's burden. But it was also thought, with good reason, that the War Measures Act – by enabling known FLQ members and supporters to be arrested – would permit the police to investigate other known or suspected *felquistes* and thereby, it was hoped, lead them to Cross and Laporte. This is the view that both governments took, and I subscribed to it fully.

Invoking the War Measures Act had another beneficial result. The written and electronic press was not controlled by the War Measures Act Regulations, except that it could not promote the FLQ or its aims, which none or very few were doing in any event. Yet the effect of the War Measures Act was to cause much of the press to act with calm and discretion for the first time. The importance of this should not be underestimated. Key to the FLQ strategy, as seen in its document *Stratégie révolutionnaire et rôle de l'avant-garde*, written by Pierre Vallières in 1968 and known to the authorities, though not released publicly until some time in November 1970,[16] is the idea that kidnappings would result in a *débrayage*, which in turn would lead to an insurrection and the overthrow of the government. Jean-Paul Desbiens, in his far-sighted editorial in *La Presse* on 6 October, the day after Cross's kidnapping, wrote: "The main thing is to keep calm. Nobody can win over people who are not so inclined. The terrorists' strength depends on an understanding with the people. There is no such understanding here. There will be more acts of terrorism, but it will not take root among our people. It is still a marginal phenomenon."[17] The War Measures Act calmed the students and the sixteen "eminent personalities." It jailed the instigators of the student demonstrations, Vallières, Gagnon, Chartrand, and Lemieux. And it calmed the press, which was in no way affected in its work.

Of course, by invoking the War Measures Act, governments were, in a sense, playing into the FLQ's hands. As with all terrorist groups, the FLQ strategy of bombings, armed robberies, murders, and finally kidnappings was intended to cause democratically elected governments to use force and, in doing so, to suspend civil rights. But was there any other choice? I think not. Bourassa said at a press conference after the crisis: "The Quebec government had only one choice to make in the face of the Crisis: to do nothing or to resort to measures which perhaps exceeded the extent of the situation." Jean Pellerin made the same point in *La Presse* on 19 October 1970:

The moment has come for each individual to ask himself if it is preferable to let the FLQ continuously assault our civil rights or to accept that the government should suspend their rights temporarily. There is much said about the trap being laid by the terrorists. But the government says it is quite aware of these traps. Prime Minister Trudeau himself has reminded us that revolutionary groups seek to provoke authorities into hard-line positions in order to justify their own violence. To prove that it has not fallen into that trap, the government must ensure that the emergency measures will only be applied for a short period. It cannot be denied that the present measures are a threat to civil liberties. We cannot, on the other hand, forget that these measures were not imposed by a repressive government but were rendered necessary by the acts of extremists.[18]

How Many Persons Can Create an Insurrection?

To those who say that the FLQ was far too small an organization to provoke an insurrection, a simple question needs to be asked: How many people does it take to bring about an insurrection? Consider what happened at the meeting of the World Trade Organization in Quebec City in 2002. At that time, the central part of the city was turned into a camp surrounded by barbwire and hundreds of troops and special police. Nevertheless, less than forty violent protestors were able to attract broad support and spark confrontations, all of which led to considerable property damage. Similar demonstrations involving the anti-globalization movement have been turned violent by a small core of organized participants. And these are cases where governments were aware of the protesters' plans months in advance and yet were unable to prevent them from causing havoc.

In October 1970, of course, we had no such foreknowledge of the FLQ's intentions. Radwanski and Windeyer describe the dilemma we then faced: "The government didn't know exactly where the frantic pace of events might lead; it knew only that the picture was growing uglier by the hour and that the possible consequences of inaction were far more grave than those of drastic measures unnecessarily taken. It decided, therefore, to clamp a lid on the whole mess and sort things out later."[19]

Just as an insurrection can be achieved by a relatively small number of people; so can a revolution. One example is Cuba, where Fidel Castro began with a band of 81 men. In 1956 this small group of fighters disembarked from a yacht in Oriente province and, within a month, had been reduced to twelve. Nevertheless, Castro managed to fight off 30,000 troops loyal to President Fulgencio Batista and trained by the Americans, and by 1958 he had 1,000 men and 7,000 clandestine urban guerrillas, a force with which he was soon to mount a revolution that succeeded in overthrowing the government.[20] And, even when revolutionary terrorist movements do not succeed in their ultimate objectives, they can be enormously destructive, as evidenced by the experiences of Northern Ireland and Spain. Were the governments of Canada and Quebec in October 1970 right to fear the worst and to take steps to guard against it? I believe so.

How many members did the FLQ have in October 1970? How many more were sympathizers who would have aided the FLQ members and its activities? How many would have carried messages, assisted and hidden FLQ members wanted by the police, not advised the police of the activities of *felquistes* or their whereabouts, and demonstrated or rioted on their behalf or for the FLQ cause? As noted in chapter 3, there were at least 180 such persons, who certainly were a large enough group to constitute a significant threat.

In any case, it is the responsibility of government officials to make decisions and take action based on the information they have at the time. The role of those in government, who must make decisions and act quickly and decisively based on the facts available, is not an easy one. Governing is deciding and for that reason there are armchair politicians, on the one hand, and active politicians, on the other. Active politicians assume the risks of office and the possibility of blame for error, failure, or delay, while armchair politicians give their views after the fact, without risk or consequences. Only occasionally do such persons dare to take responsibility and rarely do they ever hold elected office. At the time of the October Crisis, Secretary of State Gérard Pelletier, an intellectual who had nevertheless been a participant in the Asbestos strike and who in 1970 was an elected politician and a minister, believed he had good reasons to be concerned about what was happening in Quebec. He later wrote:

It is known that the probabilities of rapid deterioration in the social climate are greater in a period of crisis than in a period of calm. In 1969, at the same season of the year, the political and social situation in the province was relatively serene. Suddenly the police went on strike, and less than twelve hours later there was rioting, looting, the theft of hundreds of firearms (a theft attributed to the FLQ) and the death of one man.

...

One of my sharpest fears [in October 1970] ... was that a group of extremist students, believing the great day had come, would go out into the streets and create disturbances which, with the police and the army exhausted, might have ended in shooting. I perhaps yielded to a tendency towards alarmism: yet this kind of scenario has already been played out too often to make it necessary to argue for its plausibility.[21]

Pelletier also explained that, if we had equivocated in the face of the FLQ in October 1970, the consequences might have been dire. In this respect, he likened the politician's role to that of a surgeon: "it is not a lighthearted decision for a doctor to submit a patient to a delicate operation of whose possible complications he is very well aware. Nevertheless, if he is reasonably certain of his diagnosis he has no choice, and delay might well cause a fatal worsening of the illness."[22]

Finally, what exactly is an *apprehended* insurrection? On this point, I offer an analogy drawn from international maritime law, a subject I have taught, written on, and practised for many years. The purpose of the International Rules of the Road for Ships at Sea is to avoid ship collisions by requiring ships to, among other things, keep to starboard (the right-hand side) and to travel at a reasonable speed. International Rule 7 was changed in 1972 from compelling ships "to avoid collision" to compelling ships "to avoid a *risk* of collision." Similarly, since 1992, under the international law in respect of oil pollution at sea, a ship's officers must now act not only to avoid pollution at sea but to avoid "*the threat* of causing such damage."

In the same way, the War Measures Act wisely did not require an insurrection in order to act, but only an *apprehended* insurrection. And we acted.

Conclusion

The evidence in October 1970 pointed to an *apprehended* insurrection. It is also clear that the two governments, faced with risk of insurrection, would have been exceedingly unwise, if not dangerously irresponsible, if they had not imposed the War Measures Act Regulations on the morning of 16 October 1970. The Regulations had been carefully drafted for the situation and contained nothing that was not already in the Criminal Code.

The use of the War Measures Act snuffed out the FLQ demonstrations, which were intended to lead to confrontation and violence. Afterwards, there was no violence and no property damage (not a window broken), which was in striking contrast to the Saint-Jean-Baptiste riot of 1968, the police strike of 7 October 1969, the demonstrations over Bill 63 on 31 October 1969, and Opération Libération on 7 November 1969. It is important to appreciate as well that FLQ members were important participants, if not central players, in the above four riots, all of which took place in the two years before the October Crisis. The FLQ had plans for 16 October 1970, but it was thwarted just in time. Had we not acted, we would have been very heavily criticized by those who are criticizing us now.[23]

| Chapter 9 | # The War Measures Act and the Alternatives |

Faced with what is right, to leave undone shows a lack of courage.

Confucius

Much criticism has been directed at the federal government and the government of Quebec for the application of the War Measures Act in October 1970, but without any examination of the alternatives – if indeed there were any. The purpose of this chapter is to evaluate those alternatives. First, however, the intricacies of the War Measures Act itself must be explained.

A Brief History of the War Measures Act

The precursors of the Canadian War Measures Act were two United Kingdom statutes of 1914, entitled the Defence of the Realm Act, 1914 (4 & 5 Geo. 5, c. 29) and the Defence of the Realm (No. 2) Act, 1914 (4 & 5 Geo. 5, c. 63). The first Canadian War Measures Act was adopted in 1914 (5 Geo. 5, c. 2) and was similar to the U.K. acts. There were minor modifications in style to the Canadian Act in 1914 and 1927. In 1960, however, an important modification to the Act took place in order to exempt it from the provisions of the Canadian Bill of Rights (S.C. 1960, c. 44, s. 6).

By the time of the October Crisis of 1970, the War Measures Act (R.S.C. 1970, chap. W-2) provided for the proclamation of a state of "war," "insurrection," or "apprehended insurrection," as well as specific public-order regulations which afforded law-enforcement officials considerable powers and placed those powers in a single document.

On 5 November 1970 Parliament adopted in second reading (approval in principle) the Public Order (Temporary Measures) Act, 1970, which brought the application of the War Measures Act to an end and replaced the original regulations issued under that act (the vote was 152–1, the sole negative vote being cast by David MacDonald, the MP for Egmont, Prince Edward Island). Often called the "Turner Law," after Minister of Justice John Turner, the new Public Order (Temporary Measures) Act (S.C. 1970, c. 2) received royal assent on 3 December 1970 and was to remain in force until 30 April 1971. It was designed to be a more effective and humane instrument than the War Measures Act that had been invoked during the October Crisis. Under its provisions, the attorney general of a province could detain a person without charge for only seven days instead of the eleven days provided for under the old act.

In 1988 the War Measures Act was repealed and replaced by the Emergencies Act (S.C. 1988, c. 29). This act refers to a "public welfare emergency"

(s. 5) and a "national emergency" (s. 3), rather than an "apprehended insurrection." Any declaration of emergency under the Emergencies Act must be reviewed by Parliament, and any temporary legislation passed under the act must comply with the Canadian Charter of Rights and Freedoms.

The National Defence Act must be distinguished from the War Measures Act. It was the National Defence Act (R.S.C. 1970, c. N-4) that, on 15 October 1970, permitted Quebec to call in the Canadian army, while the War Measures Act Regulations were proclaimed by Ottawa at the request of Quebec and the city of Montreal on 16 October 1970. In particular, "Aid of the Civil Power," Part XI of the National Defence Act, allowed provincial authorities to request military assistance. In the event of a crisis, such as the October Crisis or, later, the Oka stand-off in 1990, the attorney general of a province could request military assistance under section 235. The chief of the defence staff would then determine, by virtue of section 236, the force that would be sent out in response. The army, in this situation, would act only to aid the civil authorities – it would not act on its own.

In the case of the October Crisis, the army came in to help an overworked, overstretched police force. Even when the War Measures Act Regulations were proclaimed on 16 October 1970, the Canadian armed forces could exercise only the same powers as those of the police, and they were, at all times, under the control of civil authorities.

The proclamation of a "state of apprehended insurrection" and the regulations outlining the specific powers being granted to the police and other authorities were required to put the War Measures Act into operation on 16 October 1970. The proclamation and the Regulations were by order-in-council of the federal cabinet, under whose constitutional authority the War Measures Act fell.[1] The War Measures Act Regulations of 16 October 1970 were initially drafted by lawyer Michel Côté of the city of Montreal legal department.[2] Dated 12 October 1970, the draft was then corrected and modified by lawyers of the governments of Quebec and Canada. The Regulations stipulated that the Front de Libération du Québec, as well as "any group of persons or association that advocates the use of force or the commission of crime as a means of or as an aid in accomplishing governmental change within Canada, is declared to be an unlawful association." The Regulations then authorized the arrest, detention, and imprisonment for up to five years of any person who was a member of the FLQ or of any other organization with similar aims.[3]

Six months before the October Crisis, Herbert Marx, who was an assistant professor in the Faculty of Law at the Université de Montréal and who became minister of Justice (1985–88) in the second Bourassa government, published an article in the 1970 *McGill Law Review* that provided a useful exposition of emergency powers and civil liberties in Canada and asserted that emergency powers are required in times of war, economic depression, secession, insurrection, or subversion.[4] On 7 May 1970, concerned with domestic unrest in Canada – not the least that occasioned by the activities of the FLQ – the federal cabinet formed an interdepartmental committee to consider, among other things, "steps to be taken in the event the War Measures Act comes into force by reason of insurrection." Unfortunately, "the interdepartmental committee met several times during the summer and autumn of 1970, but did not produce a report for the Cabinet Committee on Priorities and Planning until Nov. 20 – just over a month after the Government proclaimed a state of apprehended insurrection to exist and invoked the War Measures Act."[5]

The Alternatives: Martial Law, Riot Act, Criminal Code

In 1999 Rick Salutin wrote that in October 1970 "Trudeau icily declared the War Measures Act and imposed *martial rule* throughout Quebec."[6] By contrast, another commentator, Hugh Segal, claimed in 1996 that martial law was an *alternative* to the War Measures Act during the October Crisis, writing: "The War Measures Act was not the only vehicle available to authorities. Marshal [sic] law could have been imposed. The army could have been invited in."[7] Besides forgetting that the army had been sent into Ottawa by the federal government four days before the proclamation of the War Measures Act Regulations, and into Quebec one day before by the Quebec government, Segal, like Salutin, misunderstands the meaning of martial law. The same could be said of Marcel Rioux, one of the sixteen "eminent personalities."[8]

What is martial law? Herbert Marx defines it as "the action of the military when, in order to deal with an emergency amounting to a state of war, they impose restrictions and regulations upon civilians in their own country."[9] The great English jurist Lord Halsbury declared that martial law "is no law at all."[10] *État de siège*, or state of siege, "is a legal institution constitutionally foreseen (as in France) and regulated by statute; whereas, martial law is a condition in which law is temporarily abrogated."[11] Marx concedes that martial law and *état de siège* are "indistinguishable in practice." Jacques Lacoursière explains: "There is no relationship between martial law and the War Measures Act. The first suppresses all civil structures and paralyzes the courts' activities.[12] Nevertheless at the start of April 1918, Quebec City was the scene of noisy demonstrations against conscription. Because the mayor of the City opposed the reading of the Riot Act, the government of Mr. Robert Borden decreed martial law; and the army, after shooting into the crowd and killing five persons, succeeded in reestablishing calm."[13]

One may conclude from this that in October 1970 martial law was not a valid alternative to the War Measures Act. Martial law, being "no law at all," implies the absence of law. The War Measures Act Regulations, on the other hand, gave specific, limited powers to specific persons in a specific situation.

As for another possible alternative to the War Measures Act, the Riot Act, this measure has its source in an English statute of 1714 entitled "An Act for Preventing Tumults and Riotous Assemblies ... " (1 Geo. 1, Stat. 2, c. 5), which used language surprisingly similar to that of the riot provisions in the current Criminal Code of Canada (R.S.C. 1985, c. C-46), which states, in section 67, that the Riot Act may be read by a justice, mayor, or sheriff, a lawful deputy of the latter two officials, or the head of a prison or penitentiary. For this to occur, that official must be "satisfied that a riot is *in progress*" (emphasis added). The official must then command silence, and read, or cause another to read, the Riot Act in a loud voice from as close to those assembled as is safe. The precise words set out in the Criminal Code need not be used, so long as the words used are "to the like effect." Related sections are section 64 (definition of "riot"), section 63 (definition of "unlawful assembly"), and sections 32–3 ("suppression of riots").[14]

The Riot Act was used during the Winnipeg General Strike of 1919, when the mayor read it aloud and troops were called in.[15] More recently, it was used in a limited way in the Northwest Territories and British Columbia.[16] It clearly was not an alternative to the War Measures Act in October 1970, however, as Lacoursière recognized from the start: "The Riot Act only concerns an illegal grouping which starts to seriously disturb the peace (Section 65 of the Criminal Code). Thus the situation which prevailed in Quebec, in October, could not be resolved by this section of the Criminal Code."[17] The Riot Act was, and is, a section of the Criminal Code and as such is dependent on other sections of the code, the meaning of which alone or together would not be immediately clear to a peace officer. And the Riot Act required *that a riot must have already commenced, following an unlawful public assembly.* In October 1970 the use of the Riot Act would have required police officers to attend every event and meeting all over the province.

In December 1970 the well-known Winnipeg criminal lawyer Nate Nurgitz, who at the time was national president of the Progressive Conservative Party, stated that in the October Crisis the Criminal Code alone could have been used rather than the War Measures Act.[18] He pointed out that the Criminal Code and other statutes adequately covered all the powers found in the War Measures Act. In particular, he referred to section 46 ("treason"), section 60 ("sedition"), section 64 ("unlawful assemblies"), section 434 ("arrest without warrant"), section 21 ("parties to offences"), section 22 ("counselling offences"), and section 51 ("intimidating parliament or legislatures"), as well as to sections 55, 492(4), and 510 of the Criminal Code, and to sections 22 and 23 of the Quebec Coroner's Act (S.Q. 1966–67, c. 19).

Yet, in setting out his argument, Nurgitz unwittingly made the case for imposition of the War Measures Act Regulations of 16 October 1970. He did so in three ways. First, he made it clear that no part of the War Measures Act Regulations was extraordinary; all its provisions were found in the existing law. Secondly, in the very act of enumerating Criminal Code provisions, Nurgitz inadvertently demonstrated that they are longer and less clear than the Regulations. Thirdly, his analysis highlighted the value of the 16 October Regulations, because that measure dealt specifically with the FLQ and was to be found in a single document. As such, it was clearer to a policeman, lawyer, judge, elected public figure, professor, reporter, and the general public – including FLQ members and sympathizers. Using the Regulations was easier and fairer than trying to apply the various articles of the Criminal Code. If the government had proceeded under the Criminal Code, how could anyone, other than an expert like Nurgitz, have fully and clearly known his or her rights? Finally, had we employed the Criminal Code and related statutes, we would still have been obliged to define precisely, in new regulations or perhaps a statute, what exactly the FLQ was and what membership in it consisted of. This would have required considerable time.

Conclusion

The Regulations issued under the War Measures Act conferred only limited powers. As Trudeau said in the House of Commons on the morning of 16 October 1970: "The government recognizes that the powers conferred by the Act are much larger than the actual situation requires, despite the gravity of the events. For this reason, the regulations which have been adopted only permit the exercise of a limited number of these powers."[19] The Regulations proclaimed under the act were carefully prepared and did not exceed provisions found in the Criminal Code and other Canadian statutes. Admittedly it was a drastic measure, but the times were perilous. It was not perfectly democratic in theory but there was no alternative to preserve democracy in practice. Applying martial law, the Riot Act, or the Criminal Code was not practical. Nor were any of these a just and fair alternative to the Regulations of 16 October 1970.

Frank R. Scott said of the Regulations: "A shock treatment was needed to restore the balance. It was given, and it worked. There was only one death, and it was not caused by the forces of law and order. Six million Quebecers had their right to self-government restored. They can make René Lévesque Prime Minister by votes, but not by bombs. He would not want it otherwise."[20]

Chapter 10

The War Measures Act: What Went Right

We are prepared to go to the gates of hell but no further.

Pope Pius VII (1742–1823)

The proclamation of a state of apprehended insurrection and of the War Measures Act Regulations on 16 October 1970 has been heavily criticized. Yet the effect was mostly positive and the rights taken away were not extensive. This chapter is intended as a description of what went right when the War Measures Act was applied. (Chapter 11 describes what went wrong.)

One matter is not in doubt. Those persons who acted unwisely at the time of the October Crisis, either by supporting the FLQ or by not opposing the group until it was too late, today refrain from dealing with their own actions and those of the FLQ. Instead, they deflect attention from themselves by talking incessantly of the War Measures Act and the "apprehended insurrection." Such is the strategy, for example, of the Parti Québécois, its apologists, and the sixteen "eminent personalities" and their supporters. Even Pierre Duchesne, the generally even-handed biographer of Jacques Parizeau, entitles the chapter on Parizeau's part in the crisis "*La loi de la guerre*" (The Law of the War), not "*La crise d'octobre*."[1]

The Facts

Those of us in charge in Quebec had great misgivings about the imposition of the War Measures Act Regulations. Before asking the federal government to take this step, we waited until negotiations with the FLQ had broken off and we were facing the next stage of its terrorist campaign. It was fortunate that the opposition parties in the legislature, including the Parti Québécois (at the instigation of Jacques Parizeau and over the objections of René Lévesque), agreed to pass all three Medicare bills in a single day and thus end the specialist doctors' strike. If the debate over Medicare had continued for another day, or even a half-day, rather than ending just past midnight on Friday morning, 16 October 1970, the Regulations would probably not have come into effect in time. As it was, they came into force at 4:00 a.m. on 16 October 1970 and the violent demonstrations, which were the next step planned by the FLQ for Friday, 16 October 1970, did not happen. We were thus fortunate. On the other hand, we in the Quebec cabinet had prepared for action long in advance. Starting Sunday, 11 October, we had discussed the pros and cons of using the War Measures Act and by 13 October had reached a unanimous position. Ottawa and the Montreal authorities had reached the same conclusion. We had drafts of the proclamation and the Regulations finalized and ready by 15 October, after considerable work by lawyers of the city of Montreal and the governments of Quebec and Canada. This was not luck, but good governance.

Although the possibility of invoking the War Measures Act had been discussed by Herbert Marx,[2] by an interdepartmental committee of the federal cabinet,[3] and even by some newspapers,[4] the proclamation of a state of apprehended insurrection and of the Regulations on 16 October 1970 was intended to be a surprise. In this it succeeded, catching the FLQ and its supporters and sympathizers completely off guard. The *Montréal Matin* reported: "Last night, [Sunday, 18 October 1970] at 7 o'clock, 307 people were behind bars, having been arrested Friday, Saturday, or Sunday under the War Measures Act. Of this number of arrests, without precedent, 180 were carried out in the metropolis, 4 in Sherbrooke, 14 in Hull, 11 in Joliette, 3 in Rouyn-Noranda, 56 in Quebec, 13 in Chicoutimi, 24 in Rimouski and 2 in Victoriaville."[5] All of this occurred without brutality or use of excessive force by the police or violence on the part of the public.

The Greatest Myth

The greatest myth about the October Crisis is that the War Measures Act Regulations took away all civil rights. In fact, the Regulations did not prevent students, political parties, the press, and others from meeting, making declarations, or even criticizing the War Measures Act or the three levels of government. Thus, on the night of 17–18 October 1970, many of the same people who had attended the raucous meeting of 15–16 October at the Paul Sauvé Arena were present at another large gathering, which had been quickly organized by the Comité québécois pour la défense des libertés civiles.[6] At this meeting the War Measures Act was the subject of discussion and, clearly audible in the radio coverage, the news of Pierre Laporte's death was greeted with cheers. The meeting was not prohibited by the police or by the War Measures Act Regulations. Similarly, FRAP, which publicly supported the FLQ's aims, was not prevented from attacking the War Measures Act during the Montreal mayoralty election that was taking place at the same time.

The War Measures Act was again not an obstacle when the Parti Québécois National Council met on Sunday, 18 October 1970. There, PQ lawyer Pothier Ferland gave a legal opinion as to the consequences and the limits of the War Measures Act Regulations, an opinion that was reproduced in the PQ pamphlet *Pouvoir* of 28 October 1970.[7] Ferland found that the Regulations did not in any way affect the right of the Parti Québécois to go about its normal business, including the holding of meetings, the posting of notices or banners, the making of public announcements, and the criticizing of governments and their laws, in particular the War Measures Act.

Ferland wrote:

No matter how justified may be the fears we have arising from the present situation, it is no less true that the activities of the Parti Québécois were, are and intend to remain legal. We have chosen to lead the struggle in a democratic fashion by practising, more than any other political party, the democracy to be found in our aims and organization.

In the National Assembly and in the population, we have been, are and intend to remain the most fervent partisans of a true democracy, of a real social justice.

Now more than ever is the time to be proud of our objectives and methods at a moment where the society in which we live faces a very serious crisis, where even the survival of democracy could be threatened. It is time, more than ever, to show at this significant moment that we really live democracy. We have said above that the War Measures Act, and the Regulations which implement it, do not prevent us at all from pursuing any of our activities to the end, because fundamentally these activities are legal.

Therefore, as members of the Parti Québécois and as citizens, we have the right:

1)   to attend meetings of our party,
2)   to publicly express our allegiance,
3)   to publicize in printed form or orally, the ideals, goals and policies of our party,
4)   to show our allegiance by flags, stickers, flyers, signs, etc.,
5)   to criticize the governments in place and the laws that they adopt or promulgate. (E.g. Anyone may request the withdrawal of the War Measures Act or criticize its application.)

In particular, the War Measures Act did not suspend the whole Canadian Bill of Rights, 1960, but only those clauses that were incompatible with the Regulations – an effect that has been called "selective abeyance."[8] Almost immediately after the imposition of the War Measures Act Regulations, the federal government created a Committee to Aid Persons Arrested under the War Measures Act. This committee, under the presidency of Senator Jacques Hébert, a long-time friend of Prime Minister Trudeau, noted in its preliminary report:

In all honesty ... allowance should be made for certain circumstances:
- this is the first time such extensive powers had been granted to the police in peacetime;
- about 450 were arrested and of these only a small number had cause to complain of the manner in which they were interrogated. Several even emphasized the courteous nature of the interrogations and the searches;
- even if some complaints prove to be well-founded, it would seem that only very few police officers are implicated.[9]

Soon thereafter arrangements were made to enable detainees to retain legal counsel, while the Quebec ombudsman, Louis Marceau, was instructed to hear complaints by detainees, with or without counsel. The Quebec government also decided to pay up to $30,000 damages to any person unjustly arrested.[10] On 3 February 1971 John Turner, minister of justice of Canada, reported that, of the 497 persons arrested under the War Measures Act, 435 had been released and the other 62 had been charged (32 were not granted bail). Detainee complaints filed with Marceau increased from 95 on 20 January 1971 to 171 on 12 March and 238 on 6 July 1971. Of these 238 complaints, Marceau found 103 justified and meriting compensation.

Anthony Westell, a respected journalist and former director of Carleton University's School of Journalism, in referring to Quebec's and Montreal's requests for the proclamation of the War Measures Act Regulations, noted that the purpose of the Regulations was to provide the police with "powers to make arrests to prevent an escalation of violence ... If that was the intention, it worked like a charm. The night before the War Measures Act was proclaimed, Quebec was in turmoil. The day after it was calm."[11] The War Measures Act Regulations prevented demonstrations and marches in favour of the FLQ, thus avoiding confrontations with police, as well as damage to private and public property. It was astounding how the violence ended and the confrontations planned by the FLQ and its supporters and sympathizers did not take place.

Conclusion

In the circumstances of the kidnappings, the social unrest, the petition of the sixteen "eminent personalities," the often irresponsible attitude of the press and some political leaders, and our own limited knowledge of the FLQ at that time, I believe that implementing the War Measures Act Regulations was the proper course to take.

Certainly, the Regulations calmed the population, the PQ leaders, and the students, while reporters and editorialists were not directly constrained by the legislation. For the first time, however, they were obliged to exercise careful judgment as to what was appropriate.

Chapter 11

The War Measures Act: What Went Wrong

To err is human, to forgive divine.

Alexander Pope (1699–1744)

Fighting terrorism is like being a goalkeeper. You can make a hundred brilliant saves, but the only shot that people remember is the one that gets past you.

Paul Wilkinson, British expert on terrorism, 1992

On 16 October 1970 at 4:00 a.m. a state of apprehended insurrection was proclaimed, as well as the Regulations under the War Measures Act.[1] The powers available under the War Measures Act were too broad and in consequence the Regulations drafted by Quebec and Ottawa were limited in scope. As Prime Minister Trudeau said: "The government recognizes that *the authority contained in the Act* is much broader than is required in the present situation, notwithstanding the seriousness of the events. For that reason *the regulations which were adopted* permit the exercise of only a limited number of the powers available under the Act. Nevertheless, I wish to make it clear today that the government regards the use of the War Measures Act as only an interim and, in the sense mentioned above, somewhat unsatisfactory measure."[2]

I believe the imposition of the Regulations was the proper course for the Quebec and federal governments. To have failed to act would have been disastrous. Nevertheless, we made four major errors: we should have been much more careful in the choice of those arrested, they should have had the right to speak immediately to a lawyer and their families, and they should have been released more quickly. Lastly, we failed to fully inform the public of why we were acting as we did until the emergency debate on 11 November 1970.

We Were Completely Unprepared

The federal, Quebec, and Montreal governments and police had never before experienced such a concentrated terrorist action, with kidnappings and sustained confrontation. We were thus completely unprepared for the efficient kidnapping of Cross and the precision-like kidnapping of Laporte, a mere thirty minutes after Choquette had declared that we would not release terrorists for Cross. Nor were we ready for the support the FLQ received for its aims, and on occasion even for its methods, from various groups in Quebec society. No one had believed that a terrorist uprising could happen in Quebec or Canada.

It is true there had been some previous thought by the federal Cabinet, who had formed an Interdepartmental Committee on 7 May 1970 concerned with domestic unrest in Canada and, among other things, "steps to be taken in the event the War Measures Act comes into force by reason of insurrection." The committee met several times, but did not produce a report for the Cabinet Committee on Priorities and Planning until 20 November 1970.[3]

The RCMP Strategic Operation Centre (SOC), which had been in existence for years, was not much better prepared and only reported, long after the fact, on 10 December 1970. The Centre's conclusions on unpreparedness, which it should have first applied to itself, were harsh:

That little or no action *was* taken would appear to be the result of a combination of the following:

- Lack of any mechanism for proper *political* evaluation of information put forward by the R.C.M.P., and of any political input to this information.
- Lack of effective channels for communicating the information.
- Lack of any mechanism to relate this information to other politico/socio/economic developments.
- Lack of a political mechanism to *react* to this information.
- Lack of knowledge/appreciation of the "Quebec problem."
- Confusion on the part of many between the F.L.Q. and separatism.
- Following from the above, lack of appreciation/knowledge of the real nature and aims of the F.L.Q., and of the ideological affinity between the F.L.Q. and other subversive groups in Canada, in the United States, and in the rest of the world.
- Lack of knowledge/appreciation of the social change in Canada and the Western World.
- The instinctive belief that "it could not happen in Canada."[4]

Jean-François Duchaîne's comments on the SOC Report were: "That the government is squarely blamed for its refusal to take terrorism and the organizations charged with fighting it seriously. This conclusion by the S.O.C. considerably modified the attitude of the federal authorities faced with political terrorism and contributed to the excess of security services in the following years."[5] Duchaîne also noted that the Quebec and Montreal police were even less prepared for such an event than their federal counterpart. Unlike European nations, or even the United States, we had no plans to combat an uprising, nor did we have any idea of the associations, groups, or persons who could be responsible: "Quebec services were less well equipped than federal services. Neither the Montreal Police, nor the

Sûreté du Québec, possessed an information processing centre. There was only an archive where everything was classified without analysis."[6]

Being unprepared had major consequences. Not only did the police not know the names of FLQ members and supporters, but they had no accurate idea of their number. The immediate result was that we arrested many persons we should not have and no doubt missed many people we should have. Another very important but subtle consequence of lack of preparation on all levels of society was that some members of the press did not appreciate that their lack of discretion could contribute to the unrest, which was exactly what the FLQ wanted. Similarly, some political leaders were also unprepared for their role as members of the loyal opposition in a democratic society. In particular, the sixteen "eminent personalities" publicly and unwisely classified the jailed terrorists as "political prisoners."

Arrestees

The initial list of arrestees was prepared by the RCMP, but at one point members of the Quebec Cabinet had the opportunity to look at the list and to question names. I can remember scrutinizing sheets of names with one or two other ministers while sitting on a couch in an antechamber of Bourassa's office on the top floor of the Hydro-Quebec building in Montreal. None of us recognized any names. In Ottawa, Ministers Jean Marchand and Gérard Pelletier were asked by Prime Minister Trudeau to scrutinize the list and apparently a few names were removed.[7] It is clear that the police themselves later added names to the list. As I noted in my diary[8] of Friday, 16 October 1970: "No results of our raids but the War Measures Act has calmed everyone. The public, the Cabinet, the police feel better and Lemieux, Michel Chartrand, etc., etc., have all been put in jail. We had been told of 155 names to be arrested, but the police took about 300 or more. They seem to have gone too far."

The RCMP used four criteria for their initial list: "1) individuals suspected of forming part of the FLQ; 2) individuals gravitating around those in the preceding category and likely to provide them with transport, lodging, communication or any other form of assistance; 3) individuals connected with the Vallières-Gagnon group or with the *Mouvement de libération du taxi*; 4) individuals likely to publicly promote violence and those linked to various extreme leftist groups in Quebec."[9] Later, in consultation with the

Montreal Police, the names of those to be arrested were divided into three categories: "1) individuals who were likely to take action; 2) people who could distribute communiqués or other propaganda; 3) individuals who could financially assist the kidnappers."[10]

Some celebrities were unwisely arrested, including the poet Gaston Miron, Dr Henri Bellemare, journalist and poet Gérald Godin,[11] singer Pauline Julien, and Dr Serge Mongeau.[12] They were, however, founding members on 30 June 1970 of the Mouvement pour la défense des prisonniers politiques du Québec (MDPPQ), which had replaced the "Comité d'aide au groupe Vallières-Gagnon" which had been disbanded by the police.[13] They made much of their arrests and only bad publicity resulted for the governments of Quebec and Ottawa.

The MDPPQ had taken the position that the 23 FLQ terrorists, who were responsible for over 200 bombings and six deaths, were "political prisoners" and that Gagnon and Vallières were peace-loving and were not involved in the FLQ. Some of the MDPPQ members and supporters apparently had personal knowledge about the Rose brothers and other kidnappers. Could they not have helped the police? Why did they not volunteer to share their personal knowledge with the police? A single tidbit of information might have been a useful lead in saving the life of Laporte. For example, did they know the name of Paul Rose's girl friend, with whom he hid at one time? And if the MDPPQ truly believed in justice and democracy, why did they not publicly denounce the kidnappings and call on the FLQ to release Cross and Laporte? The MDPPQ was not only influential in Quebec as a whole but with some of the kidnappers as well. If the MDPPQ had spoken up, would the outcome of the Crisis have been different?

An example of individuals who were apparently arrested without cause, and without even being on the list, was a "junior producer" at CBC television Montreal (CBMT), who was working with Nick Auf der Maur on the very popular daily public affairs show *Hour Glass*. On 16 October 1970, during the daily conference in preparation for the evening's programme, Auf der Maur, who was a story editor, was telephoned by the RCMP and asked to meet them at the corner of Peel and Ste-Catherine Streets. The executive producer of *Hour Glass*, Paul Wright, asked the junior producer to accompany Auf der Maur, which he did. When they arrived they were both arrested and jailed in the Parthenais Detention Centre in Montreal. The junior producer was released three days later, never having even been questioned. Auf der Maur was released much later. The junior producer did not file a complaint or a request for compensation, while Auf der Maur, who went through varied political careers,[14] referred with pride to his arrest, which seems to have been one of the events in his life of which he was most proud.

There were occasional cases of mistaken identity. For example as described in the Montreal *Star*, Liberal Party member Jean-Pierre Charette, a Hull businessman, was released from jail after a four-day confinement in a Hull institution described as not being the "Sheraton-Hilton." He was picked up early Friday by Quebec Provincial Police, who also seized his collection of vacation slides. Mr Charette said he was interrogated by RCMP officers during his stay and that he denied any connection with the FLQ.

"An RCMP officer told me that a man with the same name as mine had hijacked a plane last year. They thought I was him. But they found out I didn't even look like him. They apologized for the mistake," he added.

Mr. Charette said he, and five other prisoners, who were released yesterday, were "not badly treated" but they did complain about not having more than a sink for washing.

Mr. Charette said he took two baths, "but l asked for them. Maybe the others didn't." He also hoped to get his slides returned "at some time."[15]

On 7 November 1970, the police even went to the home of Secretary of State Gérard Pelletier, confusing him with another Gérard Pelletier. "As the result of an unfortunate misunderstanding, five members of the Quebec Provincial Police appeared in the early hours of October 7th at the Westmount residence of Gérard Pelletier with the intention of searching the premises. They apparently were not aware that this was the residence of the Secretary of State. They were actually looking for another Gérard Pelletier, whom they later apprehended."[16]

Among the demonstrators and known FLQ sympathizers arrested were Parti Québécois members, although not the leaders – Lévesque, Parizeau, Laurin, Burns, and Charron. Some of the latter even seemed to have regretted that they had not been arrested. Parizeau was reported to have said: "We seem a little ridiculous, when our assistants are all arrested and not the big bosses."[17] There was, of course, no reason to arrest them and it was fortunate for the government that they were not arrested in error.

Many persons arrested were released within two or three days, but those detained often did not have the right to speak to their lawyers until 26 October 1970. The problem was caused by the insufficient number of lawyers, police, and staff available to study the case of each arrested person. Even worse, some families of those arrested were not advised of their arrests until 21 October 1970.

Explaining Our Actions[18]

The explanation by the governments as to why we had applied the War Measures Act was not given immediately to the public. Our reasoning was that the situation was extremely explosive, that unfortunately we had little time at our disposal, and that, in particular, we did not know how many FLQ members there were or their next planned attack. Nor, of course, did we in government wish the FLQ to know the extent of our ignorance and our plans. On the other hand, it was recognized it was imperative to inform the public as soon as possible of the reasons for our actions.[19] George Radwanski and Kendal Windeyer succinctly made the case for full disclosure:

The style in which the War Measures Act was implemented, however, leaves something to be desired. The Prime Minister gave only a terse explanation at first, then his ministers set off across the country adding highly contradictory details. When enough piecemeal explanations had been tossed out, Trudeau insisted that the nation now had full knowledge of the circumstances which had compelled his government's action. At the same time – and for weeks afterward – his Minister of Justice kept expressing the hope that some day all the information which had forced the government to act could be revealed.

Candor might have been more effective. A single statement by the Prime Minister setting forth in full the government's reasons for the move would have prevented much of the widespread speculation and rumor-mongering that came on the heels of the act.[20]

James Littleton agreed:

Only by clarifying the whole series of events since and before October 5th can the situation in this country be stabilized. If in the course of explaining the measures it has taken the Government of Canada reveals that it acted hastily and without a great deal of explicit evidence, its judgment will have to be questioned and it will have to bear the consequences of that questioning. If it can justify fully its actions then a sense of equilibrium will be restored. In either case, the real interests of democracy would be served.[21]

I wanted Bourassa to make a statement, but he wished to have more time and to be master of the facts. Nevertheless, I became so frustrated, that I made a declaration of my own. I first showed the text to Bourassa's staff, who made no changes, and it was then published in *Le Devoir* on 4 November 1970, but was refused publication by the Montreal *Star*.[22] Bourassa and the caucus were pleased with it, but it elicited criticism from Camille Laurin[23] in the National Assembly and Claude Ryan and Jean-Claude Leclerc.[24] In retrospect, I believe Bourassa's reluctance, as the Quebec government's spokesman, to give an immediate explanation of our actions was very wise. While he was aware of the public's anguish and its desire for information, his greater responsibility was for the safety of Cross and Laporte. This included not informing the FLQ of our lack of knowledge of their strength and strategy. Perhaps, however, ministers and others could have made careful personal statements, which had been vetted in advance. I suspect, however, that the press, the Parti Québécois leaders, and the intellectuals would never have been satisfied with whatever we said or did. The public and those without a personal interest, on the other hand, were to a very large extent satisfied. To my mind, the debate on the October Crisis from 11 to 20 November 1970 in the National Assembly should have satisfied the immediate concerns of the public.

Should Politicians Interfere with Police Work?

We in government had misgivings about the broad sweep of the arrests, but we also had the obligation not to interfere with the details of police work. When legislators and elected politicians meddle in individual police actions, this is fascism. Bourassa himself made this quite clear when asked by Raymond Saint-Pierre if he found it normal "that the police went to Gérald Godin's house?" Bourassa replied: "No, on the contrary. I asked what there was in this case. I was told 'a file.' The premier cannot be the chief of police. It is so easy to blame the police. It is true that there were mistakes. The case of Gérald Godin struck me as unusual, because I knew him and I could not see a revolutionary in him. So, I asked the question; but I did not go and examine the evidence in the files."[25]

If governments should not interfere in actual police work, they should, on the other hand, provide fair and just guidelines for the police and must also oversee a system of checks and balances through such institutions as Parliament, ombudsmen, and the courts.

Conclusion

The imposition of the War Measures Act Regulations was necessary and stopped the mounting confrontation just in time. Unfortunately, the governments and police of Canada, Quebec, and Montreal were completely unprepared for the crisis and the form it took. Similarly, many persons who opposed the actions taken by government were unprepared and acted badly. Unfortunately, too, the arrestees were not chosen with sufficient care, permitted to speak to their lawyers and families early on, and released quickly. Finally, until the emergency debate on 11 November 1970 we in government never resolved the dilemma of how to fully inform the public without signalling to the FLQ our strategy and our lack of knowledge of their strength.

Chapter 12

The Reaction to the War Measures Act

The lady doth protest too much, methinks.

William Shakespeare (1564–1616), *Hamlet*

... liberty and anarchy are contradictory ... our freedom is dependent upon wise restraints.

Prime Minister Pierre Trudeau, House of Commons, 9 October 1970

At the time of their application, the War Measures Act Regulations were approved of by the public at large. The small number who disapproved were FLQ members and sympathizers, who watched their hoped-for revolution collapse with hardly a whimper, some Parti Québécois leaders (not the majority of the party's members, as the polls showed), some labour union leaders, some student leaders, and some civil libertarians.

The Supporters

As a European diplomat noted:

The foreign observer raised his eyebrows. He had now spent almost a fortnight pacing the snows of Ontario and Quebec. Accustomed as he was to the CRS [Compagnies Républicaines de Sécurité], who permanently besiege certain Paris neighbourhoods, he had expected to find Montreal transformed into a police stronghold. The only representative of law and order he had encountered, apart from traffic policemen, was an official at the airport who gave his papers the most indifferent of glances. In the hotels there was no need to prove his identity, which is not the case in Europe, where the foreign traveller is requested to present his credentials at the reception desk. On two or three occasions he had seen opponents of the regime complaining with loud cries on the national television in prime time that they had been reduced to silence by the government.[1]

In a Gallup Poll published on 12 December 1970, 89 per cent of English-speaking Canadians approved of the federal government's action in adopting the War Measures Act Regulations, while 6 per cent disapproved and 5 per cent were undecided. Among French-speaking Canadians, 86 per cent approved, 9 per cent disapproved, and 5 per cent were undecided. In light of these findings, it is obvious that the Parti Québécois leaders, student leaders, and union leaders who opposed the imposition of the Regulations did not have even their rank-and-file members behind them.

Jean-François Cardin, who wrote of the crisis from the point of view of the labour unions, stated that even teachers and their unions approved of the imposition of the War Measures Act Regulations: "[public-opinion] surveys, according to *Le Devoir*, 'indicated that professors and teachers in several regions were almost unanimously in favour of the application of this same law in the circumstances.' The adoption of ... resolutions [condemning the use of the War Measures Act] were extracted with difficulty by the leadership after a long war in the trenches, where the discussions were stormy, the procedures numerous and the votes close."[2]

The students, who, caught up in the excitement of the crisis, joined FLQ demonstrations without really understanding the organization's objectives, let alone appreciating its methods, were brought to their senses by the War Measures Act Regulations and melted away, never to rejoin their leaders. Eric Bédard, author of the definitive text on the October Crisis in the universities and CEGEPS, writes: "Combined with the shock caused by the death of Pierre Laporte, the War Measures Act was the last nail in the Revolution's coffin; the brutal wakeup the day after the *Grand Soir* [of 15–16 October]. The numerous arrests, often in the middle of the night, the presence of the army in the streets ... contributed to a climate of extreme fear. Of course, there were protests and indignation. But fear rapidly took over and the large majority of students prudently got into line."[3] And again: "If one of the aims of the adoption of the War Measures Act was to calm spirits and cool the heated revolutionary ardour of certain students, and we think it was, the law without exception was a success. Divided for ideological reasons that we have already noted, the Francophone student leaders were incapable of mobilizing their troops after this show of force."[4] Another witness, Hugh Segal, a student at the University of Ottawa at the time of the crisis, wrote that "the large majority of student leaders sought to react in a reasonable fashion ... Most realized that their student constituents, like any other group of Canadians, were, at that time in our nation's history, fully prepared to give our duly elected government the benefit of the doubt. Indeed, while opposition to the government may have been more vocal among the students of the country, it would seem fair to say that their overall reaction was not far removed from the general Canadian reaction to the government's position."[5]

Most unions and their members approved the application of the War Measures Act. For example, the giant Syndicat de la Fonction Publique du Québec (SFPQ) issued a declaration expressing its approval of "the actions of the federal and provincial authorities concerning the war measures" and disassociating itself "from the statements made in the name of member unions, without preliminary consultation, by the Front Commun CSN-FTQ-CEQ."[6] Nor was the SFPQ alone. Jean-François Cardin gives countless examples of union members (CEQ, FTQ, CSN) who, in opposition to the views of their leaders, supported the application of the War Measures Act Regulations.[7] As time passed, the leaders of the three main *centrales syndicales* – Marcel Pepin (CSN), Louis Laberge (FTQ), and Yvon Charbonneau (CEQ) – became more and more vitriolic in their opposition to the actions of the federal and provincial governments, but strong support for the War Measures Act Regulations continued among the rank and file.[8] At the same time, even the leadership of the *centrales syndicales* did not speak with one voice, for a number of respected labour-union leaders took issue with the pro-FLQ views of some of their colleagues. One of these was Jean Gérin-Lajoie, vice-president of the FTQ from 1959 to 1981 and director of the normally radical Métallos Québécois from 1964, who "was opposed to the FLQ and their methods because they were contrary to the industrial union tradition of which it [the Métallos] was born. 'This position,' he affirmed, 'was generally that of the majority of his union colleagues in the Métallos, the FTQ and even the local unions.'"[9]

Like labour, the Quebec business community generally approved the Quebec government's actions taken during the October Crisis. On 23 October 1970 the Conseil du patronat du Québec (CPQ) issued a long, well-reasoned statement declaring:

Le Conseil du patronat du Québec (CPQ) wishes it to be known publicly that it gives its full support to the Quebec government as concerns the difficult decisions that it was called upon to make during the events of the last few days.

In effect, the CPQ recognizes that the government of Quebec has been legitimately and democratically elected. It is this government, and it alone, that has the responsibility, and will always have the responsibility, to make quick and extremely important decisions in the name of Quebec society, which mandated it to act in its name in these excessively difficult times that we have recently come to know.

Public reasons: In its role as an agent of the Quebec community and protector both of the individual and collective interests of this same community, the government has assumed responsibilities that it understands it must assume in the circumstances. The government must know that there has always been full support of its mandate, even if some persons are still unaware of the reasons that could justify some of the decisions taken.[10]

At the same time, the CPQ called for the repeal of the War Measures Act and its replacement by amendments to the Criminal Code and by special legislation more fitting to the situation:

The CPQ would like, at this time, to refer especially to the War Measures Act invoked by the federal government at the request of the Quebec authorities, a law which is still in force in Quebec. It is probable that the federal government did not have any alternative than to put this law into effect when called upon by Quebec to do so. It was the only law in existence which permitted the authorities to act rapidly in the interest of all citizens.

The CPQ wishes to note, nevertheless, the intention announced by the federal government of proposing short-term, special legislation, capable of attaining the preliminary goals mentioned above, without having to invoke the War Measures Act.

Finally, the CPQ called on the Quebec government to work with nongovernmental groups ("intermediate bodies, whether made up of management, unions, or other groups") to solve Quebec's social problems:

This short-term action is urgent and requires the State to find mechanisms capable of "measuring" the satisfaction or dissatisfaction of various social groups; it means finding ways of democratic and effective communication with the most dissatisfied of these groups and to assure the availability of the State to listen to these groups; it means emphasizing the use of French as the current language of work; it means the elimination of useless governmental expenses; it means the bringing of the parties together ...

For intermediary groups, made up of management, union or other bodies, this short-term action is urgently needed to bring all the leaders together. In effect, only this joining together will permit men of good will to reconcile the totally divergent ideas which animate them. Such reconciliation will lead to the realization that a social consensus will be possible only on the condition that our Quebec leaders act responsibly in social and economic matters.[11]

The United Kingdom government fully supported the Canadian and Quebec governments' conduct during the October Crisis, even when James Cross was still being held hostage. As Quebec Minister of Justice Jérôme Choquette noted: "Lord Hume, Minister of Foreign Affairs, expressed on November 13, 1970 his approval of the Canadian and Quebec governments' attitude."[12]

McGill law professor F.R. Scott, one of the country's foremost champions of civil liberties, wrote an article entitled "Global Attack on Our Institutions" in the midst of the October Crisis. In it, he argued:

the legitimate activities of the Parti Québécois, which aims to prove by democratic means that the majority in Quebec is in favour of independence, are not in question now. This party has existed for some years, it is distinct from the FLQ, and its activities are not rendered illegal by the proclamation of the War Measures Act.

It is not separatism in Quebec that is outlawed, it is a determined and well-organized revolutionary movement applying new techniques of terror aimed at the polarization of our society and the fracturing of those elements which enable Canadian federalism to exist at the moment and give assurance that it can exist in the future. It is a global attack upon all institutions in our present system.

There is at the moment in Quebec a government newly elected which clearly offered the Quebec people an option on staying within Confederation and working out the necessary adjustments without a break in the fundamental relationship. This government represents the great majority of the Quebec electorate and must be considered as the only authoritative voice of Quebec. It was this government, with the full support of the city government of Montreal, which requested Mr. Trudeau to give emergency aid.

This is the essential issue. Either Quebec is going to produce some kind of French culture in North America, of which every person in Quebec can be proud, and of which all persons outside are also appreciative and respectful, or it is not worth trying. Surely all English Canada must believe they ought to succeed in this effort. They must not be deflected from this purpose by the activities of terrorists whose primary aim is not so much the expansion of a culture as the achievement of political power for Maoist or Communist ends.[13]

The following year, Scott wrote another article, this one entitled "The War Measures Act in Retrospect," where he said:

Something had to break, and for a few dreadful days it seemed as though civil government might break. We have Claude Ryan's admission that he thought so too; he even toyed with the idea that if Bourassa was incapable of continuing,

"Lévesque is a logical possibility." René Lévesque was not even a member of the legislature. What a near victory for the FLQ!

There are plenty of differences between English and French in Canada, but not a difference as to whether violence or votes are to be the means by which we reach for solutions. I would have thought this result at least would hearten our civil libertarians, but it seems to make some of them even more afraid of the future. I do not see that poll [expressing approval of the War Measures Act] as an approval of police methods: it was rather a relief at being freed from fear.[14]

Scott, who was usually on the side of the minority, added: "I was on the side of the majority of Quebec on that question."[15]

The Opponents

In the House of Commons, only the New Democratic Party opposed the invoking of the War Measures Act. Its leader, Tommy Douglas, declared that "Right now there is no *constitution in this country, no Bill of Rights, no provincial constitutions.* This government now has the power by Order in Council to do anything it wants – *to intern any citizen, to deport any citizen, to arrest any person or to declare any organization subversive or illegal.*"[16] When one looks at the Regulations one sees that this is clearly nonsense. Douglas also said that the government "used a sledgehammer to crack a peanut." In reply, Trudeau correctly noted: "This criticism doesn't take the facts into account. First, peanuts don't make bombs, don't take hostages, and don't assassinate prisoners. And as for the sledgehammer, it was the only tool at our disposal."[17] Douglas, in a televised interview, also declared: "It is a dangerous course to abrogate basic freedoms in this manner. We have seen this course followed in such countries as South Africa, Rhodesia, and Czechoslovakia. In each of these countries people were told that their rights were being taken away temporarily for their own protection."[18] He is also quoted as saying that Quebec had been the victim of a Reichstag fire trick, referring to the fire that destroyed the German parliament building in Berlin in 1933, which Hitler had plotted and then blamed on the Communists.[19]

Like Douglas, most of the intellectuals who opposed the imposition of the War Measures Act erred as to the consequences of the Regulations and exaggerated their effects. Here are some examples of their statements, with italics denoting either error or hyperbole:

- Marcel Rioux: "in the morning of Friday, October 16, the government of Canada proclaimed *a state of martial law* under the War Measures Act ..."[20]
- Ann Charney: *"Life under emergency rule ... "police brutality"*[21]
- Alan Borovoy: *"The wholesale suspension of civil liberties"*[22]
- Abraham Rotstein: *"unprecedented repression"*[23]
- Jean Provencher: "Five hours later, it is the *overly large federal yoke* never before imposed on Quebec: THE WAR MEASURES ACT."[24]
- Richard Gwyn: "The War Measures Act *banned political rallies.*"[25]
- Hugh Segal: "... four hundred people were arrested without charge in the middle of the night, held in jail for days with not one of them ever charged with so much as double parking, with police officers deciding who was a danger to the state, and with civil liberties – *including the right to free assembly, the right to free speech, and other fundamental rights, suspended across the land.*"[26]
- Jacques Parizeau: "Since 4 o'clock in the morning, on this October 16th, 1970, *rights and liberties have been suspended in Canada.*"[27]
- René Lévesque: *"'War Measures' are brought into force by P.E. Trudeau who imprisons all those opposing his federalist ideas.* According to certain information received, this violence was remote controlled by the RCMP in the service of the politicians in power."[28]
- David MacDonald (MP for Egmont, PEI): "I cannot help but think as well, as I stand here as a member of this House, that there is a very unusual situation in this country tonight [16 October 1970] in that I am one of the 264 people left in the Dominion of Canada who still have the right to say what they feel and believe. Tragically, *none of my fellow-citizens have that kind of freedom* in this land tonight."[29]
- F. Andrew Brewin (MP for Greenwood, a Toronto riding): "Let us consider what the proclamation of the War Measures Act enables the government to do. First of all, that proclamation

suspends the constitution of the country. We are at this moment
without any fundamental law.... Secondly, the proclamation
enables the federal government to *override provincial legislatures
and provincial legislation....* The third result of the proclamation of
the War Measures Act is this: *the Bill of Rights has been torn up....*
Also, Mr. Speaker, the proclamation of the act *jeopardizes freedom
of speech and freedom of assembly* for all Canadians from one end
of Canada to the other."[30]

By the end of 1970, some critics of the federal government's response to the
October Crisis had set out their views in a forty-one-page booklet entitled
Strong and Free: A Response to the War Measures Act. Prepared by David
MacDonald[31] and his assistant, Hugh Segal,[32] it consisted of essays by
eleven Canadians. One theme of the pamphlet was that the opposition
capitulated to the wishes of the Trudeau government.

- David MacDonald: "One of the amazing insights resulting from
  the invoking of the War Measures Act was the willingness of
  most Canadians to accept, without question, *the suspension of
  many of their rights and protections under the law.*"[33]
- Patrick Watson: "... [Opposition MPs] had been put to sleep by
  the simple enormity of the government's initiative ... 'If it's that
  bad,' the Opposition seems to say, 'we'd better fall in line, at least
  until it's over' .... So now take stock. *Effective opposition in parliament has been suspended. Men and women are nervous about speaking or even reading critical words. A political party is outlawed. A
  national tolerance for suppression has been honoured by the state.*"[34]
- Hugh Segal: "[The Official Opposition] "ran for cover ... When
  the government moved to institutionalize, with no further justi-
  fication, through The Public Order Act, *the principles of authori-
  tarianism established by the War Measures Act,* the Tories and
  the New Democrats ran for cover. On second reading, men like
  [Andrew] Brewin and [Eugene] Fairweather and [David] Lewis
  and [Robert] Stanfield lost the one chance they had to salvage
  something of interminable value for what we thought Parliament
  should be. *When only one young M.P. [David MacDonald] stood to
  oppose the Public Order Act, it became clear that, the government of*

*the day had, for all intents and purposes, destroyed what was left of
the backbone of Parliament as an institution."*[35]

Another critic of the War Measures Act was Jean-Claude Leclerc of *Le
Devoir*. He wanted the act to be amended so that three categories of persons – FLQ members who had already been convicted, FLQ sympathizers
who had been "more or less active" but were now having second thoughts,
and individuals who had done nothing more than speak in favour of the
FLQ – would not be arrested. In effect, he wanted an amnesty for FLQ
members and others connected to FLQ activities in the past. He put his
case this way in the 4 November 1970 issue of *Le Devoir*:

A former member of the FLQ; a member already convicted; a more or less active
sympathizer who has kept his distance since the two kidnappings or the death of
Pierre Laporte; a speaker favourable, if not to the methods of the FLQ at least to
the "liberation of Quebec"; in short several people risk becoming guilty, by only
the will of Parliament, of acts that the same Parliament did not hold as criminal
before the adoption of this special law.

Even if a person is part of an FLQ cell, he should have a reasonable delay to
reconsider his allegiance, now that this association is illegal. *A fortiori*, a person
who has already publicly spoken in favour of the FLQ, without committing any
crimes, should be able to enjoy the same equity.

The government authorities make it a crime of the FLQ to want to control the
future of Quebec with bombs and blackmail. They themselves sink into arbitrariness and irrationality while claiming to govern the past, transforming into
crimes, acts which were not crimes, and finding guilty those people who acted in
accordance with freedoms recognized by all.[36]

The people to whom Leclerc wished to give amnesty had supported, and
even carried out, over 200 bombings and two kidnappings and had caused
six violent deaths – all part of a campaign "to control the future of Quebec
with bombs and blackmail" – *before* the imposition of the War Measures
Act Regulations. That measure added nothing to the Criminal Code and
did not change the import of the crimes the FLQ and their supporters
had committed, whether under the War Measures Act Regulations or the
Criminal Code.[37] Were these people truly deserving of exemption from
prosecution or even censure?

Nor did Leclerc explain how his proposal would be put into effect. On the announcement of an amnesty, how much time would be given those persons to whom he had referred to step forward and renounce their past? Seven days? Sixty days? Six months? Or would they be able to use the amnesty as a defence if and when they were arrested and prosecuted? Leclerc even suggested that condemned FLQ members could benefit from the amnesty simply by repenting for their actions. All in all, his proposed amnesty seems more like the amnesty accorded General Pinochet of Chile than the amnesty granted to people guilty of crimes in South Africa under the apartheid regime. In the latter case, the person seeking amnesty had to come forward and publicly admit his crimes before a special tribunal.

This was not the last time that the idea of an amnesty would be suggested. In 1985 Yvon Deschamps and the Société Saint-Jean-Baptiste de Montréal prepared a petition requesting a general amnesty for all ex-FLQ members.[38] Like Leclerc's proposal, it was to be one-directional: FLQ members would be forgiven en masse without any confession on their part and without any judgment from society; there was to be no act of contrition, no regret, no reconciliation. Fortunately, nothing came of it.

Richard Gwyn described the paradoxical situation in which civil libertarians found themselves in October 1970 when he wrote: "He [Trudeau] crushed civil liberties in 1970 to protect, as he saw it, civil liberties. One last paradox: although our civil liberties indeed were crushed, we are probably the freest, most tolerant society on earth today."[39] Some civil libertarians have difficulty accepting that a democratic government may use force, prescribed under law for a brief period of time, against terrorists. Yet what sort of a society would we be if we had given in to terrorist blackmail during the October Crisis?

Initially, many civil libertarians deplored the imposition of the War Measures Act Regulations because they expected it to cause bloodshed and rioting in the streets. When there was no bloodshed or rioting, however, they changed their focus to the loss of civil rights. "With the intervention of the FLQ," wrote Fernand Dumont, "we didn't see blood running in the gutters as had been predicted, but fear, hatred and stupidity."[40]

Actually, the public and those who opposed the FLQ were not frightened, showed no hatred, and did not behave stupidly. Matters quickly returned to normal, which would not have been the case if we had done nothing, as many intellectuals wanted. "Fear, hatred and stupidity" seem to have resided in another camp. Mitchell Sharp, secretary of state for external affairs and deputy prime minister of Canada in 1970, wrote in his memoirs twenty-four years later: "In some respects, it was the prime minister's finest hour when he appeared on television on 16 October. 'This government is not acting out of fear. It is acting to prevent fear from spreading. It is acting to maintain the rule of law without which freedom is impossible.' On this point Trudeau spoke for us all."[41] Sharp's views have been echoed by Gordon Robertson, who, as clerk of the Privy Council, was the highest-ranking civil servant in Canada at the time of the October Crisis. He writes in his autobiography: "I think that Trudeau's firm leadership, putting the preservation of law and order above any other consideration, was probably the most important single contribution he made to the preservation of peace and democracy in Canada during his time as prime minister ... the first duty of the government is to govern – which means never giving in to chaos or terror."[42]

Change of Heart

Some people who opposed the War Measures Act in October 1970 changed their minds in subsequent years, while others who supported it at the time have reconsidered. In 1998 the historian J.L. Granatstein noted that in October 1970 he had opposed the War Measures Act at a York University rally of 5,000 students and was shouted down and even threatened by the audience, which *favoured* the act. "There were other speakers, including historians Ramsay Cook and John Saywell, but in my memory I was the only one to oppose the government's actions forthrightly ... I have never before or since been afraid of a crowd, never feared being torn limb from limb, but that day I was frightened. The shouts from the students that interrupted my speech were frequent and hostile; the visceral hatred of the FLQ kidnappers and murderers, and, as I interpreted it, of all Québécois, was palpable. I was very pleased to get off that platform and into my office before I was attacked and beaten."[43] By 1998, however, Granatstein had reached the conclusion that the imposition of the War Measures Act Regulations was the proper course to follow: "Over the last dozen years I have come to believe that Trudeau acted properly during the FLQ crisis. The FLQ had been exploding bombs since 1963, attacking CBC property, armouries ... People were killed by the frustrated, angry *felquistes*." Noting further that, by October 1970, "ordinary police methods" seemed unable to control matters, he concluded: "Terrorism can never be tolerated. Advocating Quebec (or British Columbia) separatism is a legitimate political activity in a Canadian democracy, but kidnapping and murder are not."[44]

On the other hand, Eric Kierans, the federal minister of communications in 1970, wrote in his memoirs, published in 2001, that he had supported the imposition of the War Measures Act Regulations as a member of the Trudeau cabinet but later had regrets over the position he took. Kierans's account has only a short passage on the October Crisis; the violence, the bombings, the deaths, and the danger are not even mentioned.[45] What he does say is that, after the crisis, he became envious of Tommy Douglas, leader of the New Democratic Party, who "hammered the government for suspending civil liberties."

Kierans's change of heart has been cited by the small but determined band (supported by and organized by the Société Saint-Jean-Baptiste de Montréal) who, almost every October since 1970, have held a press conference to promote their opposition to the imposition of the War Measures Act Regulations. On 16 October 2003 those present were Claudette Carbonneau, the president of the CSN; Guy Rocher, one of the sixteen "eminent personalities" who signed the petition of 14 October 1970; Henri Massé, the president of the FTQ; and Bernard Landry, then head of the Parti Québécois.[46] On the same day, a long article to the same effect was published in Le Devoir and the Globe and Mail by Guy Bouthillier and Robin Philpot, president and chief researcher, respectively, of the Société Saint-Jean-Baptiste de Montréal. My reply was published in Le Devoir on 24 October 2003.[47]

Bouthillier is also responsible for one of the most exaggerated statements concerning the War Measures Act: when on 5 June 2003 he likened the use of the War Measures Act in October 1970 to the U.S. invasion of Iraq in 2003.[48] Consider the differences between the two:

- In Iraq, contrary to the Bush administration's claims, there were no weapons of mass destruction, and none of the nineteen Al Quaeda members who hijacked four planes and crashed them into the United States on 11 September 2001 came from Iraq. Nor was Iraq a threat to the United States.

- In Quebec, when the War Measures Act Regulations were proclaimed on 16 October 1970, the FLQ, which consisted exclusively of Canadian citizens and Quebec residents, sought separation of Quebec from Canada and the imposition on Quebec of a Marxist government. The organization had been responsible for over 200 bombings, six violent deaths, and two kidnappings. At the same time, sixteen critics of the provincial and federal governments had publicly advocated exchanging what they called "political prisoners" (some of whom were actually convicted murderers) for the two hostages. And a crowd of 3,000, on the eve of the day that the Regulations were proclaimed, chanted their support for the FLQ's aims and methods.
- In Iraq the war caused $22 billion dollars in damage to infrastructure (schools, office buildings, oil wells, pipelines, industrial structures, and homes) in the first few weeks, as well as resulting in the death of thousands of Iraqis and the wounding of many more.
- In Quebec the FLQ's planned confrontation with the authorities on 16 October 1970 never took place. As a result of the War Measures Act Regulations, no one was injured, nor any damage done. In all, 497 people were arrested, but those who had been arrested unjustly received compensation on application to the Quebec ombudsman.
- In Iraq, at the time of writing, the carnage continues. There is open war, and no stable government or security. And there is little or no compensation for the innocent victims.
- In Quebec, once the War Measures Act Regulations were proclaimed, the FLQ threat immediately disappeared and democracy was preserved.

Another outrageous statement in connection with the War Measures Act was made in October 2000 at a UQAM colloquium on the thirtieth anniversary of the October Crisis. There Charles Gagnon, who with Pierre Vallières had been a major figure in the FLQ, objected to the government's use of force in October 1970 under the War Measures Act. In effect Gagnon, a convicted terrorist, was complaining about his arrest and that of others, as well as the use of force by the democratically elected government he wished to overthrow.

Conclusion

The imposition of the War Measures Act Regulations was greeted with overwhelming approval, the only exceptions being the FLQ and its apologists and supporters, some intellectuals, some union and PQ leaders. Since 1970, some persons have changed their minds in both directions. Another large body of persons, who were not alive in 1970, now question the governments' actions. In my view, the questioning is not based on fact and relies on the myths surrounding the October Crisis to this day. The debate is unlikely to ever end, but perhaps the present book will provide the facts necessary to arrive at a more balanced conclusion.

Chapter 13

Provisional Government

Power tends to corrupt and absolute power corrupts absolutely.

> Lord Acton (1834–1902)

Absence of power corrupts, absolute absence corrupts absolutely.

> Pierre Trudeau paraphrasing Lord Acton, 1970

Unlimited power is apt to corrupt.

> William Pitt, Earl of Chatham (1708–78)

Power does not corrupt men; but fools, if they get into a position of power, corrupt it.

> George Bernard Shaw (1856–1950)

If someone says, that he wants to save the people, take good care to translate that to the effect that he wants power.

> Jean-Paul Desbiens (Frère Untel) (1927–2006)

One of the most intriguing aspects of the October Crisis is the issue of whether or not certain people in Quebec planned to replace the Bourassa administration with a "gouvernement de salut public," or a government of public safety. Other terms used at the time were coalition government, provisional government, or parallel government (or parallel power).

The term *gouvernement de salut public* originated in 1793, the second year of the French Republic, when a decree of the Convention Nationale, then ruling France, established a *comité de salut public* composed of citizens to supervise the government. In the twentieth century, the term usually relates to the unsuccessful 1961 putsch of four French generals, who declared themselves available, if needed, to replace the government of President Charles de Gaulle. More recently, a *gouvernement de salut public* was proclaimed in the Democratic Republic of Congo on 23 June 2000, after a long-running war in that country.

"Parallel government" (*gouvernement parallèle*) is similar to *gouvernement de salut public* and means a government, which has some sort of authority, alongside a legitimately elected government. The term "parallel power" (*pouvoir parallèle*) has the same meaning. "Coalition government" (*gouvernement de coalition*) is, of course, a more common term, signifying a government consisting of the representatives of more than one party. It can also mean, however – and this is the sense in which it was used in the October Crisis – the addition of unelected persons to a legitimately elected government. In the same context of October 1970, "provisional government" (*gouvernement provisoire*) denoted a coalition government formed to deal with the threat of FLQ terrorism. In this chapter I often use "provisional government" as a catch-all term that also encompasses the terms "government of public safety," "parallel government," and "coalition government."

It should be understood from the start that rumours of a provisional government did not affect the deliberations of the Bourassa cabinet during the October Crisis. In fact, we did not learn of such rumours until the end of October 1970, and, when we did, we were amazed and amused. As Bourassa said on 6 November 1970, "I heard about the possibility of a parallel government – I suppose some people were thinking about it but I was not able to take it seriously. After all, there was solidarity in my cabinet and in my government, there was agreement with other levels of government and we were making the decisions." Years later, in 1977, in answer to a question of Raymond Saint-Pierre of Montreal radio station CKAC, "Did you believe the thesis of a plot which aimed at constituting a provisional government?" Bourassa: replied: "personally, I did not find it realistic. Under the British system of government, to overthrow a government would have required a majority of the National Assembly. I had the loyalty of the Liberal Party. Moreover, for the whole period of my leadership of the Liberal Party, the party was on the whole, very loyal and very disciplined. It is a place where I could exercise my authority."[1]

Early References

As far as I can determine, the first reference in Quebec to the idea of a provisional government appeared in 1964, when the FLQ set out the four stages of its planned revolution: 1) preparation of the organization; 2) training, agitation, and propaganda; 3) show of force; 4) and formation of a provisional government.[2] The next reference dates to 6 October 1970, the day after Cross's kidnapping. In an editorial in *La Presse*, Jean-Paul Desbiens declared that the purpose of the kidnapping was to have the elected Quebec government negotiate with terrorists and thus give up part of its sovereignty and authority. Desbiens observed: "The example that is taking place in Jordan is conclusive. King Hussein was the only Arab leader to have recognized, in his land, *a parallel power*: that of the Palestinians. He tried to negotiate with them; he tried to limit their authority; but in the end, these two powers had to recognize the existence of one another. To this day, the confrontation has resulted in ten to twenty thousand deaths … and it has not ended."[3] Three days later, the idea surfaced again when Pierre Bourgault stated: "The government must accept the *parallel power* which the FLQ has given itself by kidnapping the British diplomat. The government must, among other things, stop the action of its police forces, it must offer immunity to the kidnappers, it must find a way to enter into contact, without danger, with this faction of the FLQ; and it must immediately commit itself to accepting this most important proposition of the FLQ."[4] Bourgault was thus acknowledging that giving in to the FLQ's demands would create a "parallel power" – something he favoured. At the time, Bourgault had considerable influence within the Parti Québécois, particularly with Jacques Parizeau, as well as in the province as a whole.

A parallel government was exactly what the FLQ wanted in October 1970 and indeed was the objective behind its actions. Robert Lemieux was explicit on this point at a student rally on 14 October 1970 and Charles Gagnon repeated the theme. In the words of a *La Presse* report, "Charles Gagnon was to endorse M. Lemieux's suggestion by asking them to organize themselves efficiently, so that the government finally recognizes the true *parallel power* – that of the Quebec people."[5]

Trudeau understood that the FLQ's aim was to establish a "parallel power" and so declared on 14 October 1970 after the army was brought into Ottawa: "We have not taken action against the FLQ as though it were a war. We have employed certain elements of the army as peace officers so that the police forces would be freer to accomplish their specific work and would not be obliged to spend their time protecting your friends from one or other form of kidnapping. I believe that it is more important to get rid of those who look to dictate their will to the government through a *parallel power* which resorts to kidnapping and extortion, and I consider that it is our duty as government to protect the members of the government and the important members of society from those who make use of these forms of extortion."[6]

Smoke and Fire: Claude Ryan

Was a plan ever *finalized* to take over the Quebec government in the event that it fell, a development that many thought was likely? I believe that there was no *final* plan, but the possibility was definitely considered even by persons who subsequently hotly denied it. The proof lies in several pieces of evidence. First, on 25 October 1970, the night of his election victory, Jean Drapeau referred to attempts to put in place a "provisional government." The next day, Peter C. Newman, editor of the Toronto *Star*, wrote an *unsigned* article which claimed that there had been a plot to replace the government of Robert Bourassa[7] – an article that was later attributed to *Star* journalist Dennis Braithwaite – and on 27 October the journalist Pierre-C. O'Neil wrote in *La Presse* of attempts to create a "provisional government" or a "government of public safety." That same day, in a press release, Robert Bourassa referred to the concept of a parallel government: "Premier Robert Bourassa formally denied, yesterday, being influenced in some way by the hypothesis 'so illusory as a supposed project of parallel government' in his decision to request the federal government for the application of the War Measures Act."

Questioned as to meaning given to the words "hypothesis so illusory," a spokesperson from the Premier's office clarified that it is necessary to understand by that "an eccentric hypothesis worked out by people working under an empire of illusions."

In a statement given to the press, the premier of Quebec specified that he was "essentially motivated in his decisions by reasons of security and public order," thus contradicting the hypothetical assertion of certain commentators.[8]

On 28 October 1970 *La Presse* stated in the same connection:

According to this rumour, a group of 11 [sic] people (René Lévesque, leader of the Parti Québécois, Claude Ryan, publisher of Le Devoir, Camille Laurin, leader of the opposition of the PQ in the National Assembly, Jacques Parizeau, PQ executive president, Jean-Marie Kirouac, UCC secretary general, Louis Laberge, FTQ president, Fernand Daoust, FTQ secretary general, Marcel Pepin, CSN president, Yvon Charbonneau, CEQ president, and Matthias Rioux, Montreal Teachers Alliance president) who, in a common statement, October 15th [sic], pleaded in favour of the government's acceptance of the FLQ conditions to save the lives of Cross and Laporte, are at the centre of this "plot."

Mr. Drapeau, who was the first to officially launch the story, has refused since Sunday night to furnish any supplementary information relative to this transition government even if he continued to hold up the threat in an interview which he gave yesterday to an international press agency.[9]

Also on 28 October 1970, Claude Ryan dismissed the rumours of a provisional government as unfounded, but two days later he backtracked and in effect admitted that these rumours had a solid basis in fact.

Ryan's shifting position deserves detailed analysis. His first statement on the issue of a provisional government, in an article entitled "The Poisoned Fruits of Panic" on 28 October 1970 in *Le Devoir*, denied all and went on the attack, speaking of unfounded rumours orchestrated by Ottawa:

In a context as hazy as this one, it was almost unavoidable that all kinds of rumours would be born. Some inevitably come from places that were carried away by panic in the heart of the Crisis.

In Mr. Trudeau's entourage, there is a typical manner of putting into circulation, then verifying, an opinion of which one is not sure, or is still a rumour, pure and simple. These come from journalist friends. One gives them a tip which promises to put them on the track of something big. One adds: make it public, specifying that it comes from very high up, but you must protect the identity of your sources. This method risks destroying reputations, aggravating panic: that is not important! What counts is that the P.M. could say, in the last analysis, "I knew things that I could not reveal" (for cases where the rumour would appear to be well founded) or again (for cases where the rumour would not be confirmed): "I cannot be responsible for all the rumours which are born in the heart of the government."

In this way, there is constructed in Ottawa the theory of a plot that had the purpose of evicting Bourassa from power and supplanting him by a *provisional government* destined to put Quebec under the supervision of the FLQ. And everything is put to work (cocktail parties favourable to the dissemination of silly rumours, calls to the left and to the right of errand-boys of the regime, etc.) in order to complete the theory.

But this instance is so barbaric, the more one seeks to support it, the more ridiculous and stupid it appears. I was going to write: malicious. I am not sure that Trudeau and his friends are out to get certain dissidents: I do not believe that they are capable of such lowness. I want rather to believe that they are carried away by panic.[10]

Ryan ended with a reference to McCarthyism: "Canada is witnessing a worrisome revival of McCarthyism. One never would have believed that this could come from the same ones who, on the faith of their old 'liberal' convictions, were elected to Ottawa to renovate Canadian policy there."[11]

Then, on 30 October 1970, Ryan, in answer to growing rumours and public commentary, finally admitted, in an editorial in *Le Devoir*, that he had actually discussed the issue of a provisional government on Sunday, 11 October 1970, with the four senior members of his staff, whom he had especially called to the *Le Devoir* offices for that purpose. There he had presented three alternatives: 1) Bourassa taking a hard line; 2) Bourassa being unable to act, which would require "the creation of a provisional government team made up of the worthiest elements of the several provincial parties, reinforced by a few political personalities from various circles" ("la constitution d'une équipe de gouvernement provisoire formée des éléments les plus valables des divers partis provinciaux, renforcée de quelques personnalités politiques des divers milieux)"; or 3) Bourassa not adopting a hard line.

Ryan went on to state that, emboldened by this meeting, and "it having been agreed that [he] should consult certain persons privately and confidentially," he immediately telephoned Lucien Saulnier, chairman of the city of Montreal's Executive Committee, that afternoon (11 October 1970). The two men then had a conversation that was "purely private, consultative and confidential." Saulnier apparently turned Ryan down but spoke to Mayor Jean Drapeau, who referred to the matter on municipal election night, 25 October 1970.

Ryan explained:

I consulted Mr. Saulnier, in my position as director of a newspaper, called to take a position on the events ... I categorically deny Dominique Clift's allegations that "Ryan has approached several important personalities" in order to evoke with them the spectre of the eviction of the Bourassa government and the prospect of a provisional government. I consulted Mr. Saulnier on October 11th in the context described above. After this date, there was no question, either in our conversations at Le Devoir, or in the conversations which preceded or followed the two joint statements, of the second hypothesis that we had conjured up at the beginning of the crisis.

Neither with Mr. Lévesque, nor with Mr. Pepin, nor with Mr. Laberge, nor with the other signatories of the "joint declaration," did I discuss at any point in time a project of provisional government. None of these people had raised this hypothesis with me.

Ryan added that, on 18 October 1970, Marcel Pepin had telephoned him and had asked him to sign a new declaration with the Front Commun leaders to the effect that the government should negotiate with the FLQ.[12]

On 31 October 1970 Pierre-C. O'Neil of La Presse replied that he more or less accepted Ryan's explanation that Ryan was acting in his assumed role of adviser to governments. O'Neil added, however:

Not content to reveal its information, Le Devoir accused those who, perhaps in an erratic way, I agree, sought to establish the facts starting with this stupid story of a plot. Not only was a Toronto journalist [Dennis Braithwaite] described as a messenger of power in this respect, but he was even summoned by Ryan to identify his sources.

The director of Le Devoir accused at the same time the government of Ottawa of spreading rumours.

The reality is different because, as far as everyone knows, the journalists who learned of this story from Ottawa did not write it. The Ottawa journalists who wrote it generally did not ascribe it to a federal source, any more than the journalists of Toronto and of Quebec who wrote this story.

With the passage of time, one wonders why the director of Le Devoir *did not explain earlier this story of a plot, since he was in the best position to do so.*

But, fundamentally, it is less a question of fixing a quarrel than shedding light on the ambiguous role which falls to *Le Devoir*, because of the importance it has in Quebec and the double role that it is called to play as consultant of the governments and as an organ of information.[13]

On 4 November 1970 Ryan blamed Trudeau again, this time for having disseminated the rumour of a plot by means of one of Trudeau's supposed docile journalist/acolytes, the Toronto *Star* reporter Dennis Braithwaite, who had written that "there was no plot, but perhaps an idea." Ryan seemed to agree with this analysis but was still upset with Trudeau. He wrote: "'No plot, perhaps, but an idea.' Here is the crime. It had to be a thick-headed Torontonian writer with a rough understanding to say it without wincing. It is now done. That which Trudeau and his acolytes would not dare admit, one of their admirers in this present crisis, the reactionary columnist Dennis Braithwaite, finally put in black and white." Claude Ryan, therefore, did not participate in any plot. There was not even a plot at all. But it was more serious than that. He dared to have an idea, "the idea, yes, that the Bourassa government would need to be reinforced by the addition of several personalities chosen outside of parliament."[14]

Michel Roy was present at the extraordinary one-and-a-half hour meeting that Ryan had in the offices of *Le Devoir* on Sunday, 11 October 1970, with his four senior staff (Roy, Jean-Claude Leclerc, Vincent Prince, and Claude Lemelin). Roy had been, quite unexpectedly, called from his home to the meeting by telephone (as had the three others) that Sunday morning by Ryan. The four staff members had been "flabbergasted" by Ryan's apparent endorsement of the idea of a "provisional government" or a "government of public safety." Various names for membership in such a government had even been discussed.[15] In his ultra-self-confident style, Ryan had apparently failed to realize that his staff disagreed with him and in fact were astonished by his position. After the meeting, Ryan drove off to see Lucien Saulnier.

The matter does not end there. On 26 October 1970 René Lévesque ridiculed the rumour of a provisional government: "This 'provisional government' is the most sinister farce I've ever heard of. Let's have no more of this sort of blackmail and calumny. This is not the way to re-establish a positive political climate."[16] In 1986, however, Lévesque declared in his memoirs that there were in fact plans to create a "coalition government": "Some honourable and well-known citizens, Claude Ryan among them, embarked on a solution. They were even ready, it appears, to envisage the perspective of a coalition government to strengthen backbones that seemed visibly yielding on the Quebec side."[17] Lévesque, in the contradictory style of which he was at times capable, then went on to state on the same page:

Alas, it was exactly from Ottawa, Toronto, and elsewhere that the final offensive burst forth without delay, its fury transforming Quebec for some time into a Gulag and responsible citizens into a panicky flock of sheep.

"Just watch me!" Trudeau had replied to journalists asking him how far he was willing to go.

As far as barefaced lying anyway, and that's the least of it, for he claimed to see, for instance, in the few meetings I have just described, "a parallel power ... that threatens the elected representatives of the people."[18]

Consider, too, the petition of 14 October 1970. That petition would have had no rational or logical purpose unless the signatories believed, or expected or hoped, that the government was falling, and, in the event that it did collapse, they wanted to offer their support in a provisional or coalition government of some sort. At the time of the petition, Lévesque wrote that there was no longer a government in Quebec.[19] Ryan, for his part, wrote that Bourassa had ceded to fear: "By requesting of its own initiative the bringing into force of the War Measures Act, the Quebec premier agreed in theory to submit his government to that of Mr. Trudeau. It established in the rest of the country's eyes the old reminder that Ottawa is the true seat of the national government and that Quebec is, ultimately, only a province a little more turbulent than the others ... Mr. Bourassa, in the middle of the crisis, yielded to fear."[20]

Jacques Parizeau explained in 1999 that he had been only the telephone operator, the "standardiste," for the petition of 14 October and was not involved with its creation.[21]

"We had the impression that the Quebec government was in the midst of falling apart ...

I think that it is what became evident in a number of people's minds: if the government falls apart, we would take up the slack. But I was not a party to these discussions ... I spent a weekend putting them in contact with one another."[22]

Note that Parizeau talks of a "weekend." That must have been the weekend that Ryan visited Lucien Saulnier in his home on Isle Bizard.

The 1970 testimony of Carole de Vault, FLQ member and petite amie of Jacques Parizeau, is intriguing. She describes how Parizeau came to her apartment at about 7:00 p.m. on what she believes was the evening of 13 October 1970 and asked for a drink. She got him his favourite scotch, Chivas Regal, and Parizeau, sitting on the couch while Carole sat at his feet on the floor, said: "You know, Carole, the Bourassa government is no longer capable of making decisions."[23] He then added that some persons were "ready to take over from the government, to set up what he called either a parallel government or a provisional government. You know, your apartment will be historic, because you will be able to say that the parallel government began here."[24] After trying unsuccessfully to reach Claude Ryan and Marcel Pepin by phone, Parizeau left about an hour later.[25] In the future, he was to call this period "the most perilous time of my life."[26] Neither the Duchaîne Report nor the Keable Report contradicted the substance of de Vault's testimony, and her book *The Informer*, published in 1982, has not been seriously challenged either.

Duchaîne's sole reference in his report to the issue of a provisional government was intertwined with the petition of 14 October 1970. His complete reporting of the two events, on which he, like Keable, did not question a single participant, was as follows:

In the meantime, the intellectuals and people linked to the political world, issue a common declaration which will cause some persons to believe that these people would like to create a parallel government. In effect, around 5 p.m., Mr. Claude Ryan, the director of the newspaper *Le Devoir*, who is one of the dominant figures in this group of intellectuals, receives a telephone call from Mr. René Lévesque, then president of the Parti Québécois. Lévesque, who had followed with interest the line defended by *Le Devoir* in this crisis, declares that he fears a hardening of Mr. Bourassa's position and asks Mr. Ryan if he would be prepared to participate, with some other people, in the publication of a common statement aiming to support the intention announced three days earlier by Mr. Bourassa to search for a negotiated solution. The leader of the Parti Québécois outlines a text that is submitted around 7 p.m. to the signatories brought together at the Holiday Inn in Montreal. During a press conference given at 9 p.m., Mr. Lévesque makes public the contents of the statement. Those persons who feared the formation of a provisional government see, in the interaction of these people, a confirmation of their fears.[27]

From this and all the other evidence, it would appear that Claude Ryan had three contradictory roles in the October Crisis: as a journalist/editor, as an adviser to governments, and as a political activist – drafter and signer of a political petition and a principal at the press conference where this petition was presented to the public. His explanations of his actions in any of the three roles seem to suggest that he may have hoped for a fourth role – as a member of some sort of provisional government.

The minutes of the PQ National Council on Sunday, 18 October 1970, shed additional light. Jacques Parizeau proposed joining with the three *centrales syndicales*, and in the ensuing discussion two council members, Guy Joron and J.-Y. Morin, suggested that it be made clear that "the common front would constitute a parallel government or a moral authority."[28] Lévesque, Parizeau, Laurin, and other leading PQ figures have dismissed the idea that a parallel government was ever considered, but they must have attended this meeting.[29]

Other Comments

Professor Dennis Smith, in the 1971 book *Bleeding Hearts ... Bleeding Country*, supported the views of Lévesque, Ryan, and the "sixteen." Smith believed that the government of Quebec, "rather than Ottawa," should have negotiated with the terrorists, but he denied there was any real talk about forming a coalition government, other than when Ryan spoke to his staff and then approached Lucien Saulnier.[30] Nevertheless, the idea of a coalition government in Quebec negotiating with the FLQ appealed to Smith, who thought the "conception ... entirely legitimate and constructive," though he conceded that "acceptance would have resulted in a profound change in the balance and direction of the Quebec provincial government."[31] Of course, this was exactly what the FLQ, Lévesque, the Parti Québécois, and the "sixteen" wanted. Their proposal was in essence, contrary to Smith, a "challenge to democratic legitimacy." Thus, Smith said what they refused to say – that they believed they were more competent than the elected governments to deal with terrorists. In effect, they wanted to form a coalition government.

Smith's frank acceptance of the concept of a coalition government is evident again when he talks, near the end of his book, about possible terrorism *in the future and creating a Quebec government of national unity*:

In the event of renewed terrorism, the alternative should thus be to contemplate what was unthinkable for the governments in October, 1970: to meet the challenge by rejecting extraordinary measures and concentrating instead on creating a Quebec government of national unity commanding the support of all sections of the population except the most intransigent terrorists and federalists. This government could negotiate terms with the terrorists without fearing for the loss of its own authority in the process. Its demonstrated confidence and authority might drive the terrorists into a relatively long period of inactivity.

Such a government would have to include René Lévesque, some other representatives of the Parti Québécois, and some Union Nationale members. Its formation would mark a dramatic change of direction for the Quebec Liberal party, for the provincial party would have to move somewhat closer to the independentist position of the Parti Québécois in order to gain its adherence. A coalition of this kind would be directed, in fact, against both federalist Ottawa and against terrorism.[32]

Again, this was exactly what the petition of the sixteen was about. And it is exactly what Ryan, Lévesque, and the sixteen were accused of. Anthony Westell observed that "if there ever had been occasion to create a provisional government to handle the crisis, the men who joined to sign the Lévesque-Ryan statement would presumably have been invited to take prominent roles."[33]

Why would such persons as Claude Ryan and René Lévesque have talked of forming a parallel or coalition government? Perhaps they did not understand Bourassa's intentions. Throughout the October Crisis, Bourassa was on the phone to a wide range of people, and, always the ultimate "spin doctor," he gave these people the impression that he was asking them for advice whereas in truth, he was more often than not using them. On Monday, 12 October 1970, Bourassa phoned Claude Ryan and had also met Rémi Paul of the Union Nationale, Camille Laurin of the Parti Québécois, and Camille Samson of the Crédit Social at the Queen Elizabeth Hotel. But his purpose was to inform them, not to consult them. Bourassa explained the consultation of 12 October this way: "There was the question of the army, the War Measures Act, and I thought I should meet the different party leaders. That exceeded the role of a party in power as such, but I do not believe, however, that it was a mistake on my part. It was not a question of forming a coalition government. It was not a question of consulting them. It was a question of informing them."[34]

In a 2000 interview with *Cité Libre*, Marc Lalonde, who was Trudeau's principal secretary during the October Crisis, spoke about the petition of the sixteen "eminent personalities" and "noises" about forming a parallel government:

Reply of Marc Lalonde: "There were grounds to take these noises seriously. This information came essentially from Mr. Saulnier, who was the president of the Executive Committee in Montreal. He said he was contacted by Claude Ryan, and in the following conversation that they had, Ryan brought up this possibility. Saulnier informed Drapeau and Bourassa about it ...

Question: "But these were rumours ..."

Reply of Marc Lalonde: "No, not rumours: Saulnier reported a conversation with Ryan where he [Ryan] told him that it was necessary to consider the possibility of constituting a new cabinet which would integrate intellectuals – probably like him! In effect, to constitute a type of 'national salvation government' under Bourassa. I do not think, however, that they would have ever suggested that Bourassa resign, in order to replace him."

Later Lalonde said, "I do not think that Mr. Saulnier lied. This was not a question of asking advice, but of putting unelected persons into the cabinet, in order to constitute a type of national front. Mr. Saulnier was not the type to invent things like that. Besides, he never subsequently said that he had been mistaken or that he had misinterpreted that which Ryan said to him."[35]

In *Les silences d'octobre*, Manon Leroux, while not mentioning any of the evidence noted above, dismisses briefly and out of hand the notion that certain people had envisaged the possibility of forming some sort of provisional government. She writes: "The same day, [14 October], sixteen political and intellectual personalities launched a resounding appeal for negotiation. This group consisted of, among others, René Lévesque, PQ leader (the movement's initiator), Claude Ryan, publisher of *Le Devoir*, and the directors of the large central unions as well as renowned academics like Fernand Dumont. This appeal will confirm a theory imagined by some, for example Lucien Saulnier, the right-hand man of Montreal mayor Jean Drapeau, according to which a parallel government was in the works with the view of overthrowing the legitimate government by a coup."[36]

I do not believe that Saulnier imagined anything at all. Ryan has said that, after discussing the proposition of a provisional government with his four leading editors, he telephoned Saulnier from the *Le Devoir* offices in downtown Montreal and then went to Saulnier's home to discuss the matter.

Of Ryan's motivation, George Radwanski and Kendal Windeyer wrote:

Although it seems quite clear that he [Ryan] never actually plotted a coup to overthrow the government, it seems equally unlikely that he would have considered himself unworthy to help bolster Bourassa's cabinet if the premier heeded that advice or to help fill the vacuum if the Bourassa government collapsed of its own accord.

Expectation isn't plotting. As long as he doesn't shake the tree, what crime does a man commit if he sits under an apple tree on a windy day waiting for a choice fruit to fall into his hands?[37]

But did Ryan, and Lévesque too, at least subconsciously, "shake the tree" with their newspaper articles, editorials, and public declarations? I think the answer is yes. Whether or not a provisional government was planned, their references — as well as those of others — to this idea illustrated, at the very least, a peculiar mindset. The same is true of their lack of discretion, calm, and judgment, to say nothing of their willingness to go first to the public rather than approach the government. What was their motivation? Did they perhaps have some subconscious self-interest as a group or individually? This was not their finest hour.

Conclusion

Again I repeat that I do not believe that a plan to create a provisional government was *finalized*, but it is clear that the possibility of such a government was seriously considered and discussed by a large number of people. Though a *coup d'état* was not envisaged, certain persons expected, spoke of, planned, and readied themselves for the government's offer of Cabinet positions or for the government's fall. Many of those involved hoped and expected they would fill the gap, contrary to democratic procedures.

Symptomatic of the planning was Claude Ryan's description of his own part, after many, many denials: "no plot, but perhaps an idea."[38]

Chapter 14

Voices of Calm, Voices of Panic

Be calm in arguing. Calmness is a great advantage.

George Herbert (1583–1648)

Il importe malgré tout de garder le calme.

Jean-Paul Desbiens, 1970

Wee, sleekit, cow'rin', tim'rous beastie, O what a panic's in thy breastie!

Robert Burns (1759–96), "To a Fieldmouse"

In his editorial of 6 October 1970, the day after the kidnapping of James Cross, Jean-Paul Desbiens wrote: "The main thing is to keep calm. Nobody can win over people who are not so inclined. The terrorists' strength depends on an understanding with the people. There is no such understanding here. There will be more acts of terrorism, but it will not take root among our people. It is still a marginal phenomenon."[1]

The Bourassa Government

Throughout the October Crisis, Bourassa stayed calm, never raised his voice, and listened patiently to everyone. In fact, throughout all the years that I knew him, from 1966 to his death in 1996, he never lost his composure.[2] In 1977 Bourassa was questioned fairly, but critically, by Raymond Saint-Pierre of radio station CKAC about his conduct in October 1970:

Question: "How did you react to the kidnapping of James Cross?"
Answer: "It was a new step in the terrorist escalation. It must be said that at that moment, we had problems. The question of the construction industry had been solved. My first hundred days had not been easy and I was in the middle of the specialist doctors' crisis. I had even cancelled part of my trip to the United States – to the west coast – as a result of the situation. These were serious problems."
Question: "On the other hand, you went to New York, even after the kidnapping of James Cross."
Answer: "Yes, I thought that all things being considered, it was preferable that I make the quick trip to New York. I was not the first Quebec leader to go to New York several months after an election. It was a trip that was nevertheless important for Quebec. We know that New York is the principal financial interlocutor of Quebec. In the economic and industrial sectors, as well, it can be very useful. Thus, as New York is an hour by plane from Montreal, I believed that it was better to accept the invitation."[3]

Later in the same interview, Bourassa stated: "Sunday afternoon [11 October 1970], we made the decision to convene the National Assembly on Medicare. The best proof that the government and its leader had kept their calm was that we took on the Medicare problem during the October Crisis. If the government had been completely overtaken by events, it would have postponed the adoption of Medicare."[4]

I too can testify that there was no panic in the Bourassa cabinet. It was a stressful time, of course, but everyone acted calmly. In 1978 François Cloutier, the minister of cultural affairs and immigration in 1970, wrote: "We are told that the premier had wanted to have all his ministers at hand so as to control them better, that many of them were faltering. That's untrue. As a whole, my colleagues, I am a witness to it, were very self-controlled. The emotional reactions were exceptional. There was certainly no panic. It was the opposite."[5] Jérôme Choquette described the situation this way:

Mr. Choquette admitted, during a press conference, that he would have had no other choice than to submit his resignation if the cabinet had not ratified his position – not to cede to the blackmail of the Front de Libération du Québec.

According to the Minister, the members of cabinet decided, after several sessions of Council, extending over a period of at least three days, that the so-called hard line must be adopted in a definitive fashion.

In addition, the Minister stated: "It is true that in a cabinet of ministers, there can be different points of view and different ways of seeing things. We discussed the Crisis for a long time and gradually reached our position and I can say that all decisions of the cabinet were unanimous."

Mr. Choquette went on, however, to specify: "I do not want to say that it is my point of view which prevailed, but the council of ministers came round to see things that way."[6]

Similarly, Claude Castonguay wrote to *La Presse* on 4 May 2001:

The minutes of the 1970 meetings of the federal cabinet were recently made public. During this time, I was a member of Robert Bourassa's government as Minister of Social Affairs. I have, therefore, lived close to the events of that sad autumn that is referred to in those minutes. Taking into account their gravity and their exceptional character, the events remain engraved in my memory.

Certain aspects of the federal minutes are at the very least contestable. The evaluation of the situation and the interpretation of the events which are reported there are far from agreeing with the reality I lived through during the period. It seems necessary for me to take a stand and give another version of the events for the benefit of those who are interested in this period of our history.

According to Prime Minister Trudeau, Robert Bourassa did not feel he was in a position, in the days that followed the kidnapping of Pierre Laporte, to preserve the solidarity of the National Assembly and of his cabinet if some action was not undertaken rapidly. He was afraid there would be resignations. In fact, the situation was completely different. The crisis, instead of dividing the members of cabinet and of caucus, had the contrary effect. We naturally felt the need to close ranks faced with the crisis and to support our prime minister during this difficult period. I had no knowledge of any resignation threat within the cabinet or the caucus. If there were any, they would surely not have gone unnoticed.[7]

Throughout the crisis, I neither saw nor heard any examples of panic or major discord within the government. We discussed the alternatives calmly, from Sunday, 11 October, to Tuesday, 13 October, and together came uanimously to the very difficult view that we could not exchange terrorists for hostages. Often, when people differ and are concerned about the position they are taking as part of a group, they make public statements – often by leaks – which they can rely on later, if need be. Among politicians, this is called "insurance." During the October Crisis, however, there were no leaks on our part, or public expressions of personal opinion, until November 1970, when the pressure was past.

The Critics

References to panic in the context of the October Crisis always seem to be made by people in one of three categories: those who themselves had panicked during the crisis; those who had, with dubious motives, tried to take advantage of the situation; or those who, years later, pointed fingers at others as a form of self-defence once their own conduct was called into question. The first person to use the word "panic" was Claude Ryan. He did so on 15 October 1970, four days after he himself had proposed the idea of a provisional government to his four senior editors and to Lucien Saulnier. He stated in *Le Devoir*: "Yesterday John Robarts [premier of Ontario] became another name to add to the numerous persons who favour the hard line. The situation created by the terrorists has degenerated, according to the premier of Ontario, into 'total war': the moment has come for each person to 'stand up and fight.' 'It is a most difficult decision,' added

J. Robarts, 'but no compromise is possible.' Robarts's diagnosis arises from panic. Matters have degenerated in Quebec in the last several days; they have not, however, reached the stage described by Mr. Robarts."[8] It is interesting that the petition of 14 October by sixteen "eminent personalities," published in *Le Devoir* on the 15th, also criticized Premier Robarts.

Others soon followed Ryan's lead. On 16 October, NDP leader T.C. Douglas called the imposition of the War Measures Act by the federal government "an action of panic."[9] Two days later, the National Council of the Parti Québécois met in Montreal, with Marc-André Bédard presiding and party leaders, including Jacques Parizeau, present. The minutes read in part:

A. Legault (Chambly) suggests that panic, which seems to be seizing the population be taken into account.

G. Grégoire suggests that the text of the proposition give to the Executive all the latitude necessary to negotiate the formation of a common front with the other groups.

Jean Doré reads the amended motion:

4th Motion: Considering that the Party's actions must not serve as a sanction of a democratic system which suppresses political and civil rights:

Considering as well that the present war measures could cause irreparable harm to individuals and to Quebec society;

Considering the panic of the population, it is moved that the National Council accept the participation of the Parti Québécois in a common front of democratic forces.

On a motion of G. Grégoire, seconded by M. Pelletier (V. – Soulanges) this resolution is ADOPTED.[10]

On 23 October 1970 René Lévesque wrote: "It becomes blindingly evident that at the three levels of government, at Montreal city hall as well in Ottawa and Quebec, there reigns the worst of counsels, a sort of hard and contracted panic, made of inhuman tension that is felt in the highest places, seasoned with a catastrophic incomprehension of the real roots of the evil from which we suffer."[11] Then, on the 26th, the following report appeared in *La Presse*: "Yesterday evening, while addressing the PQ members of Ahuntsic, Parizeau put forward the theory that the federal government took advantage of the commotion and panic created by the Cross-Laporte affair to start what he called the 'inevitable confrontation that would take place sooner or later between Ottawa and Quebec.'"[12]

The same theme surfaced in the years after the October Crisis. In 1980 Richard Gwyn wrote: "For three weeks, he [Trudeau] had to prop up Bourassa's government, frequently close to collapse, Choquette erratic and Bourassa alternately stubborn and panicked."[13] In 1996 Hugh Segal described the October Crisis as follows: "This was bad government, pure and simple. It was panic on the part of Bourassa and, in my view, the worst kind of fascist totalitarianism on the part of Trudeau, Bryce Mackasey in Labour, and Marc Lalonde, the prime minister's principal secretary."[14] Two years later, Eric Bédard wrote of panic among students "The entry into force of the War Measures Act is the crucial event of the October Crisis. This law, a veritable thunder clap in the Quebec sky, plunged many militants and sympathizers into a state of panic."[15]

Yet, despite all such talk, who really lost their heads in the October Crisis? There may have been a high level of anxiety in the population, but certainly not panic, and the invoking of the War Measures Act met with widespread support – not hysterical opposition – from the vast majority. As for the Bourassa government, it was calm and resolute throughout the crisis. Two of the opposition parties, the Union Nationale and the Crédit Social, also acted with calm and circumspection. Unfortunately, the same cannot be said of the Parti Québécois. A new political party, the PQ took public positions on every issue, while its leaders made statements, wrote newspaper articles, circulated petitions, and generally acted indiscreetly. Of no one was this more true than the party's leader, René Lévesque. Minutes of a Parti Québécois National Council meeting on 18 October 1970 include this subtle criticism of Lévesque:

6th proposition : the National Council declares its total support of the declaration and actions of the Parti Québécois Executive and must insist on the complete solidarity of all the members of the party as to the means and objectives used by the directors to face this actual crisis situation.

C. Parizé (Hull), seconded by M. Paquette (Jeanne-Mance), proposes that we support only the *last* declaration made in the name of the Party by René Lévesque.[16]

At another meeting, on the evening of 17 October 1970, when the news of Laporte's murder was announced on television, Lévesque burst into tears over the death of his friend. He spoke long and passionately of Laporte, a fellow journalist, a colleague with whom he had played tennis and with whom he had worked for years in the Liberal Party. Camille Laurin and Pauline Marois tried to console Lévesque, and the meeting was temporarily adjourned. After the adjournment, Jacques Parizeau began a monologue on strategy, in the light of the new circumstances, when Lévesque suddenly picked up an enormous ashtray and threw it at him. Parizeau was just able to avoid being hit, the ashtray crashing into pieces against the wall. The meeting adjourned for the evening.[17]

Twenty-nine years later, Pierre Duchesne noted that Jacques Parizeau still had strong feelings about the actions of the Parti Québécois during the October Crisis: "Those who lived through the events of October with great excitement nevertheless hated to see their party so completely caught off guard. After the difficult experience of the October Crisis 1970, Jacques Parizeau promised himself that in the future he would intervene so that the sovereigntist movement would never again fall into such an abyss."[18] As Parizeau himself said: "During the events of October, we behaved ourselves like amateurs. We must never again let ourselves be caught in such a way."[19]

Though it had no special inside knowledge, the PQ constantly took positions critical of the Quebec and Canadian governments. Thus, on 12 October 1970, it made a public declaration in favour of "the freeing of the political prisoners." This statement was made despite the party's admission that it was ignorant of the facts: "This is why, even though we do not possess any more information than does the general citizenry, we believe that it is our duty to make this statement."[20]

Who else lacked composure? Certainly, the sixteen "eminent personalities" seem to have lost their heads (see chapter 6) and ridden off "madly in all directions" – like Stephen Leacock's famous horseman. And those nationalists who said that the crisis was only a Quebec matter and who complained about the part the federal government was taking seemed to have lost impartiality and perspective, let alone any knowledge of the Constitution (see chapter 18). Finally, those who wrote vitriolic newspaper columns also lacked calm and judgment. During the crisis, many members of the media, especially radio commentators, competed with one another to be first with the news, magnifying each rumour and reporting enthusiastically each small morsel of information. Distinguished journalist and journalism professor Anthony Westell was critical of his profession's conduct in these difficult days: the "mass media," he said, must "share some responsibility for the crisis ... [It was] manipulated ... without the tendency of press, radio, and TV to magnify and exaggerate, a handful of terrorists could not have brought Canada to one of the great crises in its history."[21] John Saywell, dean of arts and professor of history at York University, as well as a television commentator at the time, was also critical of the media's behaviour. He stated: "For three months, the media relentlessly pursued its story, doing little to enlighten Canadians, but served as the desired publicist for the FLQ."[22]

Conclusion

It would seem that the persons who lost their sang-froid in the fall of 1970 were those who held a press conference and distributed a petition at the height of the crisis or who talked of a parallel government. They were the ones who wrote almost daily newspaper articles of a partisan and often vitriolic nature. They were the ones who ignored the fact that Canada was a federal state and that the provinces and Ottawa shared the duty under the Constitution to oppose the actions of the terrorists and to bring about a just solution to the crisis. It was these people who spoke rashly and reacted precipitously against almost every governmental decision. It also seems that, at times, they also acted opportunistically in their own self-interest.

Those who acted calmly, without panic, were the Bourassa and Trudeau governments.

Chapter 15

The Murder of Pierre Laporte

An event has happened, upon which it is difficult to speak and impossible to be silent.

Edmund Burke (1729–97)

Murder most foul.

Shakespeare (1564–1616), *Hamlet*

There have been many theories about how Pierre Laporte died and much speculation about who killed him. It is important, therefore, to try to set the record straight.

The preponderance of evidence causes me to conclude, without hesitation, that Laporte was strangled on 17 October 1970 in the house where he was sequestered at 5630 Armstrong Street, Saint-Hubert, and that only Jacques Rose and Francis Simard were with him at the time. Later, in 1982, the Chénier cell, composed of Paul and Jacques Rose, Francis Simard, and Bernard Lortie, declared that they collectively took responsibility for Laporte's death.[1]

Out of respect for the Laporte family, Justice Minister Jérôme Choquette released the coroner's preliminary report only after Pierre Laporte's funeral. *La Presse* summarized the report's findings:

The Minister of Employment and Immigration, whose body was strangled by the *Felquist* revolutionaries on Saturday night, succumbed to acute asphyxiation after having been choked by a chain that he wore around his neck.

This is what the official preliminary report revealed, which was made public at 10:30 a.m. yesterday by the coroner Laurin Lapointe, assisted by the pathologists Drs. Jean-Paul Valcourt and Jean Hould.[2]

The coroner's final report confirmed the preliminary report's conclusions.

Choquette showed the autopsy report to three ministers in Bourassa's cabinet who were also doctors – François Cloutier, Victor Goldbloom, and Robert Quenneville. Cloutier was later to write: "I saw with my own eyes the autopsy report ... There was indeed strangulation with the assistance of the chain that the victim wore around his neck and which left a characteristic mark."[3]

Public Declarations, 1970

On 6 October 1970, the day Cross was kidnapped, the FLQ's lawyer, Robert Lemieux, had said: "I have no doubt that the diplomat will be executed, if the demands of the kidnappers are not satisfied."[4] This statement may have encouraged the FLQ in the view that it would be necessary to kill one or both of their hostages. Later, on Thursday evening, 15 October 1970, at 11:00 p.m., Lemieux held his last press conference. There he announced that the FLQ had refused the final "six-hour offer" of the Bourassa government, made at 9:00 p.m., that the kidnappers could leave for Cuba, Algeria, or some other safe haven in exchange for the release of Cross and Laporte.[5] Lemieux did not call on his clients to release Laporte and Cross but stomped out in a rage, saying that the Bourassa government's position was a rejection of the petition of the sixteen "eminent personalities," whom he said represented 95 per cent of Quebec's workers.[6] He added: "Such an attitude [on the part of the Quebec government not to release prisoners] can only lead to more deaths."[7]

Thirty years later Lemieux still did not understand the irresponsibility of his words as a lawyer, in a democratic society, acting for terrorists who had already killed six innocent people. In October 2000, during the hour-long Radio-Canada TV program *Maisonneuve à l'écoute*, Marc Lalonde, Claude Ryan, Robert Lemieux, and I were interviewed. On this occasion, Lemieux stated that Laporte's death was caused by the War Measures Act. Cheerful and unperturbed before, during, and after the program, Lemieux did not exhibit an ounce of doubt, guilt, apology, remorse, or regret.

On Saturday evening, 17 October 1970, the FLQ advised Montreal radio station CKAC that Pierre Laporte had been "executed" at 6:18 p.m. and that his body was in the trunk of a car in the Saint-Hubert Airport parking lot, where it was in fact found. The FLQ communiqué of 17 October 1970 read: "Pierre Laporte, Minister of unemployment and assimilation, was executed at 6:18 p.m. this evening by the Dieppe cell (Royal 22nd). You will find the body in the trunk of the green Chevrolet (912420) at the Saint-Hubert base. P.S.: The exploiters of the Quebec people have only to behave themselves."

On 6 November 1970 Bernard Lortie was captured in a Queen Mary Road apartment. On the same day he made an unsigned admission that, on 16 October 1970, Laporte had tried to escape out the window of the house on Armstrong Street, where he was being held, and had cut himself badly.[8] Lortie further declared that on Saturday, 17 October 1970, only Jacques Rose and Francis Simard were in the house with Laporte. Laporte had again tried to escape through the window and at 4:30 p.m. was strangled in the struggle.[9]

On 28 December 1970 journalist Jacques Keable of Québec Presse received a last FLQ tape-recorded message. He summarized it as follows: "No matter what happens, no matter what could happen, we are victorious. The death of Pierre Laporte is the responsibility of a government which, by its attitude, forced the FLQ to go to the limit with its action and its influence."[10]

On 4 January 1971 an unsigned admission by Francis Simard was deposited in court. In it, Simard declared that he and the two Rose brothers were present in the house on Armstrong Street and that the three together strangled Laporte when he tried to escape. Laporte's body was then taken to the Saint-Hubert Airport parking lot in the trunk of the car used for the kidnapping. Simard's admission contained changes and corrections in his own handwriting and was admitted later at trial as evidence.[11]

On 6 March 1971 an unsigned admission by Paul Rose was admitted at trial. Rose had declared that he and his brother were present with Simard in the Armstrong Street house at the time of Laporte's death: "Two of us held him while the other tightened the chain which he wore around his neck."[12]

Blaming Ottawa

Claude Charron, Parti Québécois MNA for Jacques Cartier, blamed Ottawa for Laporte's death when he told a meeting of PQ members in the Maisonneuve constituency of Robert Burns on 17 November: "By refusing to meet the terrorists' demands, Prime Minister Trudeau is as responsible for the death of Mr. Laporte as the guys of the FLQ."[13]

René Levesque made the same argument on 18 October in his daily newspaper column: "We feel that the inflexible and uncompromising line of the State, dictated by Ottawa up until now, carries a heavy share of the responsibility for the tragic outcome we are experiencing. This is not the time to hide what we think."[14] Later, in a speech to a PQ meeting in Quebec City, Lévesque said: "I'm not making excuses for anyone and especially not for the murder that has been committed. But if an exchange had been negotiated a man would be alive today. A government does not dishonour itself by respecting human life."[15]

Post-Crisis Theories and Statements

Despite the coroner's report, many theories have sprung up as to the cause of Pierre Laporte's death, particularly by apologists for the FLQ. In particular, in 1977 Pierre Vallières wrote a long book, *L'exécution de Pierre Laporte*, attempting to show that either the army, organized crime, or the police had murdered Laporte. To my knowledge, no one has taken Vallières seriously, including the members of the Chénier cell.

Some years later, in 1982, safely free of further prosecution, Francis Simard – in collaboration with the three other members of the Chénier cell – Paul Rose, Jacques Rose, and Bernard Lortie, who had kidnapped Laporte – wrote *Pour en finir avec octobre*. Here they make it clear they were all responsible and that Laporte was murdered by one of them – which one, they do not say. They give no details of the death.

The book methodically disposes of all the conspiracy theories: "There have been many ways of 'explaining' the death of Pierre Laporte. There is one for every taste."[16] It first dismisses Pierre Vallières's theory that the FLQ had been infiltrated by its enemies, who then committed the murder: "For amateurs of mystery novels, there are idiocies, downright dishonest, of the kind found in *L'exécution de Pierre Laporte* by Pierre Vallières. It is the theory of infiltration, of the enemy coming from outside."[17] It then takes on other hypotheses, including one featuring the actions of a secret committee of the federal government: "Everything was said to have been directed by a secret committee, hidden in one of the federal government buildings in Ottawa ... There, the death of Pierre Laporte would have been decided. There, they would have wanted us to kill Laporte."[18] According to this theory, "the way to proceed was simple: act on those who kept him. The army and the War Measures Act had as their goal to push Laporte to the limit, to make him break down. Following the same logic, we would also reach a breaking point. We would lose our heads."[19] There was no manipulation, either before or during the October Crisis: "If there was any manipulation, it was afterwards. Not before, nor during."[20] The truth is that "Pierre Laporte was murdered. His death was not accidental."[21] And, finally, Simard and the others accept responsibility: "Without entering into details, we have always taken responsibility for the death of Pierre Laporte. From our arrest and through the trials that followed, we confirmed our complete responsibility, without limitation."[22] They expressed no sympathy for, and offered no apology to, Mrs Laporte and her family, or to anyone else. They considered themselves the aggrieved parties.

The Duchaîne Report of 1980 concluded that Pierre Laporte died in the presence of only Jacques Rose and Francis Simard and that the death was caused by strangulation.[23] In particular: "Our analysis of the facts and the testimonies has ... convinced us that Paul Rose was not at 5630 Armstrong at the time of Mr. Laporte's death."[24] It went on to say: "In addition, there is no hint that would permit us to connect the Mafia in some way to Pierre Laporte's death. On this point, Francis Simard and Paul Rose were explicit."[25] Duchaîne also noted that the medical testimony corroborated the version of Laporte's death given by the terrorists.[26]

It is generally accepted now that Bernard Lortie's original unsigned declaration to the police as to Laporte's death in November 1970 was correct and that only Jacques Rose and Francis Simard were with Laporte when he was strangled on Saturday, 17 October 1970.

The Funeral of Pierre Laporte

Pierre Laporte's funeral was held in Notre-Dame Basilica in Montreal on 20 October 1970. Place d'Armes was heavily guarded and access to the whole area was restricted. Before the service, I visited the Criminal Court House, a few blocks east of the Basilica, in order to pay my respects again to Mrs Laporte and her family. The darkened room was still and I could only mutter a few words of sympathy. I then walked back on Notre Dame Street to the Basilica. Instead of the usual bustle of people, tourists, delivery vans, and buses, the street was empty of even parked cars. The stores were shut tight; only the occasional soldier could be seen on the rooftops. I walked alone along the crown of the road.

My wife, Rosslyn, joined me in the great church, where parliamentarians and leaders from Quebec and Canada sat silently. The remarkable gilded carvings of the nave and altar were more beautiful than ever, but nothing overcame the feeling of emptiness for a life taken in its prime.

Chapter 16

The End of the Violence

Violence kills what it intends to create.

Pope John Paul II (1920–2005)

For me, violence is profoundly moral, more moral than transactions and compromises.

Benito Mussolini (1883–1945)

Although there were occasional FLQ bombings in 1971, terrorist violence in Quebec came to an end with the resolution of the October Crisis. The questions that now need to be addressed are: Why did the violence end? And why did terrorism peter out thereafter?

The Short Term

I believe that in the short term the proclamation of the War Measures Act Regulations on 16 October 1970 was the immediate cause of the end of the violence. The FLQ sought an insurrection, but the arrests made under the Regulations took the principal FLQ leaders and supporters off the streets, including Pierre Vallières, Charles Gagnon, Robert Lemieux, and Michel Chartrand, all of whom had been instigating the raucous student meetings and the closing of CEGEPS and universities. Without the War Measures Act,[1] the next step would have been confrontation with police, destruction of property, and out-of-control demonstrations. It is important to remember, as well, that the presence of the army, brought in the day before, on 15 October, had not calmed the students, the demonstrators, or their leaders. In the short run, therefore, it was the use of the War Measures Act that ended the violence.

Luck played a part too. On Thursday night, 15 October 1970, 3,000 students, dropouts, and others, led by Vallières, Gagnon, Chartrand, and Lemieux, were on the point of going on to their next step, physical confrontation with the authorities, the police, and the army. Fortunately, the laws that adopted Medicare and sent the specialists back to work were passed in a single day, allowing us to put the War Measures Act Regulations into force at 4:00 a.m. on 16 October 1970.

The Union Nationale and the Crédit Social had also helped us greatly from the beginning with their support of the Medicare legislation. Jacques Parizeau had lent his assistance, too, by persuading the Parti Québécois to support the government over Medicare, despite René Lévesque's public opposition and the PQ National Council's decision of 3 and 4 October 1970.[2] Together, the Union Nationale and the Crédit Social had won 30.8 per cent of the popular vote in the election held only five months before, and their strength was especially significant in rural and small-town Quebec. They could have posed problems for the government as it attempted to deal with the October Crisis, but they did not – instead, they acted with discretion and without self-interest, as responsible political parties should. In contrast, though the Parti Québécois had obtained only 23.1 per cent of the popular vote in the 1970 election, it was quick to take strident positions during the crisis, usually against the Quebec and Ottawa governments, and directly or indirectly favouring the FLQ. What would have been the outcome if the PQ had acted as responsibly as the Union Nationale and the Crédit Social, if it had called on the FLQ to release the hostages instead of advising us to exchange jailed terrorists for Cross and Laporte? This is a question that troubled me greatly at the time (see my diary) and still does so today.

We were also fortunate that, while FLQ members professed to be willing to die for the cause, in reality they capitulated at the first sign of force. They sent parcel bombs, left bombs in public places, kidnapped, and murdered – but generally at no risk to themselves. When force was used against them, they chose to accept the governments' offer of exile. And when they had had enough of living in Cuba, Algeria, and even France, they chose to return to Canada and to face the very justice system that they had earlier denigrated.

The naivete of the FLQ was another factor that helped resolve the crisis. The shock of the FLQ upon learning of the position of Quebec and Ottawa on a hostage/prisoner exchange was almost farcical: "What can you make of that, the all-out refusal, the final no of Trudeau ... Bourassa ...," said the kidnappers of Cross on tape recordings discovered after they had left for Cuba. "What has our action achieved so far?"[3] Seeing themselves as heroic figures in the mould of Che Guevara, who had fought in the jungles of Cuba and Bolivia, the FLQ chose to train in Algeria and Jordan and in the forests of Mont Tremblant Park, Saint-Boniface-de-Shawinigan, and Lac Saint-Jean (of course, only in summer) rather than in the streets of Montreal. They expected a workers' uprising, but this didn't happen, although there were sporadic resolutions by a few unions and the participation of eight Front Commun leaders in the petition and press conference of the sixteen "eminent personalities." As Gérard Pelletier said: "We came very close but the FLQ did not have clear aims. They believed in a workers' revolt for a workers' state and they hoped to get worker support, which they did not get. They did get student support, but this consisted of general student complaints as well as social grievances but none really wanted to have a workers' state. The theme of separatism was and is genuine, but the present Federal system is far from unfair and may not be far from the system that the PQ wanted."[4]

The students and professors were not really dedicated separatists or Marxists – or even socialists – so the FLQ could not count on them when the going got tough. They enjoyed the euphoria of the *Grand Soir* of 15 October 1970 at the Paul Sauvé Arena, but the application of the War Measures Act Regulations the following day brought them down to earth and they fell into line.

Another less well-known factor was the work of the police and police informers. In October 1970 we knew little about the FLQ and so the group was able to act almost as it pleased. By November 1970, however, the police had infiltrated FLQ cells and had recruited a number of informers, including Carole de Vault. Thereafter, it seems that almost every planned act of violence on the part of the FLQ was known in advance by the police.

The Long Term

In the long term, the brutal murder of Pierre Laporte was the key event that explains the collapse of the FLQ after the October Crisis. This shocking crime forced many collaborators and sympathizers to realize that the FLQ was dangerous and that its political ideas would end only in more violence and instability. For the first time, sympathizers came to understand that, in a democratic society, one cannot support the goals of terrorists without indirectly approving their methods of terror and blackmail. Thus, with respect to the FLQ's student followers, Eric Bédard notes that Laporte's murder, added to the War Measures Act, was "the last nail in the Revolution's coffin."[5]

An equally important reason for the end of the violence has to do with the nature of Quebec society. French Canadians are not, and have never been, a violent people – Quebec is not the kind of violence-plagued society that one finds in so many parts of the Third World. Compare Quebec with even Northern Ireland, where, until recently, Protestants routinely killed Catholics, and vice versa, and where a handful of paramilitary groups necessitated the maintenance of special police and troops at a cost of £3 billion per year (approximately six billion Canadian dollars). In addition, French Quebecers are extremely tolerant, as can be seen from their treatment of minorities. Consider, for example, the rights accorded Greek,

Jewish, and Muslim private schools in Quebec; there is nothing comparable in any other Canadian province or in any other country, including, in particular, Greece, Israel, and the Muslim world.

Then there are the economic factors. Since 1970, Quebec has prospered economically, despite the warnings and prognostications of the FLQ, the Parti Québécois, and innumerable intellectuals and economists. In particular, French Canadians in Quebec, through their own efforts, have attained a high standard of living. After listing seventeen dire economic statistics concerning Quebec in 1970, the respected economist Diane Cohen stated: "The imposition of the War Measures Act and its successor, the Public Order (Temporary Measures) Act, appear to be implicitly based on the assumption that a man is converted because he is silenced. Unhappily, the underlying factors that feed FLQ-type terrorism will not vanish because the FLQ has been outlawed."[6] But time has healed almost all of the economic problems noted by Cohen, evidence that the Quebec economic and political revolution has continued to the present, without the aid of terrorism.

All of these factors help to account for the disappearance of the FLQ after 1970. But we should add two others. First, as fears about the future of the French language and culture in Quebec have abated since 1970, nationalist Quebecers have had one less reason to be drawn to the kind of radical agenda promoted by the FLQ. Second, the very fact that the Parti Québécois has twice been in power since 1970 (1976–85 and 1994–2003) has alleviated the frustration of many nationalist Quebecers, although it may have disappointed many members of the FLQ. As FLQ member Gabriel Hudon said in 1977:

Will the FLQ reappear now that the Parti Québécois is in power? I think the question that must first be asked is the following: is the PQ going to achieve independence?

And then there is the possibility that one day the PQ will limit its fight to only seeking a vulgar, little, private recognition within Confederation. In that case, everything would begin again and it is strongly probable that this will lead to the birth of another generation of felquistes.[7]

Hudon may be right, but I think not. Marcel Chaput, perhaps the first Quebec separatist of our time, ended his 1961 book *Pourquoi je suis séparatiste* with the words, "The unique reason for our cause – Dignity."[8] Chaput's *cri du coeur*, however, has now been answered for many nationalists by the political, social, and economic ascendancy of French Quebec.

Conclusion

In summary we may say that, in the short run, the October Crisis ended for a variety of reasons: the decision of the Canadian, Quebec, and Montreal governments to fulfil their responsibility under the Constitution and refuse to exchange jailed terrorists for hostages; the application of the War Measures Act Regulations, at just the right moment, thanks in part to the cooperation of the three opposition parties over Medicare; the positive attitude of the Union Nationale and the Crédit Social during the whole crisis; the ineptitude of the FLQ and the unwillingness of its members to die for their cause; and the naivete of many of the FLQ's supporters and sympathizers. In the long run, politically inspired violence came to an end after 1970 mainly because of the horrible death of Pierre Laporte and the fact that French Canadians are in general a peace-loving people who respect democracy and justice. The strength of the Quebec economy and the important part that French Quebecers have in that economy, the PQ's holding of power on two occasions in the period from 1970 to the present, and the strength of the French language in Quebec are other important factors that should be taken into account.

Chapter 17

Convening the National Assembly?

During the crisis the Parti Québécois, unlike the Union Nationale and the Crédit Social, continually called for the immediate convening of the National Assembly in order to debate the government's actions. The Quebec government refused to comply until 10 November 1970 and I believe it acted appropriately.

The National Assembly was not sitting when Cross was kidnapped. It had last sat on 8 August 1970, when Pierre Laporte, as minister of Labour, had masterly negotiated, and then settled, the construction strike, to the satisfaction of all parties. The Assembly had then been adjourned until 27 October 1970.

Bourassa, as was his right as prime minister, called the National Assembly into session on Thursday, 15 October 1970, at 3:00 p.m., in order to deal with the adoption of Medicare and the specialist doctors' strike. The debate continued until just past midnight the next morning, 16 October 1970, when we adopted all three readings of all three bills on Medicare, including sending the specialists back to work. At that point the Parti Québécois presented a "motion of privilege" to debate the question of the safety of a member of the National Assembly – Pierre Laporte. In effect, the Parti Québécois wanted an immediate public debate on the crisis at the height of the crisis.

A few minutes later, at 44 minutes past midnight, the president of the National Assembly, Jean-Noël Lavoie, discussed and rejected the motion. At that point, Robert Bourassa declared:

Mr. Speaker, I have taken note of the decision that you have rendered. I believe I can well say that, in any event, the security of the state or public interest would have prevented me from commenting on the crisis, since the slightest statement could have a tragic outcome in the circumstances. This is not the time, nor the moment to play politics with the events which are presently taking place in Quebec. In conclusion, Mr. Speaker, I would like to thank all the members for the cooperation that they have brought to the adoption of these three bills.[1]

The House adjourned at 52 minutes past midnight until 10 November 1970.

The Parti Québécois

It would seem that the Parti Québécois members wanted a public debate not to find a solution to the crisis but rather to criticize the government. This latter was, of course, their right and role as members of the Opposition under our parliamentary system. In such a delicate situation, however, the Loyal Opposition has a duty to use discretion and judgment. In particular, they had to be certain that their position was the correct one and that they were not aiding the FLQ. This is especially true in parliaments, where speeches by ministers and members are made under their oath of office and the prime minister, who is also the chief executive of the government, is subject daily to probing questions during question period. Written questions answered in writing and emergency debates are other tools available to the Opposition. (Such extraordinary powers do not exist to the same extent under the American congressional system.) Nevertheless, the intelligent use of such powerful instruments in a parliament requires judgment and discretion.

The Parti Québécois members in the National Assembly were under great pressure from René Lévesque, caused by his frustrated public outbursts, and from their younger party members and their new allies, the Front Commun union leaders. The seven PQ members of the National

Assembly also rejoiced in their popularity with the press. To be cut off from the extraordinary podium, the National Assembly, was too much for most of them. Silence was impossible and discretion thrown to the winds. Unlike the Union Nationale and the Crédit Social members, many of whom had years of experience in the House and had even been ministers, the PQ members failed to see that in rallying their troops, they rallied the FLQ as well.

On radio and TV hot lines and at mass meetings, the PQ leaders often made preposterous statements. For instance at one point Robert Burns the representative of Maisonneuve said that "The true opposition in Quebec no longer lives at the National Assembly, it is here, and it lives in the prisons." Burns was speaking to a crowd of more than a thousand people, mostly students, who had come together for a teach-in on the defense of civil liberties.[2] René Lévesque also called for the immediate convening of the National Assembly in order to debate the issue, as did Claude Ryan.[3]

The Emergency Debate

The National Assembly reconvened on 10 November 1970 and the emergency debate on the crisis began on 11 November 1970, being the first real order of business, after the standard parliamentary housekeeping had been taken care of. Bourassa wisely allowed the opposition parties to proceed first and there was very little effective criticism of the government position. The Crédit Social and the Union Nationale generally agreed with the government, while the Parti Québécois conveniently ignored most of the points they had raised during the previous weeks and emphasized injustices under the War Measures Act Regulations.

All seven PQ members spoke voluminously but did not mention the PQ's negative position on the reading of the manifesto, the calling in of the army, the exchange of terrorists for Cross and Laporte, or the petition and press conference of the sixteen "eminent personalities," which included Lévesque, Parizeau, and Laurin. Instead, Lucien Lessard (Saguenay),[4] Marcel Léger (Lafontaine),[5] Guy Joron (Gouin),[6] Robert Burns (Maisonneuve),[7] Charles Tremblay (Sainte-Marie),[8] and Claude Charron (Saint-Jacques)[9] spoke almost exclusively of the War Measures Act and the economy. Only Camille Laurin (Bourget) spoke very briefly on exchanging terrorists in his very long speech.[10] I and many other Liberals did not speak in the National Assembly in November 1970 during the October Crisis emergency debate because Bourassa was keen that the Liberals say as little as possible and not become involved in arguments on the facts, especially as no one was fully informed. We were also concerned that what we might say could endanger Cross, who was still being held hostage. In addition, I had made a statement in *Le Devoir* on 4 November 1970 and that seemed sufficient, because it received considerable commentary and publicity – much more than a speech in the Assembly.[11] At that time the debates were not televised or broadcast on radio, so that there was little interest in speaking in the Assembly, except at question period and the hour or so that followed when the reporters were present. Of course, if I had been as informed then as I am now, I would have been delighted to speak at length for the record. In fact, most of the speakers during the emergency debate had very little concrete to say. It is only with time that the facts have emerged.

In 1976, when the Parti Québécois came to power, they were well aware of the weaknesses of the position they had taken in October 1970. As a result, they called for only a very private enquiry, the Duchaîne Enquiry, conducted by a single party member, who was not given powers of subpoena or public hearing.[12]

Conclusion

An emergency debate at the height of the crisis, especially, when Cross and Laporte were in the hands of the FLQ, would not have brought about calm or reflection, particularly because the FLQ was intent on proceeding with its next step – confrontation and violence. A debate at that time would have only reinforced the FLQ in its purpose.

Chapter 18 | Was the Crisis Principally a Quebec Matter?

The pure and simple truth is never pure and simple.
Oscar Wilde (1854–1900)

Opponents of the combined action of the Canadian and Quebec governments claimed that the solution to the crisis was principally a Quebec matter. To me the crisis fell almost equally under the jurisdiction of the Quebec and Ottawa governments, as even a summary study of the Constitution points out.

The Constitution

In 1970, provincial governments had authority under the Canadian Constitution (at that time the BNA Act 1867 and today the Constitution Act, 1867) over the administration of justice in the provinces, including the creation and organization of provincial courts of both civil and criminal jurisdiction, over the enforcement of provincial laws by fines, penalties, and imprisonment, and over provincial prisons at sections 92(6), (14), (15), (16), and (13). The federal government on the other hand had, and has, authority over criminal law and procedure, the appointment of superior, district, and county court judges, and the federal penitentiaries, again under the BNA Act and the Constitution Act, 1867 at sections 91 (27), (28), (29) and 96.

In particular the Government of Quebec had authority *alone* to release six of the twenty-three imprisoned terrorists by the simple procedure of *nolle prosequi*, meaning that the Crown had decided not to proceed further. Quebec had authority, as well, to recommend five others for parole. Nevertheless the federal government had constitutional jurisdiction over the armed services in virtue of the BNA Act 1867, at sect. 91(7), "Militia, Military and Naval Service and Defence," but the provinces could request the federal government to send in the Army. This was, of course, done during the 1970 crisis and the year before by the Union Nationale government during the Montreal police strike. The federal government, in virtue of its constitutional power over criminal law, adopted the War Measures Act but the provinces had authority under that same Act to request the adoption of the Proclamation and Regulations in case of war, insurrection, or apprehended insurrection. In other words the rights, obligations, and authority under the Constitution with respect to the crisis were sometimes divided between the federal and Quebec governments and at other times there was joint power and obligation.

The Appendix to the present chapter includes an impressive list of examples of instances where the federal and Quebec governments either acted alone in their jurisdictions or shared responsibilities, without controversy, in their joint search for a solution to the crisis.

Statements on Whether the Crisis was Principally a Quebec Matter

Despite the terms of the Constitution, not everyone believed the crisis fell into both federal and provincial jurisdictions. On 14 October 1970, the petition of the sixteen "eminent personalities" stated: "The Cross-Laporte affair is above all a Quebec drama. One of the two hostages is a citizen of Quebec, the other a diplomat whose functions make him temporarily a fellow citizen with the same right to respect for life and human dignity as each of us enjoys."[1] The petition also castigated Premier Robarts of Ontario for intervening in the matter: "Some outside attitudes, the most recent and most incredible of which is that of Premier Robarts of Ontario ... threaten, in our opinion, to reduce Quebec and its government to tragic impotence." The petition was referring to a declaration by Robarts the day before, where he had said: "There is no way we can yield to these terrorist demands ... By Jove, this has got to be a law-abiding country where you can bring your family up without fear ... the demands are wrong – morally wrong and socially wrong – we have to stand and fight. It's war – total war."[2] In my view, the premier of a province in the Canadian Confederation is justified in commenting on terrorists who wish to separate Quebec from Canada by other than democratic means. I wonder, however, if Robarts had to be so bellicose.

On 17 October, Claude Ryan wrote: "For Mr. Bourassa and his Government, there was more to the Cross-Laporte drama than the necessity of halting the risk of insurrection at all costs. There was also and *above all* a unique opportunity to affirm at the highest level the responsibility of the Quebec State. Giving up the inclination that he had shown in this direction, Mr. Bourassa preferred, in the final analysis, to turn to the power of Ottawa. By requesting, on his own initiative, the coming into force of the War Measures Act, the Premier of Quebec agreed in principle to subordinate his government to that of Mr. Trudeau. It confirmed, in the eyes of the rest of the country, the old erroneous vision that Ottawa is the seat of the real national government and that Quebec is only a province a bit more turbulent than the others. This rapid slide is contrary to the evolution of the past ten years. It perhaps also indicates what could happen in other fields."[3]

On 27 October, René Lévesque wrote: "*C'est notre drame. À nous d'en sortir*" ("It is our problem, it is up to us to get out of it").[4] Two days later, the Parti Québécois published an eight-page apologia entitled: *C'est notre drame. À nous d'en sortir* in a special edition of 500,000 copies of *Pouvoir*, the PQ magazine. A conclusion of the document was that Ottawa should play little part in how to solve the crisis.

On 31 October, Trudeau spoke to the nation on Radio-Canada and, in answer to René Lévesque and others who had asserted that the Quebec government of Robert Bourassa was in the process of abdicating its powers to Ottawa in the crisis, declared: "that throughout the period of the FLQ-spawned crisis there has been full agreement between the federal and Quebec governments and the Montreal municipal authorities ... A handful of small-minded persons would have you believe this is scandalous, as if any agreement between the three spheres of government was bound to hurt Quebec and help Ottawa. In fact, all that each government did was to exercise its own powers in the sole interest of collective security."

During the emergency debate in the National Assembly on 11 November, Jean-Jacques Bertrand, leader of the Official Opposition, in alluding to and criticising the position of the Parti Québécois, said: "I immediately recognize and understand – there are those who do not want to realize it – that we are in a federal regime. I know that there are responsibilities which belong to the federal government and I know that there are responsibilities which belong to the provincial government."[5]

Even the Parti Québécois report of Jean-François Duchaîne noted that it was normal that the federal authorities take the first position on the crisis, because the security of foreign diplomats in Canada was essentially a federal responsibility.[6]

The Drafting of Bourassa's Letter of 15 October 1970 to Trudeau

There has been speculation over who wrote the letter signed by Bourassa on 15 October 1970 but dated and delivered the next day, requesting that the federal government proclaim a state of apprehended insurrection under the War Measures Act. Claude Ryan, in the preface of his book *Le Devoir et la crise d'octobre*, suggested that it was Marc Lalonde, Trudeau's chef du cabinet.[7] Ryan, a normally quite equable person, disliked Lalonde, which was only surpassed by his antipathy to Trudeau. Ryan constantly repeated the story. For example, in 2000 it was the first matter he brought up when he gave me a ride in his car after the Radio-Canada TV programme of *Maisonneuve à l'écoute*, where Ryan, Lalonde, Robert Lemieux, and I were interviewed for an hour. Ryan mentioned it again when we last met at the McGill Law Faculty Library on 25 November 2003 to discuss the crisis. Claude was too sick to lunch, and soon after was diagnosed with stomach cancer, but he still was defending his position with his usual verve.

In the autumn of 2000, Marc Lalonde was questioned by Max and Monique Nemni, editors of *Cité Libre* magazine, concerning the Bourassa letter. Lalonde explained that as Trudeau's chef du cabinet, he was delegated to go to Quebec to collect a letter signed by Bourassa and to Montreal to collect another signed by Mayor Jean Drapeau:

Question: "In connection with the letters, Claude Ryan wrote 'that no one knows if the federal government (in fact, if you, Marc Lalonde) went to Quebec to find this letter at Bourassa's or to dictate it to him.'"[8]
Marc Lalonde: (Burst of laughter) "But, if he did not know, he could have asked me at the time! I would have told him everything without hesitation! Besides, the suggestion indicates a lack of knowledge of Mr. Bourassa and a lack of respect for him in order to believe that Bourassa would let such a letter be dictated by me. A first draft of this letter had been prepared by Mr. Julien Chouinard, the secretary of the Cabinet, in Quebec. We discussed it, we made several minor revisions to assure ourselves that the text of the letter corresponded exactly with the provisions required by the War Measures Act, and it was duly signed. It is obvious that we would have done nothing without that signature. And in spite of that, see how the myths continue to circulate."

Conclusion – A Federal/Provincial Matter

A study of the facts and the Canadian Constitution clearly indicates that the October Crisis and its solution was not principally a Quebec matter but fell into the jurisdiction of both the federal and provincial governments. At times it was purely federal or purely provincial and at times it was joint as, for example, when Ottawa sent in the army at the request of Quebec or when the War Measures Act Regulations were proclaimed, again at the request of Quebec.

Appendix

Herewith a compendium of various actions of the Quebec and Ottawa governments during the crisis, where they acted individually or together, but always in concert.

On Tuesday, 6 October 1970, the Bourassa government and the Trudeau government decided to work in concert. The principal demands of the FLQ were deemed unacceptable by both governments and a statement prepared by Quebec Justice Minister Jérôme Choquette was checked and amended by federal Deputy Prime Minister Mitchell Sharp and then read on the radio by Mr Choquette.

On Wednesday, 7 October, the two governments rejected the ultimatum in the second FLQ communiqué.

On Sunday morning, 11 October, Julien Chouinard, secretary to the Quebec Cabinet, called his opposite number in the federal Cabinet, Gordon Robertson, clerk of the Privy Council, at his home and "told him that the Quebec and Montreal police were making no progress in locating the FLQ cell that had kidnapped Cross." A further problem was that "any person picked up because of known or probable connections with the FLQ had to be released by the police in forty-eight hours under provisions of the Criminal Code." People under suspicion could not be held "long enough for any effective probing of stories and once they were released they 'disappeared.'" It was necessary to be able legally to hold suspicious individuals longer. The only solution they had discovered was under the War Measures Act. Robertson advised Chouinard that: "there was no chance whatever of that being done unless the premier, Robert Bourassa, could personally convince the prime minister of the utter necessity of so unprecedented an action. He accepted that and Premier Bourassa did then call Trudeau."[9]

On 11 and 12 October, there was cooperation between the authorities of Ottawa, Quebec, and Montreal in drafting the War Measures Act Regulations.[10]

On Monday, 12 October, the federal government called the army into the Ottawa region and on the same date the Bourassa Cabinet appointed Robert Demers to make contact and negotiate with the FLQ.

On Tuesday, 13 October, the Bourassa Cabinet agreed that Robert Demers, in his negotiations with the FLQ, was not to agree to exchange convicted terrorists for Cross and Laporte. Five prisoners eligible for parole would be recommended to federal authorities for parole. Robert Demers was advised of the decision but was to continue to negotiate with Robert Lemieux, negotiator of the FLQ.

On 15 October, the Bourassa government called the Canadian Army into Quebec, which was a provincial right under the National Defence Act. Duchaîne described the arrangement between the police and the Army: "The Armed Forces' headquarters will be at the Sûreté du Québec, and there will also be an inspector from the Montreal Police Force on the premises to ensure a liaison with the police. It is understood that the soldiers will have the same rights as police officers; however, it is specified that in the case of riots, the soldiers will not be able to open fire without an appointed police officer giving them the order. The dispositions that authorize a province to require the intervention of the army under the National Defence Act are that the attorney general can designate an officer responsible for a unit to accompany the troops and order the army to act. Everyone seems in agreement that the police officer, given this task, must hold at least the rank of inspector."[11]

On 15 October, negotiations had broken down between Robert Demers and Robert Lemieux and at 6:30 p.m. the Bourassa Cabinet decided to give notice that evening to the FLQ that it had six hours to comply with the Quebec government's final offer to release Cross and Laporte in exchange for sending the kidnappers to Cuba. The government would also recommend to federal authorities parole for five of the twenty-three imprisoned terrorists who were eligible for parole.

On 15 October, at 9:00 p.m., the Quebec government gave the notice to the FLQ, advising that the six-hour time limit would expire on 16 October 1970 at 3:00 a.m.

On 15 October, at 11:00 p.m., Bourassa studied and signed the final draft of the letter prepared by Julien Chouinard, the highest civil servant in Quebec, to Prime Minister Trudeau (dated 16 October 1970), which requested "emergency powers."[12] Bourassa gave it to a messenger with instructions to take it to Ottawa but not to deliver it without instructions from his office. The City of Montreal had, the day before, delivered a brief letter to Prime Minister Trudeau, dated 15 October 1970 and signed by

Lucien Saulnier, chairman of the Executive Committee, and Mayor Jean Drapeau, which asked for "the assistance of the superior governments ... to protect the society from a seditious plot and from an apprehended insurrection." To the letter was attached a long letter of 15 October by Marcel Saint-Aubin, the director general of Police of Montreal, which made the same point, but in different terms.[13]

On Friday morning, 16 October at 3:15 a.m., Bourassa's office gave instructions that the letter, dated 16 October 1970, requesting emergency powers be delivered to Trudeau.[14] Members of the federal Cabinet were assembled in Ottawa and, upon receiving Bourassa's letter, proclaimed a state of apprehended insurrection and adopted the Regulations in virtue of the War Measures Act.[15] The state of apprehended insurrection and the proclamation of the Regulations came into effect at 4:00 a.m.[16]

After the imposition of the War Measures Act Regulations, it was the Quebec government that continued to be in charge of operations taking place against the FLQ and in searching for Cross and Laporte. For example, Maurice St-Pierre, chief of the Sûreté du Québec, was in charge not only of the Quebec and municipal police forces but also of the RCMP and the army, which reported to him.[17]

On 31 October, Trudeau advised: "The troops will return to their bases as soon as Quebec makes the request."[18]

On 3 December, the flight to Cuba of the captured FLQ kidnappers was dealt with by the two governments, including federal arrangements with the Cuban government in Montreal and in Cuba to receive Cross's kidnappers.

On 14 December, the Quebec government announced that it would introduce legislation to indemnify persons who were victims of criminal acts, including Mrs Pierre Laporte.[19] Thereafter, under a Quebec law, the Quebec Ombudsman, at his sole discretion, could award sums up to $30,000 per person to those who had suffered damages because of the imposition of the War Measures Act Regulations.

On 27–28 December, Paul Rose, Jacques Rose, and Francis Simard were found in a twenty-foot tunnel in a house in St Luc, near St Jean, Quebec. Bourassa asked Dr Jacques Ferron of Longueuil to convince the three *felquistes* to surrender. Ferron visited them and they emerged from their hideout a few hours later.

Chapter 19

Federalism at Work

No government has the right to interfere with the administration of other governments in those areas not within its own jurisdiction.

Pierre Elliott Trudeau in *Cité Libre*,
February 1957, translated in *Federalism and the French Canadians*

In the previous chapter it was pointed out that the Canadian Constitution divided rights and responsibilities between the provinces and the federal government. In the Appendix to the same chapter many examples of Ottawa and Quebec acting individually and in concert are given. This, however, raises the fundamental question: Did federalism work successfully during the crisis?

The short answer is that Canadian collaborative federalism worked very well and there were no disputes between the two authorities; each acted in its own sphere and the two levels of government provided a framework of checks and balances that protected all members of society. For example it required the federal government to proclaim a state of apprehended insurrection, but at the request of Quebec. Similarly the Canadian Army was sent to Quebec, but again at the request of Quebec. And although, national defence and criminal law are of federal jurisdiction while the administration of justice is provincial, the two governments nevertheless worked as a united entity, as seen in the fact that the Army as well as the RCMP and the provincial and municipal police were under the central direction of Maurice Saint-Pierre, chief of the Sûreté du Québec, to whom they reported.[1] That federalism was effective during the crisis can especially be seen from the fact that all the wishes of the Government of Quebec were quickly complied with by Ottawa. Although Trudeau was famous for having stated some years later that "the Prime Minister of Canada is not the head-waiter of the provinces," he nevertheless responded swiftly to Quebec's demands during the crisis. Nor did he impose his ideas or his time-table during the crisis but accepted that it was the premier of Quebec who should have the principal role.

Canadian Collaborative Federalism

But what is Canadian collaborative federalism? It is a system of government wherein centralizing and decentralizing powers are balanced and federal and provincial governments are sovereign in their own jurisdictions. In Canada, matters of common interest to the provinces are usually delegated to the central government, while matters which are best handled locally are left to the provinces. Cooperative federalism requires good faith on the part of both the federal and provincial governments, so one or other government must not put its particular interests ahead of the common good.

Canadian federalism is asymmetrical, which means that the provinces need not have identical jurisdictions and may relinquish to the central government certain powers that other provinces in the federation may wish to keep. Fortunately, our federation already contains elements of asymmetry, both constitutional and administrative. Examples include the status of French as Quebec's official language, the distinct system of civil law in Quebec, and Quebec's own income tax. Of importance for the October Crisis was the fact that Quebec had its own provincial police, "la Sûreté du Québec," which only one other province has – Ontario.

Three Alternatives to Effective Federalism

If the Canadian Government had assumed all rights and responsibilities during the crisis, federalism would have failed. Yet on 13 October 1970, R.N. Thompson, MP for Red Deer, specifically requested just this under the sect 91(1) of the Constitution: "Acting upon the authority conferred upon it by Section 91 subsection (1) of the British North America Act, I call upon the government to declare that the political kidnappings in the city of Montreal are matters affecting the peace, order and good government of Canada and henceforth will be treated as a federal responsibility."[2] Had the federal government so acted, it would have spent as much time fighting the Government of Quebec as it did in trying to oppose the FLQ.

On the other hand, if the Quebec government had insisted on making most of the decisions, as the sixteen "eminent personalities" and the Parti Québécois proposed, the result would have been equally bad – an ineffective provincial force trying to face a terrorist uprising, while contesting the legitimate rights of the federal government.

And if the Quebec government had given in to the sixteen unelected personalities and allowed them to dictate terms of the negotiations with the FLQ, there would have been a descent into corporatism, if not anarchy.

Was There Intentional Polarization?

One of the persistent criticisms of Canadian collaborative federalism was that the federal government intentionally polarized the crisis on federal/

provincial lines. For my part, I believe that if there was polarization, it was not intentional but a healthy component of our federal system. It is true that under the Canadian Constitution the two spheres of government are constantly looking over their shoulders at one another, especially with respect to revenues, transfer payments, and the division of powers. In the normal course of affairs, from 1970 to 1975, as Quebec minister of Financial Institutions, Companies, Cooperatives, and Consumer Protection, I was constantly fighting over "turf" with Ottawa. We jousted, for example, over the right to legislate and control insurance companies and insurance, over the stock exchange and securities, over loan companies and consumer loan agreements, and over the lending practices of banks directed at consumers. This tension, call it polarization if you wish, was natural. The great reforms across Canada in consumer fields, incidentally, usually came from federal/provincial competition. In other words, federalism can provide healthy rivalry, which is useful when conducted fairly and without malice.

During the crisis, I found that we in Quebec and they in Ottawa first and foremost sought a just solution to the crisis, so that there was no confrontation over jurisdiction or rights or responsibilities. This did not stop commentary and even occasional accusations of intentional polarization by Ottawa.

Commentary on Intentional Polarization

It is useful to record some of the commentary on polarization.

On 14 October 1970 (two days before the application of the War Measures Act Regulations), Gilles Boyer of *Le Soleil* warned that: "The War Measures Act confers so many powers on the central government that the provincial authorities should be very reluctant, for this reason, to request its application: it will reduce the authority of the provincial government to minor matters."[3] As reported in *La Presse* on 27 October, Jacques Parizeau declared: "Ottawa took advantage of the Cross-Laporte affair to start the inevitable confrontation with Quebec."[4] On 3 November, the Montreal *Star* reported: "Party Québécois MNA Robert Burns suggested last night that the federal government sent troops into Quebec and invoked the War Measures Act in order to crush the province's separatist movement."[5]

In 1971 political science professor Donald Smiley wrote: "If we look beyond the immediate events of the October Crisis it is clear that the parallel, if not co-ordinated strategies of Messrs. Trudeau and Bourassa are directed toward reducing Quebec nationalism to impotence by polarizing the province on federalist-nationalist lines."[6] And further on: "The most dangerous possibility arising out of the present situation is that Quebec has become so polarized as to be governable only by repression."[7]

In the same year professor Marcel Rioux, one of the sixteen "eminent personalities," said: "Trudeau's Liberal team had been given a mandate to 'put Quebec in its place' and above all to eliminate the idea of independence; it suddenly realized that things were not going well in Quebec from this point of view. For these reasons, the government of Canada decided to strike a hard blow against separatism. Tarring the FLQ, FRAP, and the PQ with the same brush, it decided to have done with them all, and unleashed the police and military forces of Canada and Quebec."[8]

In 1974, Jean Provencher, despite the benefit of hindsight, was still proclaiming that "One of the dramas of the October events was this crumbling, this disappearance of the Government of Quebec, vis-à-vis the central government."[9]

On 30 December 1970, *Le Devoir*, which began publication in 1910, issued a sixtieth anniversary supplement and asked twenty-eight people to write on how Quebec had progressed in the previous 60 years. The first article was by Claude Ryan, who found, in his incisive fashion, that from 1910 to 1970 Quebec and Canada had changed from being two races to two nations. At that point, however, Mr Ryan, unlike the other contributors, left aside consideration of the first fifty-nine years and nine months, and mounted his old hobbyhorse – the October Crisis – where he found there had been a "phenomenon of polarization without precedent." In the same paragraph Ryan went further and complained of criticisms of himself for his position during the crisis and in particular: 1) his willingness to "arrive at a negotiated solution" (euphemism for exchanging hostages for terrorists); 2) "his issuing a joint opinion" (euphemism for the public press conference and the petition at the height of the crisis of the sixteen eminent personalities). The result, he declared, was that "a large number of intellectuals, youths, nationalists and syndicalized elements ... have the impression ... that the Bourassa government placed itself under the tutorship of the Trudeau Government." To his credit, however, Ryan did not believe that the federal government used the October Crisis to crush the separatist movement. "Ryan did not subscribe to the theory, according to which the federal government would have taken advantage of the Crisis to crush the separatist movement."[10]

Le Devoir and the Success of Federalism during the Crisis

Le Devoir, and in particular Claude Ryan, seemed particularly sensitive about the federalism issue. In the early days of November 1970, I wrote an op-ed piece in French and English[11] where I noted that the federal and Quebec governments had fulfilled their respective responsibilities without conflict and that the handling of the crisis was "an example of good cooperative federalism."

Claude Ryan seems to have been especially upset by this affirmation. In an editorial on Monday, 9 November 1970, Ryan wrote "Interviewed Saturday on CJAD, Mr William Tetley, Minister of Financial Institutions in the Bourassa cabinet, quietly affirmed that the way in which the three governments have acted for the past month is, in his eyes, an excellent illustration of what is collaborative federalism. Mr. Tetley was impressed by the way Ottawa, Quebec and Montreal cooperated with one another. He draws from this example encouragement and optimism for the future."[12]

Ryan, in replying, did not refer to or mention my article of 4 November 1970, published in his own newspaper, or the same arguments I had made on radio station CJAD. Rather he used the brief reference to me as a springboard to answer accusations against him made by others at meetings in the Hull region, that he was becoming more and more a *souverainiste*. Jean-Claude Leclerc of Le Devoir also wrote a similar article critical of me, again without referring to or mentioning the Le Devoir article or any of my arguments.[13]

FLQ Strategy

If federalism results in some polarization and checks and balances, it was FLQ strategy to have Quebec citizens thrust into two strongly opposing groups. As Ryan said, "The strategy of the militant revolutionaries consists, by all appearances, of bringing the citizens of Quebec to a compulsory regrouping of themselves into two radically opposed camps. Nothing would make them smile more than to see Quebecers forced to choose between their 'popular democracy' and the 'democracy' of Ottawa."[14]

Gérard Pelletier also noted that the crisis left most of Quebec's intellectuals aligned against the two governments: "It can be stated that one of the chief strategic successes of the FLQ is to have succeeded in ranging against the Government almost all the Quebec intellectuals and even a portion of the anglophone intellectuals of Canada."[15]

Conclusion

Democratic federalism divides political power among a number of jurisdictions. It requires cooperation but also permits healthy rivalry amongst the component parts. In consequence, no totalitarian regime can tolerate genuine federalism. The Soviet Union, for example, was unable to accept federalism and did not confer real authority on East Bloc satellite nations, before the fall of the Iron Curtain. It is my view that if there was a Quebec/Ottawa confrontation/polarization during the October Crisis, it was natural and not excessive.

The crisis was a demanding test of coordination, cooperation and effective federalism, and fortunately, both the Quebec and Ottawa governments acted appropriately. Collaborative Canadian federalism worked effectively during the crisis and provided a system of checks and balances that Quebec alone, or the federal government alone could not have provided.

Appendix
Article of William Tetley, published in French in *Le Devoir*, 4 November 1970 (Refused publication in the Montreal *Star*)

THE QUEBEC GOVERNMENT AND TERRORISM

Out of the terrible period of terrorism through which we have passed, have sprung a number of rumours, one of which would have it that the Quebec Cabinet was divided. Let me put that rumour to rest, once and for all and within the limits of the discretion we have imposed on ourselves let me explain some of the events.

Our Cabinet met as a full Cabinet during the whole period since the Cross kidnapping and in fact we always have so acted. We did not leave the matter to a committee and we were unanimous in all our actions. Working as a complete cabinet required long constant meetings but the fact of living and working together in the Prime Minister's offices in the Hydro Building, in Montreal, in the Queen Elizabeth Hotel and later in Quebec City, as we did, had the advantage of all of us being fully informed and of all of us having all the documents and communiqués in our hands within minutes of their being delivered. We had all police reports and background information and being fully informed we acted together, calmly and without delay. The result was that we all came to the same inescapable, inevitable conclusions.

As you know, we did not give in to the terrorists all the while trying to protect the lives of two men. The Quebec Cabinet has been discreet and has left the explanation of the acts we took to the Prime Minister of Quebec who has acted with the same discretion and in the same studied calm that he has asked of the population and of the press.

It should be noted as well that the Quebec Government decided what should be done, when and where and we did not give up our power and duties, while the Federal Government did not give up theirs and acted within their jurisdiction. This I believe to be an example of good cooperative federalism. In this regard, it should be noted that the Provincial Police Chief has controlled all Federal, Provincial and Municipal police services during this period. It should also be noted that the Quebec Government alone controlled the release of certain of the twenty-three prisoners. Besides the five persons eligible for parole there were at least six others who were before the Courts for various crimes but who had not been judged guilty. They could have been released by the signature of the Quebec Attorney-General upon his signing a simple "*nolle prosequi*" that is, that there was no suit. In effect, the Federal Government had certain prisoners within their powers and we had others within ours. The two Governments thus acted in concert and in agreement as to the reply to the terrorists.

The reasons for our decisions and the surrounding facts will be provided at the proper time and I have no doubt that the public will be proud of the Government of Quebec and especially of the Prime Minister, Robert Bourassa, and the Justice Minister, Jérôme Choquette. Ours is one of the first modern governments in the world to say "NO" to terrorists and we did so when the lives of one of our number, we knew so well, was in jeopardy. From now on, when governments are blackmailed they will have a precedent to follow; so will public and private institutions, such as universities, when their buildings are occupied.

As for the future, the Bourassa Government intends to continue to govern, to aid the population as a whole and to try to correct the injustices which are the cause of much of the social unrest. We realize that it is not sufficient to merely stand fast against terrorism; there is much more to do.

"William Tetley, M.N.A., Notre-Dame de Grâce
Minister of Financial Institutions"

Nota Bene: The English text (above) was sent at the same time to the Montreal *Star*, but was refused publication, apparently because there were not enough facts![16] (See Diary, Appendix 1 at 5 November 1970).

Chapter 20

The Duchaîne Report

Let sleeping dogs lie.

If a government wishes to avoid or at least delay the truth coming to light on a certain matter because that truth will implicate or embarrass it, the Canadian practice is to call an "independent" inquiry, even a royal commission. The custom, although not respectable, is often respected politically. The Parti Québécois, when in opposition, had called for debates and inquiries into the October Crisis, but when it came to power on 15 November 1976 it realized that an inquiry would harm it more than the Bourassa government.

Only on 18 May 1977 (six months after taking power) did the Lévesque government reluctantly and secretly call for what one may describe as "an inquiry, but not necessarily an inquiry." A Parti Québécois member and Ministry of Justice civil servant, Jean-François Duchaîne, was appointed not by the National Assembly but by Justice Minister Marc-André Bédard, and he was to report back to the minister himself.

It is useful to distinguish the Duchaîne inquiry from three other related inquiries. The first of these was an unofficial committee of inquiry begun on 12 October 1971 by ten "independent" citizens. They were to evaluate only the effect of the War Measures Act on civil liberties and the role played by the federal government, the media, and citizens in general but not the Quebec government or the Parti Québécois. The purpose, clearly, was to embarrass the Bourassa and Trudeau governments. Camille Laurin (PQ minister), Jacques Larue-Langlois and Michel Chartrand (former FLQ members), Bernard Mergler (FLQ lawyer), and a few others testified, but, evidently realizing that PQ and FLQ complaints about government misconduct were difficult to justify, the inquiry shut down in the fall of 1971 and disappeared "without a trace."[1]

The two other inquiries, the Keable Commission and the McDonald Commission, were both concerned with the issue of RCMP activity after the October Crisis per se, that is, from January 1971 on. The Keable Commission,[2] appointed by the Parti Québécois government, was chaired by Jean-F. Keable, a Quebec City lawyer at the time and a supporter of the Parti Québécois.[3] The commission had powers to subpoena and hear witnesses under oath at a public or private hearing. It did some minor investigation of the 1970 events, but was apparently wary of proceeding much further and thus implicating Jacques Parizeau. Thus when questioning Carole de Vault on the 1970 period, Keable dealt only with the activities of her "controller," Captain Detective Julien Giguère of the Montreal police.

The Keable Commission reported on 6 March 1981. It found that six RCMP operations after December 1970 clearly broke the law. Not the least was the raid on Parti Québécois headquarters and the theft of its membership lists. The Parti Québécois had long been suspicious of the RCMP and the Keable Commission's report justified that suspicion, as did the report of the McDonald Commission.[4] Created by the federal government in 1977 and chaired by Mr Justice David C. McDonald of the Supreme Court of Alberta, the commission delivered its 2,400 page report to the federal government on 27 January 1981. It was later made public – after information of a security-sensitive nature had been expunged – and its findings, like those of the Keable Commission, were highly critical of the RCMP.

A Secret Inquiry

The work of Duchaîne and his inquiry were mysterious. Even the date of appointment is not clear. Page two of the report gives the date of the letter of nomination of Jean-François Duchaîne as 18 May 1977, while Bédard declared in the National Assembly that it was 6 June 1977.[5]

The letter of 18 May 1977 reads:

To whom it may concern.

An increasing number of citizens believe that all light has not been shed on what is now called the October Crisis. Some even demand that a public inquiry be instituted. In order to have an overall picture of the events, the Minister of Justice must first assure himself that he possesses all the pieces of the file which will later be analyzed. I have charged one of our Crown prosecutors, Mr Jean-François Duchaîne, and Mr Gaëtan Lemoyne of our civil litigation department to carry out this preliminary phase of gathering data from all people, all groups, police organizations or others, which were involved in these events and who could provide us with pertinent information.

I am assured that they will be able to count on your cooperation in order to see the task through, which I have entrusted to them.

The Minister, Marc-André Bédard[6]

Thus, it was not to be a public inquiry and Duchaîne had no powers of subpoena or interrogation under oath. Rather, it was a secret investigation, not publicly announced, without any fixed deadline, with instructions to report only to the minister, and whose sole purpose was to decide if a formal inquiry was necessary.

The creation of such a body should have been announced in the National Assembly as soon as it began. Justice Minister Bédard, however, did not mention the inquiry until seventeen months later, when he was questioned in the National Assembly on 24 October 1978 by Fernand Lalonde, the Liberal justice critic and MNA for Marguerite-Bourgeoys. Bédard then declared: "In fact, Mr. Duchaîne, who was entrusted with this inquiry, was invested with powers which could be delegated by means of the Public Inquiry Commissions Act."[7] The next day Bédard corrected himself in the National Assembly: Duchaîne would not conduct a public inquiry at all but would only collect information in order to determine if such an inquiry should be called:

With your permission, Mr. Speaker, I wish to correct an inaccurate aspect of the information that I gave yesterday, when I answered a question from the member for Marguerite-Bourgeoys concerning the mandate entrusted to Mr Jean-François Duchaîne that deals with the October events. On June 6, 1977, I entrusted Mr. Duchaîne with the mandate to collect data from all persons who could provide pertinent information concerning the October Crisis. This mandate was entrusted to Mr. Duchaîne in order to evaluate if there were facts which could justify the establishment of a public inquiry, which latter has been called for at this time by many citizens.[8]

The inquiry proceeded slowly. Gaëtan Lemoyne soon left and was not replaced. Thereafter, Duchaîne acted alone, except for some assistance from Marc Duclos during the first year. He completed the main body of his work by the summer of 1978 and then presented his report (along with seven volumes of supporting documents) to the minister of justice.[9] The government, evidently embarrassed by the report, delayed presenting it for two and a half years.

On 24 October 1978 Bédard stated in the National Assembly that he had received the report in the summer of 1978 but he did not release it at that time because he was still waiting for further information from the federal government: "One part of his [Duchaîne's] report, comprising about 1400 pages, was delivered into the hands of the principal officers of the Ministry of Justice. This report relates to the steps, among others, that he carried out in relation to the different police forces, including the MUC (Montreal Urban Community) police, the Sûreté du Québec and any other persons that he believed necessary to interrogate in order to complete his mandate. The report is now at the Ministry of Justice. There is, however, a whole part of this inquiry, in respect to the October Crisis, that necessarily requires answers on the part of federal authorities, who, as you know, had a large role to play at the time."[10] Bédard repeated this explanation on 2 May 1979 when questioned in the National Assembly by Fernand Lalonde concerning the tabling of the Duchaîne Report. "Mr. Speaker, the collection of the information that we had requested from Mr. Duchaîne is effectively finished. His report has been deposited at the Ministry of Justice. I was still awaiting cooperation on the part of the federal authorities, cooperation that we have not obtained."[11] Bédard added that delay was also necessary because Duchaîne's revelations could be prejudicial to the Keable Commission. In reply, Lalonde noted that the Keable Commission was concerned with completely different matters and, in any event, being a public inquiry, could not be prejudiced if the Duchaîne Report was made public.

On 16 October 1979 the Union Nationale MNA from Nicolet-Yamaska, Serge Fontaine, stated that the new solicitor general of Canada (Joe Clark's Progressive Conservatives were now in power in Ottawa, having replaced Pierre Trudeau's Liberals) had publicly offered to cooperate with Duchaîne. He declared: "Yesterday the Solicitor General of Canada made a statement to the press and showed a much more open mind than the previous Trudeau government by declaring he was prepared to make public a large number of RCMP documents with respect to the October Crisis. In the presence of this new state of mind, can the Minister of Justice tell us, firstly, what were his comments facing this open mind, and, secondly, if he intends to prolong the mandate of the Keable Commission?"[12] Bédard did not really answer either of Fontaine's questions and Fontaine sardonically summed up the situation thus: "The Minister of Justice makes me think of a child who asks for a candy and, when he has it, he finds that the candy is not big enough. It is reported, Mr Speaker, in the media that the decision of federal Minister Lawrence to deliver the documents asked for by Quebec does not necessarily mean that Mr Lévesque and Mr Bédard are overjoyed. According to some persons, there is a reluctance to reopen old political wounds on the brink of a referendum on sovereignty-association. Could the Minister of Justice tell us what truth there is in that?"[13]

On 4 December 1979 Bédard was again evasive, when questioned by Claude Forget (Liberal MNA for Saint-Laurent), about what had been done, if anything, to obtain documents from the federal government.[14] Two weeks later, on 17 December, when questioned again in the National Assembly by Claude Forget, Bédard made it clear from his long reply that he was not keen to take up the offer of the federal government to supply any information that Duchaîne wanted from the RCMP; instead, it seemed that he just wished to keep this excuse on hand in order to refuse to table the Duchaîne's report. Forget described Bédard's strategy as follows: "The Minister tells us that the Solicitor General offered to answer questions which would be posed directly by Quebec's Minister of Justice. The Minister of Justice of Quebec tells us: 'I will not write to ask for this information,' but when one asks him what it is he waiting for in order to publish the Duchaîne report, he says: 'I am awaiting the information.' It seems to me that he is not taking the appropriate measures to obtain it."[15]

Eventually, on 24 September 1980, the report was leaked. Then, on 9 October, a preliminary report was released, followed by the final version on 27 January 1981. Entitled *Rapport sur les événements d'octobre, 1970*, it consisted of 256 pages of text and four appendices amounting to approximately 100 pages.

The Report

Duchaîne began by explaining whom he had interviewed:

In the course of the first year of our research, *we interrogated all the important actors* of the October Crisis who agreed to answer our questions, taking stenographic notes each time it was possible.

At the Sûreté du Québec, we met the officers responsible for the inquiry into the kidnapping and murder of Mr. Pierre Laporte as well as the members of the information service. We met all the officers responsible for the services of the Sûreté du Québec who participated in the operations conducted during the October events.

At the Montreal Urban Community Police Force, we met the detectives and the officers who made up the antiterrorist unit of the Montreal Police during this time. We also met with Mr. Marcel Saint-Aubin, director of the Montreal Police at the time, as well as the Chief Inspector Roland Jodoin, who assumed the coordination of security services for the three principal police forces during the October events.

Mr. Donald McLeery [sic],[16] who played a determining role in finding the place where Mr. James Cross was held, also agreed to answer our questions. We met most of the members of the Liberation and Chénier cells and some of the most active members of the Viger and Ouimet information cells. These were the four cells involved in the October events. We also met Doctor Valcourt, of the Institut médico-légal, who was charged with doing the autopsy on Pierre Laporte's body.[17]

Yet Duchaîne did not interview a number of important players. These included any member of the Bourassa or Trudeau cabinets (Bourassa had declared on 27 April 1979 that he would welcome an inquiry into the October Crisis and that he would be prepared to testify before it); Jean-Jacques Bertrand, the leader of the Official Opposition in October 1970, and Camille Samson, leader of the Crédit Social at that time; René Lévesque; Jacques Parizeau; Jacques-Yvan Morin; the sixteen "eminent personalities"; members of the Parti Québécois caucus in the National Assembly in 1970 (Laurin, Burns, Léger, Joron, Tremblay, Bédard, and Charron); Carole de Vault (who was then testifying before the Keable Commission); Robert Lemieux and Robert Demers; and Pierre Vallières and Charles Gagnon.

As for the documents that he consulted, Duchaîne first listed these:

The summary of proof in the kidnapping of the British diplomat, James Richard Cross.

The personal files of about sixty-five people involved more or less directly in these events.

All the inquiry reports and verifications carried out between October 5, 1970 and January 4, 1971 by the Montreal Police.

The police reports of meetings with informers at the time of the October Crisis and since.

The shadowing reports of the Montreal Police.

All the reports still existing at the Data and Analysis Centre, a unit created in October 1970 and formed by representatives of the three police forces.

Next, he added:

We then proceeded to the same verification compared with the information service of the Sûreté du Québec. The principal documents consulted were the following:
Personal files;
Inquiry reports;
Summaries of some meetings between members of different police forces;
Reports prepared for the Minister of Justice at the time.[18]

But here, too, there were major gaps. The documents that Duchaîne failed to examine or refer to include:

- the minutes of the national councils and executive councils of the Parti Québécois and of the Liberal Party of Quebec;
- the works of Louis Fournier, Gérard Pelletier, Jean-Claude Trait, and other authors referred to in the bibliography of this book that were available at the time;
- the National Assembly debates;
- newspaper articles written by René Lévesque during the crisis.

It is also interesting that while the Duchaîne Report cited Jacques Lacoursière's *Alarme Citoyens!* with respect to the issues of federal powers and federal/provincial cooperation, it did not do so in regard to the possibility of a provisional government, a subject that Lacoursière also addressed.[19]

The six formal conclusions of the Duchaîne enquiry were astonishingly limited in their scope.[20] The first concerned the lack of federal cooperation. Duchaîne stated: "Up until now, we had not said anything about the cooperation of the federal agencies affected by the October Crisis, namely the RCMP. In spite of several steps made, as much by the Minister of Justice as by us, this cooperation has not been granted to us. The only federal documents that we have been able to consult were those in the MUC Police or the Sûreté du Québec archives. Some others were sent to us unofficially (for example, the Strategic Operation Centre document)."[21]

The second conclusion noted that the lack of federal cooperation had not impaired the inquiry's work in a significant way: "It is certain that the refusal reiterated by the federal government to collaborate with our inquiry constituted an obstacle to the exhaustiveness of our research. We believe, however, that the consultation of federal documents and the interrogation of the RCMP officers would not have appreciably modified the version of the events that we present in this report. All our non-official meetings with members or former members of the RCMP, in effect, confirmed the information that we already possessed."[22]

The third conclusion downplayed the RCMP's role in the crisis, Duchaîne stating: "Nothing in the interrogation of the police of the City of Montreal and the Sûreté du Québec has led us to suspect that the RCMP played, during the October Events, the secret role that is sometimes attributed to it."[23]

The fourth conclusion rejected the theory that the federal and provincial authorities had used the October Crisis as a pretext to destroy the "Nationalist Movement": "The October Crisis has been perceived by several Quebecers as a plot that was aimed at definitively settling the fate of the Quebec Nationalist Movement. They saw in the development of the events the execution of a scenario intended to join terrorism and nationalism in order to discredit the supporters of Quebec sovereignty. Some have even alleged that the Crisis had been 'planned at the highest level.' We will put forward here the reasons that lead us to totally reject the hypothesis according to which the Crisis was *controlled* by the authorities, that is to say, created or deliberately prolonged by them ..."[24]

The fifth conclusion, however, agreed with those who believed that the October Crisis had resulted in large-scale repression. "All things considered," Duchaîne said, "we can only agree with this statement. The police action that followed the declaration of a state of apprehended insurrection in Quebec is a flagrant example of a police operation diverted from its primary goals. Initially, this operation was to have pursued objectives directly related to the inquiry into the kidnapping of Mr. Cross and Mr. Laporte; in its implementation, it constituted an intimidating manoeuvre towards all the opposing Quebec political groups."[25]

Building on this theme, Duchaîne's sixth conclusion asserted that certain people exploited the crisis in order to manipulate public opinion for political ends:

For example, it is clear that the statements made by Mr. Jean Marchand contributed to creating in the public opinion a hostile reaction to the separatist demands. It is also clear that Mr. Drapeau's administration used the climate that prevailed during the Crisis to discredit his adversaries in the municipal election. It should be stressed, however, that the governments did not take any steps to restrain the expression of a critical point of view on the action that they did take (only the publication of FLQ communiqués was explicitly forbidden starting on October 16). The dramatic character of the measures applied certainly did not favour the expression of impartial points of view on the events. Nothing permits to us to believe, however, that the hysterical remarks of politicians and the media were deliberately made to dramatize the situation. It rather seems to us that they were real personal reactions to a crisis whose extent and suddenness had created a certain confusion on all sides.[26]

Three of the above conclusions (2, 3, 4) supported the roles of the Bourassa and Trudeau governments, while the other three (1, 5, 6) supported the PQ position. In each case, however, the recommendations lacked enthusiasm and carried little authority. Further, the conclusions critical of Ottawa and Quebec were inconsequential to the crisis per se and were not based on fact or real investigation of the events, the people involved, or the documentary record.

Besides these six main conclusions, the report contains numerous observations that are unsupported by the evidence or questionable, all of which must be set aside because a minimum of effort would have elicited contrary evidence. For example, Duchaîne reported: "It was impossible for us to find reasons for the proclamation of a state of apprehended insurrection other than those announced by Prime Minister Trudeau and Minister Turner in the House of Commons on October 16th. The questions asked on this subject by the Opposition would also be left unanswered."[27] But on this issue Duchaîne should have consulted the official statements of, among others, Robert Bourassa and various Liberal cabinet members (Jérôme Choquette, François Cloutier, Guy Saint-Pierre, and so on), both in the Liberal caucus and in the National Assembly; Jean-Jacques Bertrand

and the Union Nationale caucus; and Camille Samson and the Crédit Social caucus, as well as other evidence referred to in this book (most of which was available at the time).

Another obvious flaw of the report was its cursory reporting of the role of PQ member and organizer Carole de Vault. De Vault was Jacques Parizeau's petite amie and had joined the FLQ at the end of October 1970. She then became a police informer at the suggestion of Mrs Parizeau, who wished to protect her husband. The police wire-tapped the telephone in de Vault's apartment and recorded conversations between Parizeau and de Vault until the end of 1970, when the relationship ended.[28] Obviously, de Vault was important to any inquiry into the October Crisis, because she was one of the few FLQ members who cooperated with the police and told her whole story. Yet, in a remarkable sleight of hand, Duchaîne managed to report a few facts on de Vault's role without once mentioning Mr or Mrs Parizeau.[29] Nor did he question de Vault herself or examine the police reports on her activities as an informer (though, like the Keable Commission, Duchaîne questioned de Vault's controller, Captain-Detective Julien Giguère of the Montreal police, on a number of occasions[30]).

Duchaîne's also passed over lightly the petition of the sixteen "eminent personalities" and the threat of a parallel government.[31] Duchaîne should have investigated whether the petition – by not criticizing the FLQ, not advising the group to release Laporte and Cross, and calling jailed terrorists "political prisoners" and advocating their release in exchange for the release of Cross and Laporte – had the effect of giving support to the FLQ cause. He did not do so. Nor did he question any of the figures involved in the talk of forming a provisional government: Claude Ryan, Michel Roy, Jean-Claude Leclerc, Vincent Prince, and Claude Lemelin or those who talked of it, including Jacques Parizeau, René Lévesque, Camille Laurin, Carole de Vault, Guy Joron, and Jacques-Yvan Morin. The Parti Québécois National Council minutes of 18 October 1970 would have shed some light in this regard, but Duchaîne ignored these too.

Summary

Given the limitations imposed on him and the pressure to comply with the exigencies of his superior, Marc-André Bédard, the minister of justice, Duchaîne was understandably superficial in his conclusions. All in all, the

Duchaîne inquiry has to be seen as a cover-up, carried out by a party anxious to conceal the story of its role in the October Crisis. Its major flaws were:

- the inquiry was a not a public inquiry under the Public Enquiries Act;
- Duchaîne had no powers to subpoena witnesses, to hold public hearings, or to examine witnesses under oath;
- the public was not made aware of the inquiry and was not invited to contribute documents and testimony;
- the reasons given for the delay in tabling the report were specious;
- Duchaîne failed to question virtually any public figure who took part in the crisis, including members of the federal and Quebec governments and the Official Opposition and Parti Québécois leaders, relying instead mainly on police documents;
- Duchaîne also failed to consult the records of the two governments and the political parties;
- the report did not analyse, in particular, the state of insurrection that existed on 13 October and thereafter;
- the report contained no analysis of the War Measures Act Regulations or their effect; and
- the report was typewritten and not widely distributed.

As far as I am aware, the Duchaîne Report has never been studied, even cursorily, by apologists for the FLQ, by critics of the Bourassa and Trudeau governments' actions, by any members of the Parti Québécois, or, incredibly enough, by any of the many articles and books on the crisis that have appeared since 1970. Nor has anyone on the Trudeau/Bourassa side analysed it. In other words, a great many people wish to let sleeping dogs lie. That is not my wish. The findings of the Duchaîne Report must be examined and questioned, and its omissions and superficialities must be held up to the light of day.

Chapter 21 — Conclusions

What's past is prologue.

> William Shakespeare (1564–1616)

Those who cannot remember the past are condemned to repeat it.

> George Santayana (1863–1952)

It is one thing to show a man that he is in error, and another to put him in possession of truth.

> John Locke (1632–1704)

While we are all wiser after the event, it is also true that after thirty-six years, one's recollection of the October Crisis is often blurred or completely inaccurate. For that reason, I have tried to rely on the written record. Yet, that record is incomplete, because many persons are silent and many secrets are still undisclosed.

If, nevertheless, the complete picture is still not available and thus may not be fully and properly analyzed, it is possible to point so some aspects of the crisis which should not be forgotten and to draw some conclusions, which I do with considerable trepidation.

Particular Conclusions

1) The seven years of violence from the formation of the FLQ in 1963 to the October Crisis of 1970 were cruel to the victims and upsetting to society in general but failed to make the public or the governments of the time sufficiently aware of the threat they posed.

2) The loss of Pierre Laporte was inestimable to his wife and family, to the Bourassa Cabinet, to the Quebec Liberal Party, to Quebec, and to Canada. His death was the result of a merciless and horrendous murder of an innocent person, who had much more to contribute as a husband, father, and political leader. Laporte was also one of those rare persons in public life who was an accomplished, published author, who kept copious notes and records for future books, all of which were lost to society by his murder.

3) The kidnapping of Richard Cross was ill-advised and unfortunate. Cross, for his part, acted with great courage, discretion, and diplomacy.

4) The heart-rending decision of the governments of Quebec and Canada not to release FLQ prisoners, convicted or charged with crimes of terror, was the correct one. No democratic government can do otherwise. The decision was eventually approved by almost every commentator and almost every newspaper in the world.

5) The public petition and press conference of the sixteen "eminent personalities" of 14 October 1970 not only failed to call on the FLQ to release Cross and Laporte but advocated "the negotiation of an exchange of the two hostages for the political prisoners." Their petition was specifically referred to and relied on by Robert Lemieux, negotiator for the FLQ, on 15

October 1970 when he cut off negotiations and refused the governments' offer to allow the kidnappers refuge in Cuba or Algeria for the return of Cross and Laporte. Would the outcome of the confrontation have been different had the sixteen condemned the FLQ and the kidnappings and called on the FLQ to release Cross and Laporte?

6) The labour movement leadership (the Front Commun) took a central and public position during the crisis but also failed to unequivocally condemn the FLQ kidnapping of Cross and of Laporte, and failed to demand their unconditional release, until the evening of 16 October.

7) The decision of the Quebec government to call in the army on Thursday, 15 October 1970, was wise in light of the growing civil unrest at the time.

8) The request to the federal government by the City of Montreal and the Government of Quebec on 16 October 1970 for the application of the War Measures Act was justified under the circumstances. After three days of widespread and increasingly raucous meetings and demonstrations, the FLQ had succeeded in holding a mass rally of 3,000 supporters, sympathizers, students, and dropouts at the Paul Sauvé Arena on the evening of 15 October 1970 and was about to move on to marches, confrontations, violence, and physical damage.

9) The proclamation under the War Measures Act on Friday morning, 16 October 1970 at 4:00 a.m., came at exactly the right moment. By midnight of 15–16 October 1970 the Bourassa government had adopted the three Medicare bills in the Natinal Assembly, one of which sent the specialist doctors back to work. This left the government free to ask Ottawa to proclaim a state of apprehended insurrection. As a result of the proclamation, violence was avoided: there was no physical damage, not a single window broken or person hospitalized.

10) The RCMP and the Quebec and Montreal police forces were not careful enough in compiling the list of persons to be arrested under the War Measures Act and the governments of Quebec and Canada were not sufficiently vigilant when scrutinizing the list. Nor were those arrested permitted to speak to their lawyers and families soon enough, while many arrestees should have been released much sooner.

11) The government of Quebec was slow to solve the dilemma of advising the public of the reasons for the governmental actions and at the same

time not tipping off the FLQ of police plans and strategy. It would have been better to have dealt with this before the emergency debate in the National Assembly on 11 November 1970, but even in retrospect it is difficult to see how the dilemma could have been otherwise resolved.

12) The Quebec government acted correctly in setting up a system whereby persons improperly arrested or treated could each be awarded sums up to $30,000 at the discretion of the Quebec Ombudsman, without government intervention.

13) The government was not acting against the wishes of the public: Canadian public opinion strongly supported the governments' vigorous response to the terrorist threat. A Gallup poll published on 12 December 1970 noted that 87 per cent of Canadians approved the imposition of the War Measures Act Regulations, with 6 per cent disapproving and 7 per cent undecided. Among English Canadians, the approval rate was 89 per cent with 5 per cent disapproving and 6 per cent undecided. For French Canadians, the results showed 86 per cent approval, 9 per cent disapproval, and 5 per cent undecided.

15) The Parti Québécois leadership, although understandably frustrated by only having 7 seats out of 110 in the National Assembly, despite 23.1 per cent of the popular vote, should nevertheless have acted with more discretion to avoid exacerbating the crisis. The PQ members of the National Assembly seem to have misunderstood their role in the crisis, as compared with the more experienced Union Nationale and Crédit Social MNAs who, incidentally, together represented 30.8 per cent of the popular vote.

16) The belief that settling the FLQ Crisis was purely a Quebec matter made little sense under the federal/provincial division of powers of the Constitution at that time and still does not make sense today.

17) Federalism, with its checks and balances, worked very successfully during the crisis, which posed problems that had never been seen in Canada. The joint efforts of the Quebec and federal governments served to bring the crisis to a proper, although painful, conclusion.

18) In the short run the FLQ threat and the crisis ended with the application of the War Measures Act and the brutal murder of Laporte. But in the long run the crisis ended because French Canadians are a democratic and rational people who have been able to avoid the kind of violence that has, for example, plagued Spain and Northern Ireland for over half a century.

19) Following the kidnappings, Vallières, Gagnon, Chartrand, and Lemieux attempted to unleash an insurrection, using giant assemblies, student strikes, and demonstrations. Bourassa and Trudeau acted to hold back and eventually stop the flood, while the sixteen "eminent personalities" unfortunately rode along on the FLQ waters, to their own and society's great detriment.

20) Those people who opposed the governments' position during or since the crisis should look at all the facts, reassess their position, and end the revisionism which has occurred since the events happened.

21) Those people who supported the governments' position during the crisis should also look at the facts and end their silence.

General Conclusions

Terrorism is counterproductive in a democratic society, if it is ever productive in any society. Given this, the public, the press, and the leaders of private and public groups (including business, labour, student, religious, and political institutions) in a democratic society should be especially judicious during a terrorist insurrection to avoid being accomplices of the terrorists. They must act on the belief that it is foolhardy, if not intellectually dishonest, to publicly support some or all of the *aims* of terrorists. This can, of course, be done while declaring opposition to the terrorists' methods. Nor should members of the public publicly second-guess the elected government by press conferences or petitions that directly or indirectly favour the terrorists.

A democratically elected government is the trustee for the electorate, responsible for the preservation of its rights and freedoms. The government has no mandate to cede its authority and responsibilities to terrorists, to the elected opposition, or to other persons or ad hoc groups, however socially prominent their members may be. Faced with terrorism a government must act firmly and, where it deems it necessary, with force. But it must always be mindful of the consequences of using that force. It should be vigilant to ensure that the measures employed are not excessive and it should ensure that injustices are properly and quickly compensated.

In times of crisis, a democratic federal system, where two levels of government are obliged to work in concert, can have considerable advantages over a centralized system. However, federal or provincial governments and opposition parties enjoying rights granted under a democratic constitution must agree to govern and act within the Constitution, with its system of checks and balances. The major lesson of the October Crisis is that governments and official oppositions must not allow their federalist or separatist options, no matter how well-intentioned, to cloud their judgment in matters of state.

The Place of the October Crisis in the History of French-Canadian Nationalism

The October Crisis was an important separatist, nationalistic, almost anarchist moment in Quebec and Canadian history. The FLQ were not, however, patriots such as those in Upper and Lower Canada in 1837 and 1838[1] or at the time of Riel in 1885,[2] who were willing to risk their lives for their cause. The FLQ fought clandestinely, with bombs, parcel bombs, robberies, kidnappings, and the "execution" of a hostage. They rarely put themselves in physical danger.

The FLQ had no plan for a democratic government. Rather, just the opposite, they opposed the democratically elected governments of Quebec and Canada. They had no social bill of rights for which they were fighting, unlike Papineau's Twelve Resolutions at St-Ours-sur-Richelieu on 7 May 1837[3] or Robert Nelson's Declaration of Independence of 28 February 1838[4] or Riel's "Revolutionary Bill of Rights" of 1885.[5] Nor was there spontaneous sympathy and support for the FLQ, such as was seen in the Conscription Riots of 1918,[6] the Winnipeg General Strike of 1919,[7] and the Asbestos Strike of 1948–49.[8] The FLQ were similar to the irrational, mostly English-speaking mob, that rioted on 25 April 1849 and burned down the Parliament building in Montreal.[9] Both groups did great harm to the society on whose behalf they were supposedly acting, with little harm to themselves.

Similarly, the sixteen "eminent personalities" who signed the petition of 14 October 1970 were not unlike those mostly English-speaking merchants who signed the petition of 20 September 1849 calling for the annexation of Canada to the United States.[10] Neither group of petitioners represented the population in general but were, in good part, promoting their own interests.

The Parti Québécois and French-Canadian Nationalists

> "Je suis un chien qui ronge lo
> En le rongeant je prend mon repos
> Un tems viendra qui nest pas venu
> Que je morderay qui maura mordu."[11]

> "I am a dog that gnaws his bone,
> I couch and gnaw it all alone –
> A time will come, which is not yet,
> When I'll bite him by whom I'm bit."

> (Translation by William Kirby in
> "The Golden Dog," published in 1877)

Some of the twenty-one chapters of the present text are quite critical of the positions taken during crisis by the fledgling Parti Québécois and by French-Canadian nationalists.[12] Yet their almost insatiable desire for sovereignty and their enthusiasm for the cause are understandable. Protection of the French language and culture and the pursuit of a separate Quebec is a bone that has been gnawed on since the founding of Quebec, four hundred years ago, and are legitimate in a democratic society if carried out by democratic means. If I am critical of some Parti Québécois leaders and of some French-Canadian nationalists, I am very sympathetic to their dedication. I appreciate that if the shoe were on the other foot and the PQ had been in power when a PQ minister and the consul general of France had been kidnapped by English federalist terrorists, the federalist opposition would probably not have immediately rallied around the PQ Government but would have equivocated, just as the PQ did in October 1970.

Appendices

Appendix 1

Diary, 30 September–28 December 1970

If my opponents stop lying about me, I'll stop telling the truth about them.

Adlai Stevenson (1900–65)

To write one's memoirs is to speak ill of everyone except oneself.

Marshal Pétain (1856–1951)

When Cross was kidnapped and then Laporte, I realized that this was history, because we would become one of the first governments in the world to say no to kidnappers, despite the possibly horrible consequences. I therefore started a diary, which I kept daily during the crisis and then during my period in Bourassa's cabinet from 1970 until I retired from politics in 1976. The diary, along with documents and clippings, fills thirty binders.

The diary was written daily, usually in longhand, usually in the evening in Quebec City. Evenings were the time when ministers read documents, reviewed newspapers, and reflected. On occasion, I wrote it at slow moments in the National Assembly or at long committee meetings or when travelling. At times I dictated it into a portable tape-recorder. It was then typed by one or other of the fine secretaries I was blessed with as a minister and put in a loose-leaf binder with relevant documents.

A diary is not a memoir, where you write what you remember or wish to remember. It is rather a chronicle of events as they happened, and your reaction – whether wise or not – to them. And a diary, unlike a memoir, is confining: you cannot revise it, either intentionally or unintentionally. Thirty-five years later, I find that there is much I wish I had and had not said.

The diary appears below, interspersed with additions in italics to set the context. It is reproduced in its original form, apart from parenthetical additions inserted for purposes of clarification and minor editorial changes made in the interests of copyediting consistency and greater readability.

WEDNESDAY, 30 SEPTEMBER 1970

I had a telephone call from Bourassa's secretary at 12:00 noon, saying he wanted to see me. I went over to his office (the second time in my life since he was P.M.) and he asked me to be the Minister of Financial Institutions. I told him I preferred to be in Revenue in order to finish the changes I was making. We were speeding up the collection of $7.5 millions per day, 7 days per week. A week was $50 millions, two weeks was $100 millions. There was also the problem of Ministry computers and sales tax. I finally said: "O.K., of course, if you want me to." He then told me he had already told Gérald Harvey that he would be the Minister of Revenue. He considered the new job bigger (which it is) and that I would replace him on his trip to California because the doctors had broken off negotiations and were striking.

I felt upset because I was putting new administrative changes into Revenue and because I thought I could really increase revenues by speeding them up. I had taken considerable time to make changes slowly but carefully to meet staff and to learn about Ministry problems.

However, I accepted gladly and especially because it will save a lot of headaches that Revenue has, especially the break down in the collection of restaurant taxes and the paying of back income tax [by persons who had done broker bail-outs up to five years before].

I called Guerci, the sous-ministre adjoint (Gauvin, the deputy minister was away), to lunch and I then phoned all the staff in Montreal and called all the Quebec staff to my office for 3:00 p.m. to announce it before the P.M. did on T.V. at 3:30. This was something they seemed to appreciate.

THURSDAY, 1 OCTOBER 1970, QUEBEC

I was sworn in [as minister of financial institutions]. The specialists [doctors] have refused to turn up to the Parliamentary Commission. We had been frightened that they would turn up but they foolishly took advice from a Parti Québécois lawyer (Ray Lachapelle who came first in our McGill law class of 1951). He, of course, told them not to come and they made fools of themselves. They think they can be above the law and still have public support.

The Parliamentary Commission continued on October 2nd and the specialists were told not to strike by their own professional body, the College of Physicians and Surgeons, and by the Hospital Association.

The province is in an uproar over the specialists. The general practitioners, dentists, and optometrists also turned up and roasted the specialists. The College and others accepted terms and government promised amendments.

We, in particular, promised what Bourassa laughingly calls "désengagement fictive" – "fictitious opting out"! Dr. Robillard, the specialist leader and illusionist, had said the money was not the issue and so we cut the ground from under him by offering a "democratic" system. They can opt out but get no more money. If they are honest and do not want money, they will not strike. We will see.

I saw Jean Lesage [the former premier of Quebec, 1960–66, and now a practising lawyer, employed in this case by the insurance industry] in the afternoon [about his request on behalf of the insurance industry]. The same antipathy still exists towards him because of his vanity and his deception of himself and of his listeners. There is a general admiration for him, however, because of his knowledge, ability, and strength. I managed to hold firm, against the demands of his clients, which are unjustified according to the Deputy-minister and his staff. [Lesage and his clients wanted the insurance industry to be independent and not to be under the deputy minister, if not the ministry.] In any event we parted on good terms.

SATURDAY, 3 OCTOBER 1970, QUEBEC

Left Dorval at 8:55 a.m. for California with Gérard Lévesque [Minister of Industry and Commerce] and various supernumeraries. I had received a first class ticket (despite asking for second class) but gave it to Paul Desrochers [Bourassa's chief adviser and his campaign manager in the April election] who was very pleased. I went 2nd class, but there was no distinction on the plane. The other Deputy-minister, Cazavant, had changed his 2nd class ticket to first and had charged the government for the difference. He is not Deputy-minister of Finance for nothing.

Jean Prieur, the P.M's assistant who bosses Cabinet ministers around, had told him to go 2nd class. I happened to be in the P.M.'s antechamber at the time. [The whole idea of ministers going economy class had been my idea and Bourassa had adopted it.]

MONDAY, 5 OCTOBER 1970, SAN FRANCISCO

James Cross, British trade commissioner, is kidnapped at gunpoint from his Montreal home at 8:15 a.m. The FLQ claims responsibility. At 4:15 p.m. the FLQ threatens to kill Cross, unless 1) the FLQ's 1970 manifesto is published; 2) the so-called "political prisoners" are released; 3) safe conduct to Cuba or Algeria is granted to the kidnappers; 4) $500,000.00 in gold bullion is paid; 5) the name of the informer who recently exposed an FLQ cell is divulged; 6) the laid-off Lapalme employees are rehired; and 7) the police investigation of the FLQ is called off.

We saw the Canadian Consul and learned of the James R. Cross kidnapping. Consternation. This really cools the trip and is catastrophic for Quebec's economy and reputation.

Lunch on the left of the President of the Bank of America, the biggest bank in the world. He did not know of the kidnapping, but was worried over Medicare. Saw more officials in the afternoon, although one interview was cancelled because of Bourassa's absence.

Dinner in the evening with Edgar Kaiser, President of the Kaiser Companies. He had heard of Cross and Medicare. Gérard Lévesque gave a speech to the thirty odd bigshots. I gave a brief speech on our government and how we had told the construction workers to go back to work. The thirty capitalistic rightists applauded, and the only question asked of any of us was concerning the construction strike. I told the whole story over again to their general delight and entertainment. I guess I have not lost my touch as to knowing what the middle class wants to hear. What the students and poor want to hear is another question. Kaiser's message was that our government should be strong in facing all problems.

TUESDAY, 6 OCTOBER 1970, LOS ANGELES
The FLQ warns that Cross will be killed unless ransom demands are met by 8:30 a.m. Wednesday.

Arrived in Los Angeles and more of the same, but more meetings cancelled because of the absence of Bourassa.

The Cross affair is célèbre. Saw Mayor Aliota of San Francisco yesterday and [Mayor] Yorty of L.A. today. Both very high power politicians. Both have kleig lights in their offices for instant T.V. pictures and Yorty is angry at Drapeau for getting the Olympics of 1976. I wanted to say that the Olympics would not help Montreal and that he was welcome to them, but I held my tongue.

WEDNESDAY, 7 OCTOBER 1970
A note signed by Cross is received, along with an FLQ communiqué extending the deadline to noon Thursday.

THURSDAY, 8 OCTOBER 1970
The FLQ deadline is further extended to midnight. The CBC French-language network broadcasts the full text of the FLQ's revolutionary manifesto. The general practitioners, dentists, and optometrists agree to amendments to the Medicare Act, which will be adopted at a special session of the National Assembly to be convened next week. The specialist doctors decide to strike.

WEDNESDAY/THURSDAY, 7/8 OCTOBER 1970
The group went to New York [to meet Bourassa] and I took time off. The P.M. and Jean Prieur [chef du cabinet adjoint] suggested a rest. [The first real one since the 29 April 1970 election and, in fact, long before then.] I was very depressed about Cross on Wednesday and Thursday.

FRIDAY, 9 OCTOBER 1970
Quebec Justice Minister Jérôme Choquette receives a note in Cross's handwriting and another FLQ communiqué setting the deadline for Cross's death for 6:00 p.m. on Saturday. The specialist doctors are on strike.

Long flight to Montreal.

SATURDAY, 10 OCTOBER 1970, MONTREAL
Federal Secretary of State Mitchell Sharp and his staff suggest changes to Justice Minister Choquette's reply to the FLQ. Bourassa returns from New York and meets Choquette; the two review Choquette's reply to the FLQ.

At 5:30 p.m., Choquette announces that terrorists will not be released in exchange for James Cross. Nevertheless, the kidnappers would be given safe conduct to the country of their choice in exchange for Cross.

Quebec Labour Minister Pierre Laporte is kidnapped at 6:20 p.m. in front of his home in Saint-Lambert, a suburb of Montreal, while playing catch-football with his nephew on the front lawn of his home.

Spent morning going around N.D.G. seeing people who had written or telephoned with difficult problems during the week. Afternoon in Dewittville, P.Q. [a tiny village between Ormstown and Huntingdon, where my parents-in-law and brother and sister-in-law live] relaxing, reading and worrying about Cross negotiations and emphasis given F.L.Q. by the news media.

Heard Choquette in the evening at 5:30 p.m. and disagreed with his hard line concerning virtually no concessions to the F.L.Q. At 7:00 p.m. heard the terrible news that Pierre Laporte had been kidnapped. Phoned P.M.'s office at Quebec and spoke to Paul Desrochers and left my number. At 2:00 a.m. was telephoned that we had a Cabinet meeting for 3:00 p.m., Sunday, October 11, 1970 in Montreal, at Hydro-Quebec offices.

SUNDAY, 11 OCTOBER 1970, MONTREAL
Claude Ryan, in his morning's editorial in Le Devoir, *describes the specialists' strike as unacceptable. He adds that, despite the claims of Dr Robillard, leader of the specialist doctors, the dispute is not over professional liberty, but over money.*

A note is found from Laporte to his wife. The FLQ set the deadline on his life at 10:00 p.m. Sunday. The police begin concentrated raids on suspected FLQ headquarters.

Rumours and everyone listening to the radio and watching T.V. The FLQ has delivered a communiqué of Laporte's kidnapping.

Ros [my wife] and her father drove me in the afternoon to Hydro-Quebec to the P.M.'s office. We used the backdoor and there was very tight security. Ros and her Dad were searched and had to sign before they got out.

The whole Cabinet is there with the exception of Gérald Harvey who is on a trip in Gaspé for Medicare and social assistance.

We read the letter from Laporte: "J'ai l'impression que j'écris la plus importante lettre de ma vie ..."

The two police chiefs report to us, Saint-Pierre and St-Aubin. St-Aubin is certain Cross is dead as promised by the FLQ. We are more impressed by St-Aubin of the Montreal Police than St-Pierre of the S.Q.

We try to find a code in Pierre's letter. Apparently Cross has used the signal Ω for an island. Pierre speaks of "l'endroit où je suis détenu."

I am for negotiating and so are most of the others; so is Bourassa. I pronounce a long speech in English (the first time ever to the Cabinet) to say "we have a life at stake."

Choquette says he will quit the Cabinet, if we give in. He is in a minority.

We are all angry with the federal government and Trudeau for taking a high-minded position. They do not know the personal feelings towards Laporte. Nor do they have the decision to make.

Both Bourassa and Choquette cool us with ice water.

We pay for our own chicken charlie at night, $2.00 each. This ought to please the electors. We are still meeting in Hydro.

We decide to delay and Bourassa puts out a vague statement which leaves the door open but does not contradict Choquette. It calls on the FLQ to name a negotiator. The police tell us there is a big raid tonight which could turn up Cross or Laporte. Men are being watched who enter and leave buildings carrying rifles, etc.

MONDAY, 12 OCTOBER 1970, MONTREAL

Discussions begin between FLQ nominee, lawyer Robert Lemieux, and Quebec government nominee, lawyer Robert Demers. The FLQ communiqué is to the effect that Cross will be released if police activity is ended and "political" prisoners freed.

The federal government calls in the army for service in Ottawa.

We go to bed Sunday night very late in the Queen Elizabeth Hotel. I sleep until noon Monday. The police raid last night was a failure.

No news of Laporte or Cross except that they both write Bourassa thanking him for saving their lives.

We get more police reports and details of a general conspiracy which make us all the more hawkish. The Choquette side is winning us over.

The police promise a big raid tonight and we agree to hold out until tomorrow. We will delay and talk. For the negotiations we name lawyer Robert Demers to meet with lawyer Robert Lemieux.

We are on the 20th floor of the Queen Elizabeth Hotel and Mrs. Bourassa and family are there.

Mrs. Laporte and children are on the 19th floor. Bourassa sees them often. Their son writes a letter to Bourassa: "Please save my daddy."

The public supports our strong view – we must not give in to terror, but newspapers and radio announcers are very pro-FLQ. They revel in the news as it unfolds.

The police promise another big raid tonight – 3 chances out of 4 of success, they tell us. We are optimistic.

I meet Jean-Jacques Bertrand [leader of the Official Opposition and of the Union Nationale] and Camille Samson [leader of the Crédit Social] in the corridor on the 20th floor. Apparently they have been called in to a briefing by Bourassa. Camille Laurin [parliamentary leader of the PQ] was there too and all agree with Bourassa's position.

Jean Lesage turns up at the Q.E. Hotel immediately after a Cabinet meeting. He bursts in and asks to be briefed in his autocratic fashion. Two or three of us are there – Claude Castonguay [minister of health], François Cloutier [minister of cultural affairs] and myself and we are all taken aback. I say that I wonder if we can tell him what we have been told. He blows up and asks if I think he has come all the way from Quebec without being invited. I don't reply, that is his style, but merely say that the P.M. speaks for us and will undoubtedly do his own briefing. Lesage stalks out and says he is leaving for Quebec City. He only goes two doors down the hall however. Paul Desrochers says: "You did right, Bill. It was time someone put him in his place." Later I try to apologize to Lesage and try to placate him but he is rude and vulgar as he can be at times, although usually rarely.

TUESDAY, 13 OCTOBER 1970, MONTREAL
Parliament opens in Ottawa. The army had been called in to Ottawa by the federal government on the previous day.

We meet in Hydro again in the P.M.'s office. The big raid of last night was a flop.

Our negotiator, Robert Demers, is continuing to stall and will not comply with all the FLQ demands. We only offer: a) safe conduct to the kidnappers; b) recommend parole [for the five FLQ terrorists eligible for it], but we do not want to do even this.

The papers are howling and the French press is calling us down. Lemieux is having press conferences every few hours and is the darling of the noisy press.

(Medicare, which was for yesterday in the House, was put off.)

Bourassa is wavering still. I am hawkish and want to call in the troops, impose martial law, etc. I have completely changed in two days. Bourassa kindly reminds me that two days before I was for releasing all 23 prisoners. Bourassa is calm, fair and human. He is remarkable for his composure and handling of the matter. Choquette threatens to resign. As the discussion continues, he walks out of the room. I go after him and bring him back or at least get him to stop in one of the outer offices where we talk. Later he comes back.

Trudeau has made an excellent speech on "bleeding hearts" and holding the line. It is taped and is going to be played to us in Cabinet. Jean Prieur calls me out of Cabinet and with Guy Langlois [Bourassa's chef de cabinet] says that it is very important that the importance of "bleeding hearts" be made clear, that it is not Laporte's heart but our weakness that is referred to. Prieur and Langlois want to shake up the Cabinet and have them hold fast.

I return to the Cabinet and Charles Denis [Bourassa's head of communications] plays the tape but leaves out the bleeding hearts part. We seem pretty hawkish and I make another statement.

Bourassa talks about phone calls with Trudeau, Claude Ryan and others. Bourassa is very calm, although he drinks three glasses of milk at our meeting which goes on afternoon and evening.

The police promise another sure raid. We are all very doubtful of their efficacity [sic], especially of the Chief of the Quebec Police.

We speak to Demers and tell him to stall as long as possible, i.e. 10:00 p.m. or 10:30 p.m. He says Lemieux has a press conference for 11:00 p.m. and nothing will deter him.

We decide to call in the Army and to have Demers give our two conditions, which we know will be refused, although we have an idea the liberation cell holding Cross will give in, or would like to give in.

Sunday night, another cell "Nelson Vengeur" had sent us a communiqué which said they will shoot someone every 48 hours and gave a list of names including ours.

Georges Tremblay [minister of transport], who was sick again, was absent today. I had phoned Harvey Sunday night to come but to guard his family in Jonquière.

We all agree to hold fast and decide to meet in Quebec the next day. We leave in police cars from the basement of Hydro with reporters on the street and the radios blazing away.

As we drive to Quebec, Maurice Tessier [minister of municipal affairs], Gérald Harvey, me and two police officers at the Sûreté du Québec, hear the press conference of Robert Lemieux at the Nelson Hotel. He is late, it is about 11:20 p.m. and he is very angry because we have not given in. The crowd of reporters and others are excited and are cheering Lemieux. "The blood of Laporte and Cross will be on our hands, etc.," they say. The reporters and the French press are hysterical and have lost their perspective, let alone any objectivity. As all news passes through them they are enormously important but they have no sense of responsibility. They not only report, but comment the news, which is their right, but it should not be classified as news. They are trying to scoop one another, their voices are high. They are active participants in an attack on democracy and they are acting like children. It will be the low point in the history of the Quebec Press.

A foreigner reporter at the press conference tries to ask a question in English and there is a hot argument. Lemieux and the radio announcers make a great to do about their dignity, how disgusting his question is, etc.

Such blindness, acting and colossal hypocrisy. I am very depressed. Tessier is calm and so is Harvey; they understand perhaps better, the excitability of their compatriots and discount it. I am probably too Anglo-Saxon to understand.

WEDNESDAY, 14 OCTOBER 1970, QUEBEC

Premier Robert Bourassa offers to recommend the parole of five FLQ members, who are eligible for it, in exchange for the release of Cross and Laporte. The kidnappers would have safe conduct to the destination of their choice. Robert Lemieux rejects the offer.

At 9:00 p.m., sixteen "eminent personalities," apparently solicited at the instigation of Claude Ryan and René Lévesque, hold a press conference and sign a petition directed to Bourassa, counselling the exchange of Cross and Laporte for the jailed terrorists and adding that this is a Quebec matter not a federal one.

I am in the Château Frontenac near Tessier. We arrived about 1:45 a.m. at top speed. The constables are in a room in between us.

Today we found out the police raid was to no avail. All faith in the police is lost.

I call for force, the troops and preventive detention. We must have the War Measures Act because it would take too long to act through lesser provisions of the law. It is the only way to control the 200 or 300 FLQ who exist. It will put them out of circulation and lead us to those who are holding Cross and Laporte.

We decide to call the troops in and I suggest that Bourassa make a state of the Union message. He is playing it all by ear and agrees and disagrees. He has a little press conference but nothing much.

More FLQ threats and deadlines.

We plan to have a special session for Medicare tomorrow. We can get the whole thing through in two hours. The Opposition parties agree. The specialists are still striking and even more so now. They seem maddened and especially Dr. Robillard, their leader. Castonguay says even the emergency wards are now crowded and the situation is dangerous. The doctors won't come back. They make an offer; if we hold off Medicare, they will come back. It is lovely blackmail during the FLQ crisis. It is said that only a few doctors agree with their leaders. I suspect only a few know what is happening. This is the lowest point in Quebec medical history. The fault is that neither the public, the government nor the doctors were ready for Medicare. The federal government forced it on us. On the other hand, we would never have got it otherwise, if the federal had not forced it.

THURSDAY, 15 OCTOBER 1970, MONTREAL

An editorial by Huguette Roberge in La Patrie *states that concessions to the FLQ will result in more threats, more bombs, more kidnappings. Robert Lemieux, Pierre Vallières, and Michel Chartrand convene a rally of Université de Montréal students and convince nearly 1,000 to sign the FLQ manifesto.*

Bourassa rises in the National Assembly to announce that we have called in the army. All three opposition party leaders – Jean-Jacques Bertrand, Camille Samson, and Camille Laurin – rise in turn to voice their approval of the decision. Even Robert Burns, parliamentary house leader (leader parlementaire) of the Parti Québécois, rises and does not voice any objections.

Less than two hours later, Parti Québécois parliamentary leader (chef parlementaire) Dr Camille Laurin changes his mind and criticizes the premier for making a dangerous gesture that could spread panic among the population.

At 9:45 p.m., 3,000 students at the Paul Sauvé Arena cheer Pierre Vallières, Charles Gagnon, Michel Chartrand, and Robert Lemieux, shouting their support for the FLQ.

We have the session and still no great speech by Bourassa. He cuts off all talk at the opening and we pass special rules. Gérard D. Lévesque is not bad as parliamentary leader, but he is not Laporte. No one is.

We have a Cabinet meeting in the little office of the P.M., behind the speaker's chair and decide to invoke the War Measures Act at 5:00 a.m. tomorrow and to give a six hour deadline to our terms, i.e. until 3:00 a.m. We have decided this before, but this time it is the real thing. Bourassa, who delays often, by intuition and is usually right, is going ahead. The situation is getting out of hand. I believe Bourassa is right to go ahead. It is incredible what we are doing in one single day – Medicare, the end of the strike and the War Measures Act all at once. I wonder if we would have imposed the War Measures Act if we did not have the strike? or vice versa? I would have but I wonder about whether Bourassa would have. He is less rash than I am. His judgment is usually better.

The reasons for putting in force the War Measures Act are as follows:

a) The Police are exhausted.
b) There is disorder and loss of control of the population or at least
   a small part has got out of hand.
c) If the known FLQ sympathizers are arrested, we will get leads to
   Cross and Laporte through questioning.
d) The absence of other FLQ persons will cause us to follow them
   up to Cross and Laporte.
e) We do not intend to control the press and radio – they will have
   to use their discretion. Something they should have been doing
   for a long time.

The Medicare debate goes on and the doctors refuse at the last minute
to give in. We pass Bills #39, #40 and #41 [i.e., no. 39 being amendments
to Medicare, allowing opting out; no. 40 bringing Medicare into force 1
November and mandating that both sides must negotiate; no. 41 forcing
doctors back to work now without delay].

At 12:30 or 1:00 a.m. Thursday the three Medicare Bills finally pass. The
P.Q. tries to raise the question of terror and our calling in of the troops.
They are voted out of order. Outside the Assembly there is a group of French
reporters around Claude Charron, the P.Q. member from St. Jacques. He
says that we are responsible for the death of the hostages which he proph-
esies. He is excited, passionate, smiling.

I spend some time contradicting him and arguing. I hope nothing will
appear in the papers. I have gone too far, but he went much too far the
other way. We must not escalate matters.

A reporter asks what is going to happen at 3:00 a.m. I feign ignorance
and go home to bed.

FRIDAY, 16 OCTOBER 1970
*At 3:00 a.m., letters from the government of Quebec and the city of Montreal,
requesting the application of the Regulations under the War Measures Act, are
received in Ottawa by the federal government.*

*The War Measures Act Regulations are put in force at 4 a.m. Police through-
out Quebec round up more than 250 suspects by evening.*

Another 150 "personalities" are listed in an unsigned article, appearing in
Le Devoir *on 16 October, as supporting the petition of Lévesque, Ryan, etc.*
the day before. Almost all are students, the majority from Dawson College.
Only one lawyer signs – Richard B. Holden. Seven persons oppose the petition,
including lawyer Louis-Philippe de Grandpré.

No results of our raids but the War Measures Act has made everyone calm.
Everyone (the public, the Cabinet, the police) feels better and Lemieux,
Michel Chartrand, etc., etc., have all been put in jail. We had been told of
155 names to be arrested but the police took about 300 or more. They seem
to have gone too far.

I drive to Dewittville, P.Q., where the family has been all week.

It is restful.

SATURDAY, 17 OCTOBER 1970, DEWITTVILLE
An FLQ *note is found at 9:30 p.m. saying that Laporte had been "executed" at*
6:18 p.m.

Quiet all day, arrests, etc. and the federal N.D.P. talk about injustices, etc.,
not releasing prisoners. Everyone feels better, although the press, now feeling slightly guilty, has another bone to gnaw on.

At about 12:30 a.m. Saturday/Sunday night we learn on T.V. that Laporte's body had been found, not far from his home. Rumours of Cross'
body being in Rawdon are false.

Terrible feelings of sadness. Do not feel that the blood of Laporte is
on our hands, but terribly depressed. Would there have been murder if
the press, the Claude Ryans, the René Lévesques, the labour union leaders, Yvon Charbonneau [CEQ], Marcel Pepin [CSN] and Louis Laberge
[FTQ] had come out against the kidnappings and the violence? They all
indirectly backed the FLQ with their talk. In each speech, however, they
always left an escape hatch (where they criticized violence) for history.

SUNDAY, 18 OCTOBER 1970, DEWITTVILLE TO MONTREAL
On Sunday morning, just after midnight, Laporte's body is found in the trunk
of a car south of Montreal. He had been strangled. Police issue warrants of arrest
for Paul Rose and Marc Carbonneau, charging them both with kidnapping.

7:00 p.m. Go to New Court House, i.e. Criminal Court House where poor Laporte's body is lying in state. I am taken into a small room where Mrs. Laporte is present with the whole family. I am too overcome except to say "mes sincères sympathies."

Caucus at night and a brief Cabinet meeting. We think Cross must be dead.

Go back to home at 112 Cornwall Avenue. It has had three soldiers on it since Wednesday, October 14, 1970.

There are reports that Michel Chartrand had apparently gone to Laporte's home ... and had a tantrum. I cannot believe that this person represents the Quebec worker. He should be fired by his Union and would be if it were democratic.

MONDAY, 19 OCTOBER 1970, MONTREAL
The federal parliament votes, 170 to 17, in favour of the decision to invoke the War Measures Act. Police broaden the search for kidnap suspects to Bernard Lortie, Francis Simard, and Paul Rose's brother, Jacques.

Work in Montreal. N.D.G. Medicare meeting cancelled. Specialist doctors angry and the Gazette is printing stupid editorials. Apparently, it is Charles P who is off his rocker. He lives in the 19th century. He supported Duplessis – he is at least consistent.

TUESDAY, 20 OCTOBER 1970, MONTREAL
Funeral of Laporte. Simple and sad. Everyone is very guarded, no problems. One of the Ministers' wives wore a pants suit – slightly gaudy or at least I thought so. Ros noted that at least she had come to the funeral, while Jean Bienvenue was disgusted. Poor Laporte.

Laporte's death is not only a loss for his wife and family (who were apparently quite devoted) and to the Cabinet (who can only replace him with difficulty as Leader in the House and as Minister of Labour) but also for what he could have produced as a writer. He had filing case upon filing case of documents, letters, clippings and had something to write about. All this has been lost. It would have been an important nationalist but non-separatist documentary. This loss is also a terrible tragedy.

WEDNESDAY, 21 OCTOBER 1970, QUEBEC

Off to Quebec. Work in office and Cabinet. Normal problems. Tension relieved. Lunch with everyone and supper. Have membership in Winter Club – free – hurrah. Will get some exercise, if time permits.

FRIDAY, 30 OCTOBER 1970, QUEBEC

We had a very tough caucus yesterday afternoon. Bourassa told the 72 members that he was going to name Jean Cournoyer [minister of labour in the previous Union Nationale government] Minister of Main-d'Oeuvre. The whole caucus opposed. Bourassa wanted Cournoyer because labour problems are so <u>complicated</u> now and so <u>urgent</u>. I suggested in an aside to Bourassa a soupape [consolation] for Gérard Cadieux [MNA for Beauharnois] and Alfred Bossé [MNA for Dorion] for Ministre d'Etat and Parliamentary Assistant respectively.

Bourassa, in the very difficult times of terrorism, keeps putting off a statement to the people despite our agreement in Cabinet. Drapeau and Trudeau keep getting the credit for standing up while there is talk of a provisional government. Claude Ryan denies this, but he made the offer and has made a complete ass of himself.

The English-speaking population is up in the air over Medicare and A.B. [a schoolmate in the Town of Mount Royal High School graduating class of 1943] phoned me yesterday. As usual his thinking is uninformed and woolly.

The Cabinet Wednesday was not very enthusiastic over Cournoyer's appointment. Georges Tremblay walked out in a huff and has done this before.

30 OCTOBER 1970, QUEBEC TO MONTREAL

Gave the ministry staff a pep talk on working together and their general attitude. Prepared speech on the terrorism and how we did not give in. Speech for Monday. Bourassa did have press conference last night but not much to it. He wants to go slow in case the War Measures Act turns out really badly. He is also concerned about the federal-provincial rights and the influence of the intelligentsia. It is his intuition again. He is probably right but I would prefer him making the strong statements rather than Trudeau getting all the glory. Actually the Trudeau government did not make the real decisions in the crisis or even the timing. We did all the hard and dirty work. The public will never know or believe this.

It looks as though Bourassa will get away with the Cournoyer thing. He is a real gambler but it is the beginning of the inevitable division between a P.M. and the troops. This is true because Bourassa is not a glad hander, although fun to know and sincere.

SUNDAY, 1 NOVEMBER 1970, MONTREAL

Spent yesterday and today in Montreal. Yesterday in visiting the riding and seeing people about Medicare who are uninformed and uptight. The rich and middle rich city dwellers in Montreal will lose their privilege of having special medical care quickly which they could insure against in the past. The doctors will lose their high incomes and are also worried about the unknown. Medicare starts today with a lot of doctors saying they are leaving because of loss of income, because they were forced back to work and because of the terrorist action which forced them back to work. They don't mention income tax which they will be paying in many cases for the first time.

Today I prepared a paper on how our Cabinet was not split over terrorism which is rumoured and written up in the papers and is also the reason given by Claude Ryan for trying to form a provisional government.

Trudeau's paraphrase of Lord Acton is the laugh of the nation in respect to Ryan. "Absence of power corrupts – absolute absence corrupts absolutely."

Ryan is really in the doghouse but I am not going to try to knock him. He means well, is a great writer but his vanity and his hatred of Trudeau have led him astray.

MONDAY, 2 NOVEMBER, 1970, MONTREAL

Justice Minister John Turner tabled new legislation in the Commons to be used in place of the War Measures Act.

Denis Chaput, the new particular secretary, arrived at the office and I worked him hard all day to 11:00 p.m.

Lunch with Investment Dealers. Speech for 4:00 p.m. Speech for B'Nai Brith at 6:30 p.m. N.D.G. Liberals at 9:00 p.m.

Police officer of the Sûreté du Québec still following me around.

Two soldiers at home but are supposed to leave soon.

Dominique Clift has another article [Montreal *Star*, 2 November] about a provisional government implicating Bourassa badly. Clift's facts seem wrong.

I had my article on the Cabinet read by Guy Langlois of the P.M.'s office and approved by him.

Chaput is trying to translate it.

Claude Ryan in his explanations of his non-part in the provisional government goes too far and, to save his own neck, imparts confidences.

TUESDAY, 3 NOVEMBER 1970

Left Montreal by car after working in the office until 10:30 a.m. Drove the long north shore road to Three Rivers to visit the Caisse Populaire as planned but Mr. Caron, the President, had gone to hospital with ulcers and had not given me notice. Had lunch in a hamburger stand. The driver, Mr. Godbout, is hopeless and the provincial police officer is terrified and dismayed.

Worked on administration all day and had a long meeting with Bouchard, the Deputy-Minister, and Lajeunesse, the Securities Commission President and have cleared up some disputes, between them. Much more pacifying work to be done. Had dinner with another functionary tonight. They appreciate it, but it is tough on me.

Spent the evening in my room in Victoria Hotel reading many, many reports.

There is a report Gilles Houde [MNA for Fabre] was nearly kidnapped today. It may not be true.

The P.Q. and others are still yacking that Trudeau killed Laporte as much as the FLQ.

My article, despite all the effort, was not published in the *Star*. More rumours on a split, etc.

Geo. Springate [MNA for Sainte-Anne] foolishly said publicly he is against Cournoyer's nomination. He was not at the Caucus [on 29 October].

American elections tonight and Agnew seems to have failed to aid the Republicans with his law and order policy. The people are concerned about unemployment. This is a warning to us.

WEDNESDAY, 4 NOVEMBER 1970, QUEBEC

Tried to clear up administrative problems all day. Lunch and dinner – two more functionaries. Very interesting and useful for me. First time they had ever met a minister.

Cabinet meeting 3:00 p.m. to 7:00 p.m. We still have not got down to 100,000 jobs or social problems but Bourassa is aware of the job to be done.

At last, caught some terrorists yesterday.

Choquette ticked off for speaking of Cabinet in newspapers. Bourassa understanding, nevertheless. He is the easiest boss to work for and inspiring.

Cabinet and caucus have great leaks. Not me anyhow, my article appeared in *Le Devoir* [4 November] and was praised by many. It was discreet and was passed by the P.M.'s office.

THURSDAY, 5 NOVEMBER 1970, QUEBEC

More organizations and lunches, etc.

Jessop, sous-ministre adjoint, has good ideas on how to help the economy and the 100,000 jobs and also social investment. Perhaps by cooperatives (medical clinic cooperatives) such as Ste-Marie. The only hospital that is working in Quebec – no deficit. The doctors are on salary at $40,000 per year in Bellechasse.

The *Star* refused to publish my article on terrorism but never told me. There were not enough "facts," I found out later. Where will they ever get a Cabinet minister to make a statement again? [They never did for the next six years.]

Took train at night to Montreal. Could not stand poor Godbout's [my chauffeur's] driving.

FRIDAY, 6 NOVEMBER 1970, MONTREAL

Kidnap suspect Bernard Lortie is arrested in west-end Montreal apartment.

Worked in the office all day trying to clear up administrative problems created by my predecessors. Union Nationale appointments and even Choquette's appointment of S.N. [a fine person, but subject to depression. An old friend of Choquette's and an acquaintance of mine].

The R.C.M.P. Chief Higgitt makes stupid statements in Ottawa about FLQ case being broken shortly and is criticized by Ottawa and Choquette.

Our best worker in the Securities Commission section of analysis is the worst paid. I want to promote him but find out he was a P.Q. organizer and official agent in the last election. I had him in – his name is D. and we had a good talk with Lajeunesse, Chairman of the Securities Commission. [He got the promotion.]

The police are apparently on to leads and have made a number of arrests of importance of FLQ members.

SATURDAY, 7 NOVEMBER 1970
The inquest into Laporte death begins.

SUNDAY, 8 NOVEMBER 1970
Preparation of diary – going backwards. This proves I must do the diary daily.

It seems clear that Claude Ryan is going separatist, out of choice and out of hate for Trudeau.

Played bridge with the girls and had fun. They are growing up. Last night saw poor George Petrie [college friend, who was a paraplegic from the Second World War. He was confined to Queen Mary Veterans' hospital and I usually visited once per week.] He has great courage. Went to the Cenotaph in the afternoon and spent rest of day working. The hours of an MNA are long.

MONDAY, 9 NOVEMBER 1970
An article in *Le Devoir* this morning about my "precedent." It is a bit dishonest trying to make out that I had said that it was the first time a government had not given in. It is also unfair and suggests I am heartless. It is by a former priest who has certainly given up on Christian charity.

I had actually said it was "one of the first governments," and "a precedent."

Denis Chaput is very good and Miss Montpetit excellent.

The guard from the provincial police is getting on my nerves. He is a baby face who is always late. Yesterday at the Cenotaph he asked if he could sit in the car as he was cold. The car was parked over three hundred yards away.

TUESDAY, 10 NOVEMBER 1970, QUEBEC

Came to Quebec last night by train with Chaput. Long debate continues in Ottawa and Canada and in public over Mesures de Guerre Act and also whether we should give in to terrorism.

Claude Ryan had a little crack at me yesterday, but not much. He is not giving up.

At caucus this morning, we planned to speak on the economy and terrorism. I will try and speak on both.

Jacques Roy, Proulx and Chaput are preparing speeches.

Bourassa at the caucus said again that my article in Le Devoir was excellent last week and then, surprise, said the argument about the release of 6 people under our control was excellent. He did not know about this during the crisis evidently. I explained it was actually 9, but some might be affected by parole violations. Bourassa was acting from intuition based on his broad knowledge of the facts, but this important fact was not known at the time. [Actually, Bourassa had known but had forgotten.]

Jacques Roy, Proulx, Chaput [my personal staff] and I discussed my role as a député and the terrorism debate. Roy, says to be quiet for a while until we see how the wind blows. He is concerned about the reaction from the full story of the FLQ.

Gradually, I am getting the Ministry under control. Today lunch and supper with two functionaries who enjoyed themselves. Mr. Camaraire [superintendent of insurance in the ministry], who still wants to be free of the Ministry or who at least wants to agree with the insurance industry, presented a document signed by Piper [of the Insurance Association] asking for autonomy. It was really written by Jean Lesage and Camaraire.

WEDNESDAY, 11 NOVEMBER 1970, QUEBEC

Treasury board in the morning. The same old fights over the emphasis on France, on studies of fecundity, etc. We at least cut off the "bourses" of three persons [professors] from France who wanted to continue their studies in Quebec.

The debate was a little wild in the House over the question of terror. We allowed an emergency debate but Bourassa let Bertrand speak first. This has its advantage as they don't know what to say. Bertrand really agreed with us but the newspaper (Le Devoir, le 11 novembre 1970) makes out we were divided and that the federal government took over. Bourassa spoke from a few very rough notes on two or three pages. He again asked me for the exact spelling of "nolle prosequi," that I had told him about yesterday. He put it into his speech.

More lunches (this time the four secretaries) and a supper.

At the Cabinet meeting I was weak, Bourassa read my report in part.

I am taking up with Choquette the question of who does what in Consumer Protection. We will meet tomorrow but his having the service is wrong. He is quite stubborn and does not realize he is overworked.

THURSDAY, 12 NOVEMBER 1970

Denis Chaput, my new assistant, all of a sudden went home with my documents on terrorism. I spoke to him roughly on the phone and phoned him later to say not to worry.

A big debate today and tonight on terror. Laurin, the P.Q. leader (they elected their weakest member as leader) read a speech prepared for him. It was the party line. He attacked me for "glorifying" the death of Laporte as per Le Devoir article. I replied badly but not too badly so he withdrew his remarks. Bourassa spoke at length and got really strong. He was also strong in the answers to questions and I will tell him so.

Met Bourassa in the shower at the Winter Club. We both swim there but usually at different times. The club was swarming with police. He is relaxed and like me is in best shape when working under pressure.

My guard was such a pest that I am glad he has been replaced. I often walk around without a guard anyhow.

My article in Le Devoir was cold. I will have to change the French one for the Manoir Express [NDG weekly newspaper]. I emphasized the unity of the Cabinet but failed to emphasize the loss of Laporte which I feel and which is great.

FRIDAY, 13 NOVEMBER 1970

The papers, particularly French, give all the debate to the P.Q. as though Bourassa had not spoken well. The French reporters are for the most part young, inexperienced and ultra-nationalistic.

Went back to Montreal with the new guard Denis Leblanc. The other guard put me off, in large numbers.

The debate went on. As Choquette answered, I sneaked out.

SATURDAY, 14 NOVEMBER 1970, MONTREAL

Spent the morning and afternoon in the riding seeing people and 6 bazaars (count them). A poor group is starting up and I went to see the organizers. The organizers keep the names of the members secret for the most part as they want to control them. They want me to help but to get no credit. That is political life.

A Mrs. A .... wants to start a boy's club. I am putting her in touch with the Y.M.C.A.

The political troubles are much deeper engrained than most people realize. Our troubles will continue in Quebec for 50 years.

FRAP, the separatist people's organization in Montreal municipal affairs, is now divided between Racist terrorists and Socialist democrats. The same split exists in the Parti Québécois and the whole province. Drapeau who for the first time was to have opposition, will now have none at all as FRAP is breaking up. The P.Q. will divide at some time.

There is also the rich/poor split and the French Canadians who believe the English are colonial oppressors. The problem is "humiliation." There is a good article this week in the papers on humiliation and that the problem in Quebec is not poverty. The problem of humiliation on racial grounds is only a problem for a few people. They do not realize that every country has other groups in it. They do not realize that they have control of so much in Quebec.

I learned today that the guard, I did not like, was a fervent Pequiste. He was always late and always asking if he could disappear. At the Cenotaph, last Sunday, he asked to sit in the car as he was cold.

SUNDAY, 15 NOVEMBER 1970, MONTREAL

Tried to relax all day – read and prepared speeches. Still have pain when tired in my left wrist.

Speech tomorrow at Loyola and a radio program tomorrow night at CJMS.

Everyone in the press is attacking our government. Things are going to be tough.

Bourassa took the same view on television as I had in my article in Le Devoir, that it was a precedent. He is worrying about being called weak. Our position is very difficult, part of the population wants us to look strong and the other part wants us to be soft on demonstrators. Bour-assa, the pragmatist, was able to do what was necessary at each particular instant. A rigid person such as Agnew, Goldwater or even Nixon would have made a mess of the situation. So would have Claude Ryan, Alfred Rouleau [president of Assurance-vie Desjardins] and the N.D.P. who have no strong view on anything – they have a broad general view usually fair and very democratic on everything which causes them to fail to take decisions when necessary. Trudeau is flexible and strong when necessary. He can take decisions.

MONDAY, 16 NOVEMBER 1970, MONTREAL

Spoke at Loyola on federalism. Lots of reporters and 3 T.V., 3 radio. Questions on everything else.

Feel tired and sleep badly.

Bourassa is reported in papers as saying that we had created a "precedent." He will regret it, or it will come back to haunt him, like me, although he is right.

TUESDAY, 17 NOVEMBER 1970

Came up on the train and read an article in Le Devoir on the page opposite the editorial which article is terribly against me and my previous article concerning unity of the Cabinet and our discussion re terrorism. The article said I was not modest, etc. in being so proud of declaring we had been the first government in the world to say NON to the terrorists, forgetting poor Laporte. This really hurts.

Worked on the unity of the Ministry all day and also in the House. Phone calls and complaints all day.

Rotten day, expected questions in the House re reports in the newspapers of my speech yesterday which was reported everywhere, but nothing in the House.

Staying at the hotel Victoria in order to stay in a different hotel each week.

Convinced Bourassa and Choquette to leave consumer protection in my Ministry. By not fighting too soon, I was right and the apple fell, on its own, into the basket.

I don't really want the Protection of Consumers anyway, but it should be in our Ministry.

I will go to the Grey Cup because of a federal-provincial conference. What a break!

WEDNESDAY, 18 NOVEMBER 1970

The Gazette had an excellent report on my views on the ministry by a girl named Joan Fraser [later editor-in-chief of the *Gazette*]. She had interviewed me briefly on Monday.

A group of political assistés sociaux wanted to see Castonguay, but filled up my office at about 2:00 p.m. They would not leave, but for once I handled them properly. I was very firm to their questions most of which were stupid or vain. I let them sit at my desk – I could not prevent it actually. I took their demands to Castonguay in the House. They had my secretary type a letter to me in the House and generally took over using the long distance phone, etc. There were seven in all – mostly from Ste-Anne's riding but had given up on George Springate [their member] whom they could never see and with whom they seem to have no rapport.

I got Castonguay's secretary and assistant to agree to see them, but Castonguay was tough and when he is right, he is unwilling to discuss anything. He never did see them.

Cabinet meeting today – long and tough for me: old problems, chauffeurs, particular secretaries.

THURSDAY, 19 NOVEMBER 1970

Very, very tired today, all day. Slept badly in the hotel room at lunch and at supper.

Tried to explain to the three deputy-ministers that many of the structural problems in our ministry were caused by a lawyer being at the crux of the situation. Left the matter in Bouchard's [the deputy minister's] hands.

He told me Mr. M.L. [head of the Quebec Securities Commission] made a bollix of some speech. Is this jealousy?

I am getting too excited and too tired from the work. Must keep my cool.

FRIDAY, 20 NOVEMBER 1970 (QUEBEC)

Wanted to speak on Consumer Protection but the War Measures debate drags on. The reporters are taking a blast for what they did during the crisis, no self-control.

I will go to Toronto and everyone wants to go for the Grey Cup, the fun, etc. Tough to choose.

The remarks I made for T.V. at Loyola were seen by everyone. The remarks were only "fair." I must be very careful to be "good" in the future.

The speech to Westmount Ladies is cancelled for Sunday. It seems they meant January 22, 1971, not November 22, 1970 or was my office at fault?

Spoke at Pointe Claire Chamber of Commerce and was a great success. I turned the speech that Proulx and I had prepared, completely around.

Then went to a party at Nipper's [the artist John C. Little, a friend since school days], which was great fun. Leblanc, the Quebec policeman, would not go home, he enjoyed himself so much.

The question of guards is embarrassing to me. They make people believe that you believe you are important. They hang around, but don't protect you and are never there when you want them.

SATURDAY, 21 NOVEMBER 1970, OTTAWA
Letter is received from Cross saying he is alive and "well treated."

Went to Ottawa after Billy [my son and fourth child, age nine] had his hockey game at 8:00 a.m. They won 8 to 4; their goaler had only 4 shots – missed them all. Billy scored a goal.

The Federal Liberal Conference of Canada was on in Ottawa and I hung around the lobby of the Château Laurier and met everyone. Was the only Quebec Liberal there from caucus or Cabinet.

Ann Marie Kelly [of Trudeau's staff] told me of a [Mount Royal constituency] tea party given by Trudeau at 4:00 p.m. in the Château Laurier. She gave me her engraved invitation. There were about 40 federal Mount Royal riding members pressing around the P.M. and being obnoxious and familiar to poor Trudeau. How he suffers fools gladly – at least from his riding – not in the House. Trudeau came over and we spoke to one side on the terror situation, but a few clucks noisily rushed in. I complimented him on what he did and he replied "With some good help from you." Actually I think we did the good work and he helped, but he is charming and fair.

Trudeau said he wanted to discuss the current situation some time and to call his assistant when I was next in Ottawa.

I said federalism was stronger as a result of our joint actions in Quebec and in the Cabinet. This pleased him. It is very, very true and I think history will show it to be so.

I also said that much federal-provincial trouble was caused by civil servants. He said yes, the only recourse was to fire them as had been done in the CBC.

Dale Thomson was there and seemed very interesting and fun. I had a ball.

We stayed at the Lord Elgin with Ros, Priscilla [daughter, age eleven] and Pauline [daughter, age fourteen]. Jane [daughter, age thirteen] stayed in Montreal and Billy [son, age nine] stayed at Fraser's [Ros's brother's] home.

At night, we went to the Château Laurier grill with Pauline and Priscilla and had a lot of fun. There was a fine dinner and an orchestra – the girls were impressed.

I insulted two people. D. L., the battle-axe from Robert Baldwin riding, who is not leaving Quebec after all. I told her I was sorry to learn this. Ros asked why I bothered with her. She does it to make me sore. D.W. [from Mount Royal riding] had a few words on language, but I did not take her up on it. She attacked our recent declaration on the use of the French language in government.

One of the businessmen here is also against the language declaration. He says it will stop investment. I told him to stop complaining and to learn French. As a millionaire, he might do something for his country. He is a member of the Liberal Party with the patent aim to keep taxes down and business moving. By taxes he means "taxes on business." He is one of the group which supports John Turner but wants John locked into his 19th century ideas.

About five people told me about Marcel [Lajeunesse; chairman of the Quebec Securities Commision] making a lot of fool[ish] statements at a C.A.'s dinner. He is sick and occasionally far out of line.

SUNDAY, 22 NOVEMBER 1970

An excited, stupid concerned woman phoned tonight about her papers which were only photos that I had sent to Warren Allmand [MP for NDG]. I really had not handled her case well, considering her situation. Actually I had done all I could, but I had not reassured her.

Chaput, my assistant, needs more instruction on handling files.

S.R. [an NDG voter] phoned as usual. He is decoding the latest Cross letter. There is definitely a code in it, according to him.

MONDAY, 23 NOVEMBER 1970, MONTREAL

All day in Montreal. Saw Charles Neapole [president of the Stock Exchange] about Marcel Lajeunesse and his inappropriate speech. He advised me to do nothing, but that he would speak to Perrier, president of the C.A.'s.

Mrs. D.L. is talking against me as is K.R. [businessman and old squash partner] about Medicare. I must learn to say nothing strong to these people. I cannot convince them and they are unfair.

This is written Wednesday at the Treasury Board and it is surprising how things, which seem important Monday, are unimportant Wednesday.

The doctors continue to have all sorts of letters in the Gazette. The rich English rage and the rest of the world ignores the problem. The French press is silent.

A meeting of the NDG's citizens' society. It is a very small group of unimportant, self-important people.

Preparation of speech tomorrow night for the Assureurs.

TUESDAY, 24 NOVEMBER 1970

More fights between various members of the ministry, Lunch with A. who wants to be a Commissioner of the Quebec Securities Commission.

Claude Ryan continues to write about his peculiar position on the terror situation. Choquette had said that only two newspapers had taken Ryan's position, Le Devoir and a journal in Algiers. Ryan has found one or two other reporters in some obscure newspaper in France. He really is pathetic.

I foolishly accepted to speak on French radio at 4:00 p.m. It was good but it killed me to get home in time to change and to get back to speak at the Q.E. Hotel.

Speech to the Insurers was one of the best French-English speeches I have ever made but not necessarily very good. 700 persons present and lots of publicity but nothing in the Gazette.

Drove to Quebec from Queen Elizabeth to Hotel Victoria in 2 hours. 1 hour 40 minutes between bridges!!!

WEDNESDAY, 25 NOVEMBER 1970

In Quebec for the House all day and then by the "jet," "le jet à Lesage" to Toronto with our team for the Consumer Protection Conference.

Still fighting Jérôme Choquette for Consumer Protection. I know I will regret it when I get it.

Walked around Toronto at night and met George Springate M.P.Q. [MNA] for Ste-Anne in a bar. He is also kicker for the Alouettes.

Grey Cup fever building up.

THURSDAY, 26 NOVEMBER 1970, TORONTO

The Consumer Protection Conference all day. The Bill we presented and prepared by Jérôme is very weak [i.e., Bill 45]. It will have to be modified.

The N.D.P. minister from Manitoba stole the spotlight by a long boring dull speech which the newspapers dutifully reported. I got in a few licks however at capitalism and saving the poor people.

We all go to the Grey Cup game Saturday at the expense of the Ontario government. Ros comes up tomorrow.

I gave it right back to a reporter today, Greer of the Star, as to our objectives in Quebec.

FRIDAY, 27 NOVEMBER 1970, TORONTO

More Consumer Protection. Maurice Marquis [classmate in law at Laval, 1949–51 and now ministry lawyer for consumer protection] knows his stuff but the rest of the lawyers are quite weak.

More tough press conferences. We convinced Jérôme in Quebec to have the Consumer Protection Bill come under my Parliamentary Commission. Now to get him off the Bill and me on the Commission.

Grey Cup fever very high. The Royal York is jammed. Kids jumping around.

Rosslyn is here and thinks our suave hotel is something – the Sutton Place. Trudeau is here at the hotel. All the clucks are at the Royal York.

SATURDAY, 28 NOVEMBER 1970

Als win Grey Cup. Great game. First time I ever saw one.

Saw all the big shots after. One thing about this job, we get invited around.

Jean Chrétien said that he also opposed Medicare for January 1, 1968 when he was Sharp's assistant.

The head of [a large federal crown corporation] at the party with his mistress. She looks a little dowdy, but interesting.

SUNDAY, 29 NOVEMBER 1970

Came home by train and gave the sermon at United Church on Queen Mary Road at 1:00 p.m. One doctor very angry. I spoke on Medicare.

Bob Godin, President of the N.D.G. Association, nicely controlled Dr. McKeown today at an executive meeting. Dr. McKeown wanted to have a debate with Robillard.

I must try to take it easy.

MONDAY, 30 NOVEMBER 1970

Worked in Montreal all day and went to Quebec by train at night. Very slow.

Had lunch with Conrad Harrington, President of the Royal Trust Company and easily let him pick up the cheque. I am going to have to learn to do this with more grace if I am to stay solvent. Had the first overdraft in my life today – $2,000.

Harrington explained the Brinks movement the Sunday before the April 29th, 1970 election.

a) No press were called by them.
b) One client asked to move some stuff.
c) There were many trucks because Brinks has to have double trucks and also double crews after passing the town of Belleville. Double trucks in case of a breakdown.
d) Brinks made the arrangements for daylight all at the same time.

TUESDAY, 1 DECEMBER 1970, QUEBEC

Came to Quebec last night by train for meetings in the morning. Find I am spending more and more time away from home. Bourassa does not want us to give up guards but I find them painful.

Saw people all day and then sat in the House. Had my first question ever as a Minister [of financial institutions] in the House on the French/English labelling problem from a P.Q. [member] (Marcel Léger) [MNA for Lafontaine]. I was not listening but answered easily and well. The fact that I was questioned, surprised me. Choquette, who thinks I cannot answer or debate, said "It's your department, you must answer," as though he thought I did not want to answer or was afraid to.

At first, I did not want Consumer Protection but it is nice to know that someone else not me, was the person who messed up the bill. This is the way to take over.

My other bills will be prepared with great care. I got Madame Thérèse Casgrain to be speaker with me at the next meeting of the Association at N.D.G. Wesley Church, December 14th.

Had a caucus at 10:00 a.m. where we discussed the 17 protected counties or really 19. We must convince the effected members, especially Glen Brown and Ken Fraser to give up their seats. I whispered to the P.M. to promise them both jobs if they lose out. I think he is going to do so.

WEDNESDAY, 2 DECEMBER 1970, QUEBEC
Quebec provincial police say they are "making headway" in Cross case.

The Parliamentary Commission on the Consumer Protection [Bill 45] started badly. Jérôme has done no work on the bill, its preparation or its presentation. This makes it difficult to plan the budget, prepare the staff, etc. It is very annoying. Nor did the bill have the language proposals in it as [François] Cloutier [MNA for Ahuntsic] noted at Cabinet last night. Jérôme's excuse was that he was going to report it soon. Finally at the end of the session "he" announced it. He will be getting us into trouble.

I know quite a lot about the law in Bill 45, to Jérôme's surprise. I hope to bring down considerable amendments.

My only claim to fame is that my ministry seems to be organized.

Met Yves Caron [McGill Law professor] at the Parliamentary hearings. He is the son of the ex-Dean of Law at University of Montreal.

At Cabinet we questioned Jérôme about Cross and the FLQ. Either Jérôme does not know or is not telling us [he knew, but was not telling us].

THURSDAY, 3 DECEMBER 1970
A three-storey house is surrounded in Montréal-Nord and police say Cross is inside. The Cuban consul arrives on Île Sainte-Hélène at 11:30 a.m. The island was designated earlier by the Quebec government as the site the Cross kidnappers could use in taking advantage of safe-conduct offer to Cuba.

Shortly after 2 p.m., a fast-moving cavalcade roars away from the house towards the former Expo '67 grounds. Premier Bourassa's office confirms that

Cross and two suspects – Marc Carbonneau and Jacques Lanctôt – are in the cavalcade. Carbonneau drives the car, with Cross in the back seat.

At Expo, Cross is delivered to a Cuban embassy official, apparently in good health and spirits. He talks by phone with his wife in Switzerland, Prime Minister Trudeau, Premier Bourassa, and Prime Minister Edward Heath of Great Britain.

A Canadian Armed Forces four-motor Yukon aircraft takes Jacques Lanctôt, his wife and child, Jacques Cossette-Trudel and his wife, Marc Carbonneau, and Yves Langlois (alias Pierre Séguin) to Cuba. Upon their arrival there, the Cuban consul in the Canadian pavilion at Expo formally releases James Cross.

Cross is being released – his hiding place in a triplex in Montreal East has been found. Everyone is excited and the newspapers are full of it.

Everyone is very happy.

Having two Chefs de Cabinet – Jacques Roy and Raymond Proulx (Choquette's old chef in the Ministry of Financial Institutions) is difficult. Picard, the second assistant with Chaput has arrived and seems good. Everyone's English is terrible.

I gave a briefing before the budget meeting to the heads of departments. Not expecting me to be there, they all arrived late. "A quelle heure, votre réunion de 9 h 30"? Mr. Bouchard the Deputy Minister runs around to get them there on time.

Bouchard, Lacombe and Jacques Roy want to protect G... [a civil servant], principally because he is a civil servant. There is a feeling after a few years in governing that one protects one's own. This presumably applies even in G.'s case where:

a)   he had $18,000 per year and did not work;
b)   arrived late and was a trouble maker;
c)   had no competence for the job;
d)   made no effort to learn the securities commission work and took only part of the course and then quit.

They want him changed to information officer:

a)   despite the fact the job does not exist;
b)   his qualifications for the job have never been really investigated. He has never done it before but has some CBC theatrical and speaking experience;

c) mutation to another ministry, i.e. information would break all the rules of:
    i)   exams;
    ii) the job being there;
    iii) they want him.

I decided to fire him and this will shake everyone up.

FRIDAY, 4 DECEMBER 1970

More preparation of the speech for tonight with Proulx. The fact that the House sits at 3:00 leaves me free time to work in the morning.

Proulx has made a very intelligent basis for his speech, but the English and some ideas are dreadful. Generally, however, the work is excellent. He is quoting Kenneth Boulding, now the grand poo-bah of consumerism, and formerly my professor at McGill. Proulx was impressed that I had known Boulding. The speech is only to 75 persons however and never will really see any publicity because of Saturday being so crowded newswise.

Cross has been released and is going home. The papers are full of it. Apparently at 10:00 p.m. Wednesday when we were discussing this in Cabinet with Jérôme, Jérôme knew that the F.L.Q. had realized they were surrounded and had informed Cross. At 2:00 a.m. the next morning, the electricity was turned off and the police who had been occupying the premises above saw a note thrown out the door in a piece of steel pipe. That was yesterday and finally arrangements were made to send seven persons to Cuba. The FLQ really got the worst of it, because their six conditions were not realized and they themselves leave the country after threats, bravado, etc. which have proven hollow.

I went to N.D.G. at 6:30 p.m. after going to the Gazette to deliver my speech to Hal Winter. Then spoke at the Mount Royal Hotel and was quite good, lots of press but they will undoubtedly write little or nothing. The speech is not newsworthy and there is no central theme. It is also Friday.

SATURDAY, 5 DECEMBER 1970, MONTREAL

Did not do much in the constituency today. Had my hair cut, picked up mail and played squash but left the guard at his home.

James R. Cross flew home today after 60 days of confinement. He was 28 lbs lighter but in good health. He had been kept in one place and did not know where he was. The F.L.Q. controlled him much more severely than Laporte. There was no code in his letters. This makes one laugh when one realizes that experts from Quebec, Ottawa and Scotland Yard (flown over) tried to decode them and presumably found leads. Laporte's letters did have leads.

Now our strategy seems to have paid off. It was unfortunate that we did not find Laporte in time or that they were not convinced to give him up. If Lévesque, Claude Ryan and others had called on the F.L.Q. to give up Laporte and Cross, Laporte might have been saved.

My speech last night hardly made the papers at all. As usual Friday night is no good at all, while the speech had no "main theme."

I have been reading John Kenneth Galbraith's "India diary." He talks of a "main theme" in a speech for Kennedy. He advised on everything before the inauguration. His diary is very polished however and he also spoke of doing it "everyday." This I must do.

Went to a party at Lauchie Chisholm's next door which was fun after going to see "Scrooge" and Chinese food with the kids.

27–28 DECEMBER 1970

Three of the kidnappers of Pierre Laporte – Paul Rose, Jacques Rose, and Francis Simard – are found in a twenty-foot tunnel at Saint-Luc, near Saint-Jean, Quebec. (Earlier Bernard Lortie had been captured in an apartment near Queen Mary Road.) Bourassa wisely does not order the police to force them out, but calls on Dr Jacques Ferron (who has the confidence of the terrorists) to convince them to come out peacefully. Thus, injury and violence are avoided and the terrorists are to stand trial.

Appendix 2

The twenty-three "political prisoners" whom the FLQ
wished to be released in exchange for James Cross and
Pierre Laporte and their crimes

The names (not the crimes of or the charges against) were made public by
the FLQ on 6 October 1970. After the kidnapping of Pierre Laporte, the
same list was referred to.

Pierre Boucher, age twenty-five – sentenced to sixteen years for three armed
robberies, joined the FLQ after these.

Cyriaque Delisle, age twenty-five – sentenced to life imprisonment for the
murder of two employees of International Firearms in Montreal during a
hold-up.

Pierre Demers, age twenty-one – sentenced to twelve years in prison for
FLQ armed robberies intended to finance the FLQ.

Serge Demers, age twenty-five – sentenced to eight years for bombings and
robberies as a member of the Vallières-Gagnon cell.

Marcel Faulkner, age twenty-five – sentenced to six years and eight months
for holdups and bombings as a member of Vallières-Gagnon cell.

Marc-André Gagné, age twenty-five – sentenced to twenty-five years for participation in FLQ-related armed robberies.

Pierre-Paul Geoffroy, age twenty-six – sentenced to life imprisonment after admitting his participation in some thirty bombings, including the bombing of the Montreal Stock Exchange in 1969.

Edmond Guénette, age twenty-six – sentenced to be hanged, later commuted to life imprisonment, for his part in the International Firearms hold-up.

Gabriel Hudon, age twenty-eight – sentenced to twelve years for manslaughter in connection with the killing of night watchman Wilfrid (Wilfred) O'Neil (O'Neill).

Robert Hudon, age twenty-six – sentenced to eight years for the theft of weapons from armories in Quebec.

François Lanctôt, age twenty-one, brother of Jacques Lanctôt – arrested on 21 June on charges of planning the kidnapping of Harrison Burgess, the American consul general in Montreal.

Gérard Laquerre, age twenty-eight – sentenced to six years and eight months for manslaughter in the parcel-bomb killing of Thérèse Morin at the La Grenade Shoe Company.

André Lessard – charged with FLQ armed robberies and on bail at the time of the crisis, previously condemned to two years, six months, for having taken a police officer hostage in 1965 near Mont Laurier in an FLQ-police gun battle.

Robert Lévesque, age twenty-nine – sentenced to seven years for various crimes committed in Vallières-Gagnon cell, in particular for manslaughter in the La Grenade bombing.

Michel Loriot – sentenced for arson, although his connection to the FLQ was not clear.

Pierre Marcil – charged with conspiracy to kidnap the Israeli consul general on 26 February 1970 in Montreal (on bail at the time of the crisis).

Rhéal Mathieu, age twenty-two – sentenced to nine years for manslaughter in connection with the deaths of Jean Corbo and Thérèse Morin.

Claude Morency, age nineteen – on trial at the time of the crisis on charges of possession of dynamite.

André Ouellette, age thirty-one – sentenced to ten years for armed robberies, later joined the FLQ.

André Roy, age twenty-three – facing charges relating to the planned FLQ kidnapping of Harrison Burgess, the American consul general in Montreal, by an FLQ cell.

François Schirm, age thirty-eight – sentenced to life imprisonment for the armed robbery at International Fireworks, later commuted to life imprisonment.

Claude Simard, age twenty-three – sentenced to five years, ten months, for manslaughter in the bombing at La Grenade.

Réjean Tremblay, age twenty-seven – charged with an FLQ-related armed robbery (on bail at the time of the crisis).

Appendix 3

Translation of "Petition of the Sixteen Eminent Personalities," delivered at a press conference, Wednesday, 14 October 1970 at 9:00 p.m, at the Holiday Inn, Sherbrooke St. West, Montreal, and published in *Le Devoir* on 15 October 1970

The Cross-Laporte affair is above all a Quebec drama. Of the two hostages, one is a citizen of Quebec, the other is a diplomat whose functions make him temporarily a fellow citizen with the same right to life and personal dignity that each of us enjoys.

The members of the FLQ, on the other hand, are a tiny fraction of this same Quebec, but they are still a part of our reality, because extremism is a part of society in general. At the same time extremism denotes a major problem and may put us in mortal peril.

The fate of two human lives, the reputation and the collective honour of our society, the danger of social and political degeneration, makes it self-evident to us that it is Quebec which has responsibility for finding and carrying out a solution and must put it into effect.

Some outside commentaries, the most recent and most incredible of which is that of Premier Robarts of Ontario,[1] adding to the atmosphere of virtual military rigidity that can be detected in Ottawa, in our opinion threaten to reduce Quebec and its government to tragic impotence.

Faced with every threat to the equilibrium of the society that they are charged with maintaining, it is natural that the authorities should make

---

1 John Robarts had issued a call for "a general war" against the FLQ and at the same time had made a biting attack on the Parti Québécois.

a superhuman effort to negotiate and arrive at a compromise. We believe that Quebec and its government have indeed the moral mandate and responsibility to do so, particularly because their familiarity with the facts and of public opinion will enable them to decide wisely and well.

We are reinforced in our position by the fear that, especially in some non-Quebec circles, there exists the terrible temptation of "the policy of the worst course" [politique du pire], which is to say that Quebec in a chaotic and ravaged state will be easy to keep under control. That is why, leaving aside our differences on a whole panoply of subjects, and keeping in mind, for the moment, the unique fact that we are vitally concerned Québécois, we wish to give our most urgent support to negotiating an exchange of the two hostages for the political prisoners, which necessarily implies, despite any obstruction, that may come from outside Quebec, the cooperation of the federal government.

And we immediately invite all citizens and groups who share our point of view to make known their approval, within the shortest delay.

(The signatories of the petition are Messrs. René Lévesque, président du Parti Québécois; Alfred Rouleau, président de l'Assurance-vie Desjardins; Marcel Pepin, président de la C.S.N.; Louis Laberge, président de la F.T.Q.; Jean-Marc Kirouac, président de l'U.C.C.; Claude Ryan, directeur du DEVOIR; Jacques Parizeau, président du Conseil exécutif du P.Q.; Fernand Daoust, secrétaire général de la F.T.Q.; Yvon Charbonneau, président de la C.E.Q.; Matthias Rioux, président de l'Alliance des professeurs de Montréal; Camille Laurin, chef parlementaire du Parti Québécois; Guy Rocher, professeur de sociologie à l'U. de M.; Fernand Dumont, directeur de l'Institut supérieur des sciences humaines à l'Université Laval; Paul Bélanger, professeur de sciences politiques à l'université Laval; Raymond Laliberté, ex-président de la C.E.Q.; Marcel Rioux, professeur d'anthropologie de l'U.de M.)

Appendix 4

Sentences of FLQ members involved in the crisis

The eventual sentences of FLQ members involved in the October Crisis 1970 were as follows:

Jacques and Louise Cossette-Trudel: two years imprisonment for the kidnapping of Cross. Freed conditionally in April 1980.

Jacques Lanctôt: one year imprisonment for the Cross kidnapping.

Marc Carbonneau: twenty months in jail, three years probation and 150 hours of community work for kidnapping Cross, forcible confinement, conspiracy, and extortion.

Yves Langlois (alias Pierre Séguin): two years imprisonment less one day for the kidnapping of Cross. Freed conditionally in July 1983.

Nigel Barry Hamer: suspended sentence.

Paul Rose: two terms of life imprisonment for the kidnapping and murder of Laporte. Conditional release in December 1982.

Francis Simard: life imprisonment for the murder of Laporte. Freed conditionally in September 1982.

Bernard Lortie: twenty years for kidnapping Laporte. Freed conditionally at the end of 1978.

Jacques Rose: eight years (after his fourth trial) for complicity in the death of Laporte. Freed conditionally in July 1978.

Michel Viger: eight years for complicity. Freed conditionally in July 1978.

Robert Dupuis: two years imprisonment. Freed conditionally after one year.

Denis Quesnel: one year imprisonment.

Louise Verreault: one year imprisonment.

Richard Therrien: one year imprisonment.

Francine Belisle: nine months imprisonment.

Hélène Quesnel: six months imprisonment.

Yves Roy: six months imprisonment.

Françoise Bélisle: six months imprisonment.

Lise Balcer: six months imprisonment.

Lise Rose: six months imprisonment.

On 1 November 1984 Raymond Villeneuve, one of the three founders in 1963 of the FLQ and the person who gave it its name, became the last FLQ member to return from exile. He spent eight months in prison.

Notes

1 De Vault was a PQ organizer who joined the FLQ and subsequently became an informer in the employ of the Montreal police.

2 See, for example, the Parti Québécois National Council minutes of 18 October 1970, reproduced in http://www.mcgill.ca/maritimelaw/crisis, appendix O, and the Duchaîne Report, discussed in chapter 20.

3 See, among other works, Fournier, *FLQ: Histoire d'un mouvement clandestin*, 308; Leroux, *Les silences d'octobre*, 13; and the CBC's *Black October*, 2000, accessed on CBC's website but no longer posted

4 See http://www.mcgill.ca/maritimelaw/crisis, appendix N, which reproduces Parti Québécois lawyer Pothier Ferland's legal opinion to this effect. Ferland also gave the same opinion at the Parti Québécois National Council meeting of 18 October 1970 (see appendix O at the above-mentioned website and chapter 10).

5 Such websites include http://www.mlnq.net (MLNQ); http://www.vigile.net/pol/flq (Vigile); http://membres.lycos.fr/quebecunpays/OCTOBRE-70.html (Québec un Pays); http://www.independance-quebec.com/flq/plan.php (Site Historique du FLQ); http://membres.lycos.fr/frq/flq.htm (Front Révolutionnaire du Québec); and http://www.cvm.qc.ca/glaporte/metho/a01/a109.htm (a paper on the FLQ and the October Crisis).

6 See http://www.mcgill.ca/maritimelaw/crisis, appendix X.

7 Fournier, *F.L.Q.: The Anatomy of an Underground Movement*, 9. He made the same statement fourteen years later in *FLQ: Histoire d'un mouvement clandestin*, 6.

8 Manon Leroux, *Les silences d'octobre*, 14.
9 *Journal des débats*. Assemblée nationale, 1970, November, 1524–25, 1527, and 1528.
10 René Lévesque, *My Quebec*, 175–6.
11 René Lévesque, *Memoirs*, 245. French edition, *Attendez que je me rappelle*, 327.
12 *Le Devoir*, 30 October 2002.
13 Desbiens, *L'Actuel et l'actualité*, 282–3. See http://www.mcgill.ca/maritimelaw/crisis, appendix G.

CHAPTER ONE

1 *Le Devoir*, 16 October 1970.
2 In power, the Parti Québécois has not been as generous. In 1994 the PQ won 77 seats but only 44.7 per cent of the popular vote, while the Liberals, with 44.4 per cent of the vote, won only 47 seats. The discrepancy reflected the disproportionate weight accorded rural as opposed to urban ridings, an imbalance the PQ did nothing to correct. Four years later the PQ, with only 42.9 per cent of the popular vote, formed the government with 76 seats. The Liberals had 43.5 per cent of the vote but only 48 seats. Again, the PQ government was happy with the status quo.
3 Lacoursière, *Alarme citoyens!* 198.
4 Cardin, *Comprendre octobre 1970*, 67.
5 *Journal des débats*, Assemblée nationale, 11 November 1970, 1494.
6 Ibid., 1714.
7 Leroux, *Les silences d'octobre*, 126.
8 *Le Devoir*, 14 October 1970.
9 Montreal *Gazette*, 16 September 1970.
10 *Le Devoir*, 13 October 1970.
11 Saywell, *Quebec 70*, 111–20.
12 An "informal organization" that has existed since 1995 under the name "*Intellectuels pour la Souveraineté*" (IPSO) included three hundred people at its formation. Among these, there were few, if any, elected politicians. (One member, Daniel Turp, now the MNA for Mercier, was not holding office at the time of the group's creation.) Of the three hundred, 175 were professors or teachers, 39 were students, and 86 were almost exclusively employed by the Quebec government, usually in various roles at the universities. See Sarra-Bournet, *Manifeste des intellectuels pour la souveraineté*, 23–32.
13 F.-A. Angers, *Le Devoir*, 16 October 1970.
14 *La Presse*, 31 October 1970.

CHAPTER TWO

1 Organisation de l'Armée secrète, involved in an attempted 1961–2 putsch against French President Charles De Gaulle.

2 See Savoie, *La véritable histoire du F.L.Q.*, 41–6.

3 See http://www.mcgill.ca/maritimelaw/crisis, appendix H.

4 It is interesting that the Parti Québécois, too, has never resolved the contradiction between seeking economic well-being of the people, on the one hand, and the desire to separate from Canada at any cost, on the other. We federalists, however, have not solved the problem of federalism. We often fail to appreciate the difficulty of governing Canada as a single economy from coast to coast and at times we fail to recognize the strains of cooperatively administering one federal and ten provincial governments.

5 Cardin, *Comprendre octobre 1970*, 61. "CEGEPS" stands for "Collèges d'enseignement général et professionnel, intended for high school graduates prior to entry into university. The full name of the FLP was the Front de libération populaire.

6 Cardin, *Comprendre octobre 1970*, 62.

7 Bédard, *Chronique d'une insurrection appréhendée*, 55.

8 *Format 60*, Radio-Canada, 20 October 1970; Pelletier, *The October Crisis*, 187. In 1964, one FLQ member, Pierre Schneider, wrote from prison: "In Canada, democracy never existed." See Comeau, Cooper, and Vallières, *FLQ: Un projet révolutionnaire*, 33. Schneider, however, benefited from Canadian democracy and justice. After his trial, where he was ably defended without expense to himself, he was condemned to three years in prison but was released long before his sentence had expired. Presumably, he now takes part in all municipal, provincial, and federal elections and enjoys the benefits of Quebec and Canadian society and democracy.

9 Comeau, Cooper, and Vallières, *FLQ: Un projet révolutionnaire*, 33–4.

10 Ibid.

11 Compare appendices W and H at http://www.mcgill.ca/maritimelaw/crisis.

12 *La Cognée*, 30 April 1964; Bédard, *Chronique d'une insurrection appréhendée*, 52.

13 See http://www.mcgill.ca/maritimelaw/crisis, appendix C.

14 Communiqué from the FLQ on 8 October 1970. See Pelletier, *The October Crisis*, 92.

15 Simard, *Pour en finir avec octobre*.

16 See http://www.mcgill.ca/maritimelaw/crisis, appendix G.

17 *Le Devoir*, 24 March 1981; Leroux, *Les silences d'octobre*, 70.

18 Gellner, *Bayonets in the Streets*, 67.

CHAPTER THREE

1 Savoie, *La véritable histoire du F.L.Q.*, 14–15.

2 Ibid., 33.

3 Ibid., 14.

4 Fournier, *FLQ: Histoire d'un mouvement clandestin*, 485.

5 On 7 November 1969, the Comité d'aide au groupe Vallières-Gagnon had not only demonstrated in support of the FLQ but had also launched incendiary bombs against Montreal city hall, the Montreal police headquarters, and a number of banks. See Fourner, ibid., 484.

6 Mongeau, *Kidnappé par la police*, 33.

7 Ibid., 36.

8 Cardin, *Comprendre octobre 1970*, 59.

9 Ibid., 59–60.

10 Lina Gagnon, *Le Devoir*, 16 October 1970.

11 *La Cognée*, May 1965.

12 Fournier, *FLQ: Histoire d'un mouvement clandestin*, 507.

13 *Hansard*, 16 October 1970, 224.

14 *Journal des Débats*, Assemblée nationale, 26 November 1970, 1812.

15 Pelletier, *The October Crisis*, 113.

16 Ibid., 50.

17 Ibid., 51.

18 Rioux, *Quebec in Question*, 176.

19 Lacoursière, *Alarme citoyens!* 26.

20 Laurendeau, Marc, *Les Québécois violents*, 222–4.

21 Duchaîne, *Rapport sur les événements d'octobre, 1970*, 20; Bédard, *Chronique d'une insurrection appréhendée*, 108; Fournier, *FLQ: Histoire d'un mouvement clandestin*, 288.

22 See http://www.mcgill.ca/maritimelaw/crisis, appendix X.

CHAPTER FOUR

1 Comeau, Cooper, and Vallières, *FLQ: Un projet révolutionnaire*, 13 (first manifesto), 210 (second manifesto), and 234 (third manifesto).

2 See http://www.mcgill.ca/maritimelaw/crisis, appendix H, for the text of the manifesto.

3 Laurendeau, *Les Québécois violents*, 50–1.

4 Ibid., 57.

5 Fournier, *FLQ: Histoire d'un mouvement clandestin*, 306.

6 Trudeau, *Memoirs*, 135.

7 *Journal de Montréal*, 10 October 1970.

8 Pelletier, *The October Crisis*, 57.

9 Bédard, *Chronique d'une insurrection appréhendée*, 67.

10 *Le Devoir*, 13 October 1970.

11 Montreal *Star*, 14 October 1970.

12 Special Issue of *Le Devoir*, 30 December 1970.

13 Ibid.

CHAPTER FIVE

1 Fournier, *FLQ: Histoire d'un mouvement clandestin*, 262.
2 *Le Soleil*, 9 October 1970. Emphasis added.
3 *Le Devoir*, 3 November 1970.
4 *Journal des débats*, Assemblée nationale, 13 November 1970, 1557.
5 Saywell, *Quebec 70*, 129–34.
6 *Hansard*, 13 October 1970, 67. Long after the October Crisis, U.S. Secretary of State Henry Kissinger declared that he had advised us at the time not to give in to the terrorists' demands. I have found no reference, however, in any public or private record of Kissinger actually having given such advice.
7 Winnipeg *Tribune*, 7 October 1970, translated and reported in *La Presse*, 14 October 1970, and translated back into English by the author.
8 Winnipeg *Free Press*, 12 October 1970, translated and reported in *La Presse*, 14 October 1970, and translated back into English by the author.
9 *Le Devoir*, 6 November 1970.
10 Ibid. It is interesting that Leclerc's 6 November 1970 editorial is not among the collected editorials published by Claude Ryan in *Le Devoir et la crise d'octobre 70*). That volume contains editorials by Ryan, Claude Lemelin, Paul Sauriol, and Leclerc himself.
11 Emphasis added. See the complete editorial in http://www.mcgill.ca/maritime-law/crisis, appendix G.
12 *Journal de Montréal*, 10 October 1970.
13 Lacoursière, *Alarme Citoyens!*, 197–8; *Journal de Montréal*, 13 October 1970.
14 See chapter 6 and http://www.mcgill.ca/maritimelaw/crisis, appendix J.
15 Duchaîne, *Rapport sur les événements d'octobre, 1970*, 151. See also the minutes of the PQ National Council reproduced in http://www.mcgill.ca/maritimelaw/crisis, appendix O.
16 Montreal *Gazette*, 17 October 1970.
17 *Journal des débats*, Assemblée nationale, 12 November 1970, 1524–31.
18 Ibid., 1524. See also 1527 and 1528.
19 See ibid.: Lucien Lessard, 1561–2, 1571–5; Marcel Léger, 1596–9; Robert Burns, 1627–31; Guy Joron, 1655–60; Claude Charron, 1706–11; Charles Tremblay, 1690–4.
20 Duchaîne, *Rapport sur les événements d'octobre, 1970*, 20.
21 Trait, *FLQ 70*, 26–8.
22 *Le Soleil*, 14 December 1970.

CHAPTER SIX

1 Montreal *Star*, 15 October 1970. See appendix 3 for the English text. The French text of the petition is reproduced in http://www.mcgill.ca/maritimelaw/crisis, appendix J.

2 Duchesne, *Parizeau*, vol. 1, 566.

3 The day before the petition, Trudeau said in the House of Commons: "It is a mistake, I believe, to give them publicity, which is the thing they hope for the most. I also think it is a mistake to encourage the use of the term 'political prisoners' for men who are bandits." *Hansard*, 13 October 1970, 52.

4 *La Presse*, 15 October 1970.

5 Duchesne, *Parizeau*, vol. 1, 565.

6 Rioux, *Quebec in Question*, 172.

7 Pepin, preface to Cardin, *Comprendre octobre 1970*.

8 Ibid., 99.

9 Pelletier, *The October Crisis*, 59.

10 Rioux, *Quebec in Question*, 169. Emphasis added. In the French edition *La question du Québec*, 1976 at p 236 the wording was "M. Jérôme Choquette, un poids lourd à la machoire carrée ..."

11 See http://www.mcgill.ca/maritimelaw/crisis, appendix S.

12 Cohen and Granatstein, *Trudeau's Shadow*, 303. Emphasis added.

13 *Le Soleil*, 16 October 1970. Emphasis added. See also *Le Devoir*, 16 October 1970, to the same effect.

14 Montreal *Gazette*, 16 October 1970. Emphasis added.

15 Léon Dion, 20 October 1970, *Format 60*, Radio-Canada; Pelletier, *The October Crisis*, 22.

CHAPTER SEVEN

1 Cabinet minutes, 15 October 1970, 2:30 p.m.

2 R.S.C. 1970, c. N-4. There have been two other instances. Premier Jean-Jacques Bertrand of Quebec tardily called the army into Quebec in October 1969 during a strike by the Montreal police. Decades later, in January 1999, Mayor Mel Lastman of Toronto was to call in the army for assistance after unprecedented (for Toronto) snowstorms, known by some of his critics as Lastman's "quelques centimètres de neige."

3 Montreal *Gazette*, 16 October 1970.

4 Ibid.

5 *Journal des débats*, Assemblée nationale, 15 October 1970, 1380.

6 Ibid.

7 *Le Devoir*, 16 October 1970.

8 Montreal *Gazette*, 16 October 1970.

9 *Le Journal de Montréal*, 30 October 1970.

10 *Le Devoir*, 16 October 1970.

11 *Le Soleil*, 16 October 1970. Boyer, in his reference to the "real insurrection (but one which could be apprehended)," was referring, of course, to the application

of the War Measures Act, of which the public and the press had been speaking openly for some time, although it was not implemented until 16 October 1970.

12 *Le Devoir*, 15 October 1970; Duchaîne, *Rapport sur les événements d'octobre 1970*, 106.
13 Duchaîne, *Rapport sur les événements d'octobre 1970*, 251–2.
14 *Le Devoir*, 10 November 1970.
15 Ibid.
16 Segal, *No Surrender*, 23.
17 Lévesque, *Memoirs*, 246.

CHAPTER EIGHT

1 Pelletier, *The October Crisis*, 117–25. See also 225–33 of the French version for a list of FLQ bombings, robberies, and violent deaths from 1963 to 1970.
2 Fournier, *FLQ: Histoire d'un mouvement clandestin*, 476–85.
3 Ibid., 484.
4 For newspaper accounts of student walkouts and demonstrations in support of the FLQ at UQAM, U.deM., CEGEP du Vieux Montréal, CEGEP de Jonquière, the secondary schools of Saint Stanislas and Pius IX and in Quebec City at Université Laval and the CEGEPs of Limoilou and Sainte-Foy, see *Montréal Matin*, 16 October 1970, and *Le Devoir*, 16 October 1970.
5 *La Presse*, 15 October 1970. Emphasis added.
6 Bédard, *Chronique d'une insurrection appréhendée*, 184.
7 *La Presse*, 16 October 1970.
8 MacDonald and Segal, *Strong and Free*, 36.
9 Radwanski and Windeyer, *No Mandate but Terror*, 123–4.
10 Westell, *Paradox*, 256.
11 Pelletier, *The October Crisis*, 127.
12 Claude Beauchamp, *La Presse*, 17 October 1970.
13 *Journal des débats*, Assemblée nationale, 12 November 1970, 1534.
14 Ibid., 13 November 1970, 1558–9.
15 See http://www.mcgill.ca/maritimelaw/crisis, appendix K.
16 Comeau, Cooper, and Vallières, *FLQ: Un projet révolutionnaire*, 193.
17 See the full text of the editorial in http://www.mcgill.ca/maritimelaw/crisis, appendix G.
18 Butler and Carrier, *The Trudeau Decade*, 179, quoting *La Presse*, 19 October 1970.
19 Radwanski and Windeyer, *No Mandate but Terror*, 124.
20 Marc Laurendeau, *Les Québécois violents*, 197.
21 Pelletier, *The October Crisis*, 115.
22 Ibid., 15.
23 I must comment here on one allegation in particular. On Tuesday, 28 January 1992, commissioner W. Len Higgitt of the Royal Canadian Mounted Police,

declared that on Wednesday morning, 14 October 1970, he had advised the federal cabinet committee on security and information that, relying on the counsel
of John K. Starnes, head of the RCMP security service, he believed the use of the
War Measures Act was unnecessary. He told the government at the time that the
number of persons who should be arrested in order to undermine the FLQ was
188 and that only 68 of these were considered to be hardliners. He also indicated
that the RCMP had someone under surveillance who, it hoped, would lead to the
kidnappers (*La Presse*, 30 January 1992).

In this connection, it first needs to be pointed out that Higgitt and the Quebec
and Montreal police chiefs had made erroneous predictions of arrests to the
Quebec cabinet on the evenings of 11–14 October, and Higgitt had done so again
in Ottawa on 6 November. That aside, I believe that the advice of Higgitt (based
on Starnes) on Wednesday morning, 14 October, on the use of the War Measures
Act was not valid by the night of 15–16 October, if it ever was. A great deal had
happened between the morning of 14 October and the early morning of 16 October, including meetings of FLQ sympathizers, strikes around the province, and a
giant pro-FLQ rally. I also wish to note that Starnes, in his 1998 memoir *Closely
Guarded*, writes: "I was unable to be an active player [during the October Crisis],
for the simple reason that I was struck down with a severe bout of pneumonia on
October 8 and remained out of the picture until November 23, when my doctor
pronounced me sufficiently recovered to return to work." By the time Starnes was
feeling better, the crisis was over! Clearly, since he was out of the picture at the
time, Starnes was not the best-placed person to deliver an opinion on whether
or not the crisis qualified as an apprehended insurrection or whether reports of
FLQ activity and the civic unrest it engendered were exaggerated. In particular
in October 1970 Starnes thought that the situation was sufficiently dangerous
for him to have "a team of armed members of the RCMP Security Service ... dispatched to act around the clock to guard ... him and his wife and our property ...
in a relatively remote region in Quebec" (158–9).

CHAPTER NINE

1 See the proclamation, dated 16 October 1970, the War Measures Act, and the
   Regulations in http://www.mcgill.ca/maritimelaw/crisis, appendix L.
2 A first draft of the "Public Order Regulations, 1970" (the official English name of
   the War Measures Act Regulations) can be seen in annex B of Duchaîne, *Rapport
   sur les événements d'octobre, 1970*. In the official French text, the Regulations were
   designated in the singular as the "*Règlement de 1970 concernant l'ordre public*," and
   this at times causes confusion.
3 See http://www.mcgill.ca/maritimelaw, appendix L.
4 Marx, "Emergency Power and Civil Liberties in Canada."

5 *Globe and Mail*, 23 December 1971.

6 Cohen and Granatsein, *Trudeau's Shadow*, 181.

7 Segal, *No Surrender*, 23. Emphasis added.

8 Marcel Rioux, *La question du Québec*, 176.

9 E.C.S. Wade and G.G. Phillips, *Constitutional Law*, 5th ed. (1955), 422, as cited in Marx, "Emergency Power and Civil Liberties in Canada," 43.

10 Marx, "Emergency Power and Civil Liberties in Canada," 43.

11 Ibid.

12 Lacoursière, *Alarme citoyens!* 248.

13 Ibid.

14 See *Martin's Annual Criminal Code, 1970*, 64–5, which contains the sections applicable at the time of the crisis.

15 *R. v. Russell* (1920), 1 W.W.R. 624 (Man. C.A.) at para. 142.

16 See *R. v. Brien* (1993), 86 C.C.C. (3d) 550 (NWT Supr. Ct.), and *R. v. Loewen* (1992), 27 W.A.C. 42 (B.C.C.A.).

17 Lacoursière, *Alarme citoyens!* 248.

18 MacDonald and Segal, *Strong and Free*, 16–23.

19 Duchaîne, *Rapport sur les événements d'octobre, 1970*, 120; *Hansard*, 16 October 1970, 193.

20 Scott, *A New Endeavour*, 132.

CHAPTER TEN

1 Duchesne, *Jacques Parizeau*, vol.1, 535–91.

2 See chapter 9.

3 See chapter 9.

4 Gilles Boyer, *Le Soleil*, 15 October 1970.

5 *Montréal Matin*, 19 October 1970; Duchaîne, *Rapport sur les événements d'octobre, 1970*, 127.

6 Leroux, *Les silences d'octobre*, 129.

7 See http://www.mcgill.ca/maritimelaw/crisis, appendix N.

8 Scott, "The War Measures Act, s. 6(5) and the Canadian Bill of Rights," 344.

9 Pelletier, *The October Crisis*, 184.

10 A minister's salary was $24,000 at that time.

11 Westell, *Paradox*, 255.

CHAPTER ELEVEN

1 See the Proclamation and Regulations at http://www.mcgill.ca/maritimelaw/crisis, appendix I.

2 *Hansard*, 16 October 1970, 194; Duchaîne Report, 1981, 120–1. Emphasis added.

3 *Globe and Mail*, 23 December 1971.

4 Duchaîne Report, 26–7. N.B.: The italicized words in this quotation are emphasized in the text of the Duchaîne report.

5 Ibid., 27.

6 Ibid.

7 *Le Devoir*, 8 October 1981.

8 See appendix 1 at 16 October 1970.

9 Duchaîne Report, 94.

10 Ibid., 99–100.

11 See Godin's account of his eight days of detention in Daniels, *Quebec/Canada and the October Crisis*, 87–93.

12 See Serge Mongeau, *Kidnappé par la police*, 1970.

13 See Foisy, *Michel Chartrand*.

14 Journalist, author, and broadcaster Nick Auf der Maur ran under various banners in municipal, provincial, and federal politics between 1974 and 1994.

15 Montreal *Star*, 23 October 1970.

16 *Le Devoir*, 7 November 1970; Pelletier, *The October Crisis*, 142.

17 Duchesne, *Parizeau*, vol. 1, 556.

18 As Lord Hewart said in *Rex v. The Sussex Justices* [1924] 1 K.B. 256 at p. 259: "it is not merely of some importance but is of fundamental importance that justice should not only be done, but should manifestly and undoubtedly be seen to be done."

19 The dilemma was described on 22 October 1970 in an article entitled "*Les faits justifiaient-ils la décision du gouvernement?*" by the Canadian Civil Liberties Association. See *Le Devoir*, 22 October 1970.

20 Radwanski and Windeyer, *No Mandate but Terror*, 124.

21 James Littleton in MacDonald and Segal, *Strong and Free*, 11.

22 See Appendix to chapter 19.

23 *Journal des débats*, Assemblée nationale, 12 novembre 1970, 1525.

24 See chapter 19.

25 Raymond Saint-Pierre, *Les années Bourassa*, 29–30.

CHAPTER TWELVE

1 Jean Egen, *Le monde diplomatique*, Paris, January 1971, 12; Pelletier, *The October Crisis*, 160.

2 Cardin, *Comprendre octobre 1970*, 118.

3 Bédard, *Chronique d'une insurrection appréhendée*, 160.

4 Ibid.

5 MacDonald and Segal, *Strong and Free*, 30.

6 *Le Soleil*, 29 October 1970.

7 Cardin, *Comprendre octobre 1970*, 117–23.

8 Ibid., 122–3.

9 Ibid., 39.

10 *Le Devoir*, 28 October 1970.

11 Ibid.

12 Jérôme Choquette, *Journal des débats*, Assemblée nationale, 13 November 1970, 1559.

13 Scott, *A New Endeavour*, 127–9.

14 Ibid., 132.

15 Ibid., 135.

16 T.C. Douglas, *Hansard*, 16 October 1970, 199.

17 Trudeau, *Memoirs*, 143.

18 *Canadian News Facts*, vol.4, No. 19 16–31 October 1970, 531; on-line at http://www2.marianopolis.edu/quebechistory/docs/october/douglas.htm.

19 See *Le Soleil*, 29 October 1970, page 20, editorial by Amédée Gaudreault, "Colonels de chocolat," which concludes: "On entend même M. Tommy Douglas raconter que le Québec a été victime du coup de l'incendie du Reichstag. On se souvient que l'incendie du parlement allemand avait été tramé par Hitler et mis sur le dos des communistes, avant la dernière guerre. Voilà donc M. Trudeau en train de manipuler le FLQ. Ça bat l'histoire des colonels de chocolat, qui peuvent donc aller se rhabiller."

20 Rioux, *Quebec in Question*, 174.

21 Ann Charney in Abraham Rotstein, *Power Corrupted*, 17.

22 Alan Borovoy in ibid., 99.

23 Abraham Rotstein in ibid., 123.

24 Provencher, *La grande peur d'octobre*, 62.

25 Gwyn, *The Northern Magus*, 109.

26 Segal, *No Surrender*, 22.

27 Duchesne, *Parizeau*, vol. 1, 554.

28 Lévesque, *My Québec*, 175. Emphasis added. The foregoing is the complete description and, in fact, the only discussion of the October Crisis – and René Lévesque's part in it – in a book that covers Lévesque's life until his election in November 1976. For those interested in October Crisis revisionism, this is a good example.

29 D. MacDonald, *Hansard*, 16 October 1970. N.B.: Immediately after MacDonald uttered these words, the Hon. H.A. ("Bud") Olson, Minister of Agriculture, interjected: "Nonsense, read the regulations." (H. Olson, *Hansard*, 16 October 1970, 243)

30 *Hansard*, 16 October 1970, 234 and 235.

31 The Prince Edward Island MP who, on 5 November 1970, had cast the sole vote in second reading (approval in principle) against the Public Order (Temporary Measures) Act, which replaced the War Measures Act used in October 1970.

32 At the time president of the Students' Council at the University of Ottawa and was named a senator in Ottawa in 2005.

33 David MacDonald in MacDonald and Segal, *Strong and Free*, 39.

34 Patrick Watson in ibid., 1–2.

35 Hugh Segal in ibid., 32.

36 Jean-Claude Leclerc, *Le Devoir*, 4 November 1970. Emphasis added.

37 See also Nurgitz in MacDonald and Segal, *Strong and Free*, 16–23.

38 *Le Devoir*, 22 March 1985; Leroux, *Les silences d'octobre*, 127.

39 Gwyn, *The Northern Magus*, 109.

40 Lévesque, *Memoirs*, 248, citing Dumont, *The Vigil of Quebec*.

41 Sharp, *Which Reminds Me*, 197.

42 Robertson, *Memoirs of a Very Civil Servant*, 264.

43 Cohen and Granatstein, *Trudeau's Shadow*, 297–8.

44 Ibid., 301–2.

45 Kierans, *Remembering*, 181–4. Kierans left the Trudeau cabinet on 29 April 1971 over a difference of opinion on economic policy and took up a career of university teaching.

46 *La Presse*, 16 October 2003.

47 See Appendix to chapter 19.

48 As reported on 29 March 2004 at http://www.vigile.net/ds-histoire/index/octobre70.html.

CHAPTER THIRTEEN

1 Saint-Pierre, *Les années Bourassa*, 33.

2 *La Cognée*, 30 April 1964; Bédard, *Chronique d'une insurrection appréhendée*, 52.

3 *La Presse*, 6 October 1970. Emphasis added. See http://www.law.mcgill.ca/maritimelaw/crisis, appendix G.

4 *Le Soleil*, 9 October 1970. Emphasis added.

5 *La Presse*, 15 October 1970. Emphasis added.

6 *Le Devoir*, 15 October 1970. Emphasis added. Also: Duchaîne, *Rapport sur les événements d'octobre*, 106.

7 Duchesne, *Parizeau*, vol. 1, 564–5. Thirty-four years later, in his memoirs, *Here Be Dragons* (Toronto: McClelland and Stewart 2004), Newman admitted and regretted his actions, but then, without any study of the facts revealed since 1970, blamed the talk of a plot on Prime Minister Trudeau. In so doing, Newman ignored or confused the difference between an actual plot and various suggestions, visits, phone calls, meetings, discussions, and attempts – not by the Trudeau government but by assorted players in Quebec – to have the plan of a provisional government available, in case it should be needed. After Newman's original story, his claim was picked up by others eager to suggest that Trudeau had used the threat of a provisional government as an excuse to proclaim the state of apprehended insurrection.

   Author Larry Zolf, who knew the origins of the rumour, set the record straight in 2001 on the CBC (http://www.cbc.ca./news/indepth/october/zolf2.html).

After the murder of Pierre Laporte, a new and intriguing explanation for the invoking of War Measures appeared in the Toronto *Star* in a story with no byline. The story told of a dinner party at the home of deputy ministers Bernard and Sylvia Ostry. Trudeau cabinet ministers were present and engaged in some strange table talk.

According to Ottawa insiders, that table talk was leaked to Peter Newman, Canada's foremost journalist, then with the *Star*. The Newman story talked of War Measures being invoked because of an attempted provisional government of Quebec coup; the story was an immediate national sensation. The story seemed to play right into the hands of the Left in Canada.

Toronto journalist Ron Haggart and Toronto lawyer Aubrey Golden could now be taken seriously when in *Rumours of War* they said: "The War Measures Act was invoked ... to suppress a legitimate political movement," i.e., Quebec separatism.

With Newman's story out, John Turner, justice minister at the time, was now freer than ever to say that some time in the future his secret papers would reveal the true reasons for invoking War Measures. These true reasons obviously would not be the same apprehended insurrection reasons Trudeau had given.

This past week the "dean of the Ottawa Press Gallery," Douglas Fisher, said he was waiting for Turner's secret papers to be released. Fisher added ominously that of the two men, Trudeau and Turner, Turner was "the truthful one."

Trudeau himself went on the record during the October Crisis saying there was a vast difference between the terrorist FLQ and the democratic Parti Québécois. Said Trudeau: "This country is only held together by consent. If any part of our country wants to leave Canada, I don't think that force of arms will be used to keep them in the country."

But by this time the media were buying all the rumours of war, and all the rumours of provisional Quebec government coups. The media were buying anything that made the Trudeau government look trigger-happy, as if it were capriciously playing with people's lives.

This media recklessness led to a bunker mentality in Trudeau and his people. The media were shunned like lepers. Right after Newman had done his provisional government coup story, I came up with a strategy to get the Trudeau response to it.

Trudeau's principal secretary, Marc Lalonde, and his press secretary, Romeo Leblanc, were approached. It was suggested that if they gave me a briefing I would write their point of view on Newman's provisional government story. They could then check what I wrote. In return I would read what I wrote on air, first telling Canadians that what I was reading was the Trudeau government view and not my view and that my script had been cleared with the Trudeau government.

Leblanc and Lalonde agreed to the briefing, to my terms and to my script. At least six major CBC executives were in the studio as I delivered my script to videotape. That tape never hit the air.

In 1972, two years later, Tony Westell, one of Canada's legendary journalists, in his book, *Paradox: Trudeau as Prime Minister*, argued that my censored script proved fully and completely that there was no "plot to establish a provisional government and that was not the real reason War Measures had been invoked."

Westell then quoted this portion of my script:

"In a sense Prime Minister Trudeau sees Quebec democracy today facing the same dangers the Third Republic of France found in the 1930s when the Popular Front threat from the Left and the Fascist threat from the Right produced the collapse of the French democrats in the middle. Claude Ryan's mustering of the Left elites in Quebec could have led to a countervailing mustering of Quebec's conservative authoritarian elites. In the middle, in an exorable bind, would be Robert Bourassa's Liberal government and the process of democracy in Quebec."

This far from incendiary piece of political analysis failed to hit the air because by this time the CBC too had been a bit affected by the general media chill towards Trudeau. Despite the prevailing myth that the CBC was in Trudeau's back pocket, the CBC was in fact desperately trying to prove that they were doing everything possible to keep Trudeau at two arm lengths or more away.

Shortly after the October Crisis, everyone in the media was doing War Measures math. Over 400 arrested, fewer than four convicted. Very few in the media factored into that equation a murdered Laporte and a kidnapped Cross.

Fewer still in the media cared that 85 per cent of the public, French and English, supported Trudeau. [Emphasis added.]

8   *La Presse*, 28 October 1970.

9   Ibid.

10 *Le Devoir*, 28 October 1970. Emphasis added. Also: Ryan, *Le Devoir et la crise d'octobre 70*, 112.

11 *Le Devoir*, 28 October 1970; Ryan, *Le Devoir et la crise d'octobre 70*, 113.

12 *Le Devoir*, 30 October 1970; Ryan, *Le Devoir et la crise d'octobre 70*, 113–18.

13 *La Presse*, 31 October 1970. Emphasis added.

14 Ryan, *Le Devoir*, 4 November 1970.

15 Author's interview with Michel Roy, 27 August 2000.

16 René Lévesque, *La Presse*, 27 October 1970; Pelletier, *The October Crisis*, 170, and *La crise d'octobre*, 194.

17 Lévesque, *Memoirs*, 245.

18 Ibid.

19 *Journal de Montréal*, 15 October 1970.

20 Claude Ryan, *Le Devoir*, 17 October 1970.

21 Duchesne, *Parizeau*, vol. 1, 566.

22 Ibid., 565.

23 De Vault and Johnson, *The Informer*, 94.

24 Ibid.

25 Ibid.

26 Duchesne, *Parizeau*, vol. 1, 546.

27 Duchaîne, *Rapport sur les évenements d'octobre, 1970*, 101.

28 Excerpt of the minutes of the National Council of the Parti Québécois, 18 October 1970. See also http://www.mcgill.ca/maritimelaw/crisis, appendix O; and Duchesne, *Parizeau*, vol. 1, 564.

29 In *Alarme Citoyens!* Jacques Lacoursière produces, without any mention of his source, the following record of a conversation between Robert Bourassa and Guy Joron, the Parti Québécois MNA from Gouin, on Thursday, 15 October 1970, during the National Assembly's dinner-hour break:

"What do you want me to do?" Bourassa asked him point blank.

"A *coalition government* must be formed immediately," answered Mr. Joron. "You must first force the members of your cabinet who refuse *to take their responsibilities to resign. They must be replaced at once by agreeable members of Parliament from the opposition parties or of your own party, adding representatives from intermediary bodies, the unions.* This must be done very quickly, since they are nearly all in Parliament right now. This *coalition government* would rebel against Ottawa and negotiate with the FLQ to save the lives of Cross and Laporte. We do not have a moment to lose. It is your last chance."

Mr. Bourassa: "I know. Besides, I have already thought about it. But, it is too late."

Mr. Joron: "No, it is not too late."

Mr. Bourassa: "I cannot do it." (231)

Jacques Lacoursière, when questioned by me on 11 August 2003, said that he could not remember his sources for this passage in his book and that his notes for the conversation were missing.

On 17 February 2005 Guy Joron told me that he did not believe he had spoken to Lacoursière; what likely happened is that he spoke to someone else who then spoke to Lacoursière. Joron does remember talking to Bourassa, an old friend, in the premier's small office close to the National Assembly at the dinner hour on 15 October 1970. At that time, Bourassa discussed the situation with Joron but was firm about what he intended to do.

On 24 February 2005 Joron wrote me this letter:

J'ai bien lu la page 231 du livre de Monsieur Lacoursière *Alarme Citoyens* (Editions La Presse, 1972) et je n'ai pas du tout le souvenir d'avoir tenu à Monsieur Bourassa les propos précis qu'on m'y prête.

Je me souviens plutôt avoir tenté de le réconforter dans ce moment difficile, l'avoir exorté comme chef du gouvernement québécois à assumer la responsabilité de gérer cette crise sans l'intervention d'Ottawa et lui avoir dit pouvoir compter sur nous (les députés du Parti Québécois) si l'Assemblée Nationale était appelée à se prononcer unanimement en ce sens. Voilà le souvenir qu'il me reste trente-cinq ans plus tard.

J'en profite pour vous redire le plaisir que j'ai eu à vous revoir la semaine dernière.

There clearly is an honest misunderstanding between Lacoursière and Joron, two men whom I like and admire.

30 Smith, *Bleeding Hearts ... Bleeding Country*, 29–30.
31 Ibid., 28.
32 Ibid., 148.
33 Westell, *Paradox*, 248.
34 Bourassa, 6 November 1970, quoted in Lacoursière, *Alarme citoyens!* 167.
35 Lalonde interviewed by Max and Monique Nemni, *Cité Libre*, autumn 2000, 47–8.
36 Leroux, *Les silences d'octobre*, 14.
37 Radwanski and Windeyer, *No Mandate but Terror*, 97–8.
38 *Le Devoir*, 4 Novembre 1970.

CHAPTER FOURTEEN

1 *La Presse*, 6 October 1970. See http://www.mcgill.ca/maritimelaw/crisis, appendix G. Claude Castonguay, minister of social affairs in the Bourassa cabinet in October 1970, expressed similar views in a letter to *La Presse* on 4 May 2001 commenting on the petition of the sixteen "eminent personalities." See http://www.mcgill.ca/maritimelaw/crisis, appendix S.
2 In my view, Bourassa's calmness and resolution were again on display in 1974, when FTQ workers, with the compliance of their leaders, destroyed a great part of a James Bay project on the La Grande River, causing $30 million in damage. The Bourassa government not only took legal action against the FTQ – resulting in large awards against the union – but created the Cliche Commission, which found evidence of corruption against union leaders. (Compare this to the Lévesque government, which, soon after coming to power in 1976, began negotiating the wiping out of the FTQ debt, no doubt as a reward for electoral support from the unions.) Consider, too, how Bourassa acted in the Oka Crisis of 1990: he resisted illegal force with the authority of his democratically elected government and, in the end, prevailed. Compare this with the capitulation of the Charest Government in 2004, when a mob burned the home, in Kanesatake, of the democratically elected Grand Chief James Gabriel. The same mob then ousted the police force and put themselves in charge, yet the Charest Government did not

oppose them. Instead, Public Security Minister Jacques Chagnon tried to negotiate with the illegal native government. At the time of writing, the dangerous and unsatisfactory situation has not been solved. It is very difficult to put the genie back into the bottle.

3 Saint-Pierre, *Les années Bourassa*, 12.
4 Ibid., 21.
5 Cloutier, *L'Enjeu*, 105.
6 *L'Action*, 4 November 1970.
7 See http://www.mcgill.ca/maritimelaw/crisis, appendix S, for the complete text of Castonguay's letter.
8 Claude Ryan, *Le Devoir*, 15 October 1970. Also, Ryan, *Le Devoir et la crise d'octobre 70*, 39.
9 *Hansard*, 16 October 1970, 200.
10 The complete minutes are in http://www.mcgill.ca/maritimelaw/crisis, appendix O.
11 *Le Journal de Montréal*, 23 October 1970.
12 *La Presse*, 27 October 1970.
13 Gwyn, *The Northern Magus*, 119.
14 Segal, *No Surrender*, 22.
15 Bédard, *Chronique d'une insurrection appréhendée*, 116.
16 The full text of the Council minutes is in http://www.mcgill.ca/maritimelaw/crisis, appendix O.
17 Duchesne, *Parizeau*, vol. 1, 563.
18 Ibid., 609.
19 Ibid., 609.
20 Lacoursière, *Alarme citoyens!* 198.
21 Westell, *Paradox*, 257–8.
22 Saywell, *Quebec 70*, preface.

CHAPTER FIFTEEN

1 Simard, *Pour en finir avec octobre*, 191–3.
2 *La Presse*, 22 October 1970.
3 Cloutier, *L'Enjeu*, 98.
4 *Le Soleil*, 7 October 1970. See also *La Presse* and *Le Journal de Montréal* for the same date.
5 Gérard Cellier, *Montréal Matin*, 17 October 1970.
6 *Le Soleil*, 16 October 1970. See also *Le Devoir*, 16 October 1970, to the same effect.
7 *Le Soleil*, 16 October 1970.
8 Duchaîne, *Rapport sur les événements d'octobre, 1970*, 132.
9 Ibid., 131–49.

10 Trait, *FLQ 70*, 229.
11 Leroux, *Les silences d'octobre*, 17, 22.
12 *Le Journal de Montréal*, 13 March 1971. See also Leroux, *Les silences d'octobre*, 20.
13 Montreal *Star*, 3 November 1970. See also my diary, appendix 1, 15 October 1970.
14 *Le Journal de Montréal*, 18 October 1970; Fournier, *FLQ*, 257.
15 Fournier, *FLQ*, 257.
16 Simard, *Pour en finir avec octobre*, 191.
17 Ibid.
18 Ibid., 192.
19 Ibid.
20 Ibid., 193.
21 Ibid.
22 Ibid., 192.
23 Duchaîne, *Rapport sur les événements d'octobre*, 136–49.
24 Ibid., 137.
25 Ibid., 139.
26 Ibid., 149.

CHAPTER SIXTEEN

1 "a veritable thunderclap," Bédard, *Chronique d'une insurrection appréhendée*, 116.
2 Duchesne, *Parizeau*, vol. 2, 545.
3 Saywell, *Quebec 70*, 129–34.
4 Pelletier, *The October Crisis*, 57.
5 Bédard, *Chronique d'une insurrection appréhendée*, 160. Bédard goes even further, arguing that the events of October 1970 represented a *permanent* defeat for the student left, as evidenced in the dissolution of the two radical student associations, Union générale des étudiants du Québec and the Association générale des étudiants de l'Université de Montréal. He cites the Marxist Jean-Marc Piotte's statement that "'middle class' (petit bourgeois) students will never be part of the forces of history," 161.
6 Diane Cohen in MacDonald and Segal, *Strong and Free*, 13.
7 Hudon, *Ce n'était qu'un début*, 171.
8 Chaput, *Pourquoi je suis séparatiste*, 149.

CHAPTER SEVENTEEN

1 *Journal des débats*, Assemblée nationale, 16 October 1970, 1456.
2 *La Presse*, 27 October 1970.
3 *Le Devoir*, 29 October 1970. "Mr. René Lévesque has underlined, with reason, the non-existent role of the National Assembly during the crisis caused by the Cross-Laporte drama."

4 *Journal des débats*, Assemblée nationale, 13 November 1970, 1561–2, and 17 November 1970, 1571–5.
5 Ibid., 17 November 1970, 1596–9.
6 Ibid., 19 November 1970, 1655–60.
7 Ibid., 18 November 1970, 1627–31.
8 Ibid., 20 November 1970, 1690–4.
9 Ibid., 20 November 1970, 1706–11.
10 Ibid., 12 November 1970, 1524–31 at 1524, 1525, 1527 and 1528.
11 See Chapter 19.
12 See Chapter 20.

CHAPTER EIGHTEEN

1 See appendix 3 for the text of the petition.
2 Toronto *Star*, 15 October 1970; Smith, *Bleeding Hearts ... Bleeding Country*, 33. The federal Cabinet minutes of 15 October 1970 at 2:30 p.m. have an interesting reference to Robarts' declaration: "The Prime Minister further said he had received a call from Mr. Robarts who was enquiring whether his statement had been helpful. The Prime Minister answered him affirmatively and Mr. Robarts said he would support legislation preceded or followed by police action in Quebec."
3 *Le Devoir*, 17 October 1970.
4 *Journal de Montréal*, 27 October 1970.
5 *Journal des débats*, Assemblée Nationale, 11 November 1970, 1496.
6 Duchaîne Report, 1981, 57.
7 Ryan, *Le Devoir et la crise d'octobre*, 18–19.
8 *Cité Libre*, Automne 2000, 46–7.
9 See Gordon Robertson's understated, but beautifully written biography, *Memoirs of a Very Civil Servant*, 262.
10 Duchaîne Report, 1981, 103–4.
11 Ibid., 80.
12 Lacoursière, *Alarme Citoyens!* 246.
13 See http://www.mcgill.ca/maritimelaw/crisis, appendix K.
14 Document 146, dated 18 December 1970, in answer to a question of Claude Charron, Member of the National Assembly.
15 See http://www.mcgill.ca/maritimelaw/crisis, appendix L.
16 Duchaîne Report, 1981, 118.
17 *Le Devoir*, 17 October 1970.
18 *La Presse*, 2 November 1970.
19 *Le Devoir*, 14 December 1970.

CHAPTER NINETEEN

1 *Le Devoir*, 17 October 1970.

2 *Hansard*, 13 October 1970, Debate on Address in Reply.
3 Provencher, *La grande peur d'octobre*, 49.
4 *La Presse*, 27 October 1970.
5 Montreal *Star*, 3 November 1970.
6 Donald Smiley in Rotstein, *Power Corrupted*, 33–4.
7 Ibid., 35.
8 Rioux, *Quebec in Question*, 177.
9 Provencher, *La grande peur d'octobre*, 48.
10 Leroux, *Les silences d'octobre*, 72; *Le Devoir*, 29 September 1975.
11 See the appendix to this chapter. The French text is available at
    http://www.mcgill.ca/maritimelaw/crisis, appendix P.
12 *Le Devoir*, 9 November 1970.
13 *Le Devoir*, 6 November 1970.
14 *Le Devoir*, 16 October 1970.
15 Pelletier, *The October Crisis*, 155.
16 See appendix 1, 5 November 1970.

CHAPTER TWENTY

1 *Le Devoir*, 14 and 15 October 1971; *La Presse*, 14 and 15 October 1971; Leroux, *Les silences d'octobre*, 38, 39.
2 Its formal name in French was the Commission d'enquête sur les opérations policières en territoire québécois.
3 Years later, in 2002, he would be appointed a judge of the Court of Quebec in Montreal by another PQ government.
4 Its full name was the Commission of Inquiry concerning Certain Activities of the Royal Canadian Mounted Police and the Question of Governmental Knowledge.
5 *Journal des débats*, Assemblée nationale, 25 October 1978, 3287.
6 Duchaîne, *Rapport sur les événements d'octobre, 1970*, 1–2.
7 R.S.Q. c. C-37. *Journal des débats*, Assemblée nationale, 24 October 1978, 3205.
8 *Journal des débats*, Assemblée nationale, 25 October 1978, 3287.
9 Ibid., 24 October 1978, 3205.
10 Ibid., 24 October 1978, 3205 and 3206.
11 Ibid., 2 May 1979, 1018 and 1019.
12 Ibid., 16 October 1979, 2894 and 2895.
13 Ibid., 2895.
14 Ibid., 4 December 1979, 4006.
15 Ibid., 17 December 1979, 4591.
16 His name was actually McCleery.
17 Duchaîne, *Rapport sur les événements d'octobre, 1970*, 3–4.

18 Ibid., 4–5. Duchaîne did not claim to have consulted the Quebec Cabinet minutes of 1970, although one reference at p. 76 of his Report suggests that in fact he did so.

19 Lacoursière, *Alarmes Citoyens!* 231.

20 Duchaîne, *Rapport sur les événements d'octobre, 1970*, 215–19.

21 Ibid., 5.

22 Ibid.

23 Ibid.

24 Ibid., 215. Emphasis in original.

25 Ibid., 218.

26 Ibid., 218–19.

27 Ibid., 128.

28 Detective Julien Giguère of the Montreal Police, who was de Vault's "controller," declared that the conversations between de Vault and Parizeau "would have been sufficient to arrest him [Parizeau] during the period of the application of the War Measures Act, but as he was not the type of person who was going to act in any way, it was not worthwhile. He was of no use to us. What he could have told us, we already knew." (Duchesne, *Parizeau*, 552–3)

29 Duchaîne, *Rapport sur les événements d'octobre, 1970*, 162–3 and 176–7.

30 Ibid., 66, 82, 177, and 210.

31 Ibid., 101. For the full text of this excerpt from the Duchaîne Report, see chapter 13: "Provisional Government."

CHAPTER TWENTY-ONE

1 See http://www.mcgill.ca/maritimelaw/crisis, appendix Z.

2 Ibid.

3 Ibid.

4 See http://www.mcgill.ca/maritimelaw/crisis, appendix W.

5 See http://www.mcgill.ca/maritimelaw/crisis, appendix U.

6 See http://www.mcgill.ca/maritimelaw/crisis, appendix Z.

7 Ibid.

8 Ibid.

9 Ibid.

10 See http://www.mcgill.ca/maritimelaw/crisis, appendix V.

11 The plaque of the Chien d'Or, bearing the above inscription, in its original French spelling, and a bas-relief of a dog gnawing a bone was originally placed over the door of the very large home of surgeon Timothée Roussel, built in rue du Fort, Quebec City in 1688. The plaque is presently to be found over the porch of the former Post-Office, now the Louis St. Laurent Building in Quebec City.

12 My relations with the Parti Québécois, too, have always been friendly, perhaps because two of the first modern laws to contain provisions intended to protect the

French language were laws which I presented as minister – the Consumer Protection Act, 1971 (all consumer contracts must be in French, but may also be in English) (S.Q. 1971, c. 74) and the Companies Act, 1973 (all company names must be in French, but may also be in English) (S.Q. 1973, c. 65). Both provisions are to be found in Bill 22 (S.Q. 1974, c. 6) adopted by the Bourassa government in 1974 and Bill 101, better known as the Charter of the French Language, adopted by the Parti Québécois Government in 1977 (S.Q. 1977, c. 5 (now R.S.Q., c. C-11)).

Bibliography

Arnopoulos, Sheila McLeod, and Dominique Clift. *The English Fact in Quebec*. Montreal: McGill-Queen's University Press 1980.

Bédard, Éric. *Chronique d'une insurrection appréhendée: La crise d'octobre et le milieu universitaire*. Sillery, Que.: Les Éditions du Septentrion 1998.

Bergeron, Léandre. *The History of Quebec: A Patriote's Handbook*. Toronto: NC Press 1975.

Bourassa, Robert. *Gouverner le Québec*. Montreal: Éditions Fides 1995.

Butler, Rick, and Jean-Guy Carrier. *The Trudeau Decade*. Toronto: Doubleday Canada 1979.

Cardin, Jean-François. *Comprendre octobre 1970, le FLQ, la crise et le syndicalisme*. [Montreal]: Éditions du Méridien 1990.

Cardinal, André. "Quebec and the Intellectuals." In Dimitrios I. Roussopolos, ed., *Quebec and Radical Social Change*. Montreal: Black Rose Books 1974.

Chaput, Marcel. *Pourquois je suis séparatiste*. Montreal: Les Éditions du Jour 1961.

– *Why I Am a Separatist*. Toronto: Ryerson Press 1962.

Chodos, Robert, and Nick Auf der Maur. *Quebec: A Chronicle, 1968–1972*. Toronto: James Lewis and Samuel 1972.

Cloutier, François. *L'Enjeu: Mémoires politiques, 1970–1976*. Montreal: Stanké 1978.

– *La mémoire vagabonde*. Montreal: Stanké 1995.

Cohen, Andrew, and J.L. Granatstein. *Trudeau's Shadow*. Toronto: Random House 1998.

Comeau, Robert, D. Cooper, and Pierre Vallières. *FLQ: Un projet révolutionnaire, lettres et écrits felquistes (1963–1982)*. Montreal: VLB Éditeur 1990.

Dagenais, Bernard. *La crise d'octobre et les medias: le miroir à dix faces*. Montreal: VLB Éditeur 1990.

Daniels, Dan, ed. *Québec/Canada and the October Crisis*. Montreal: Black Rose Books 1973.

Desbiens, Jean-Paul. *Les insolences du Frère Untel*. Montreal: Les Éditions de L'Homme 1960.

– *The Impertinences of Brother Anonymous (Frère Untel)*. Montreal: Harvest House 1962.

De Vault, Carole, and William Johnson. *The Informer: Confessions of an Ex-Terrorist*. Toronto: Fleet Books 1982.

Dion, Gérard. *Rapport au ministre de l'éducation*. Quebec: Government of Quebec, 15 March 1971.

Dion, Germain. *Une tornade de 60 jours: La crise d'octobre à la Chambre des Communes*. Hull, Que.: Éditions Asticou 1985.

Duchaîne, Jean-François. *Rapport sur les événements d'octobre, 1970*, 2nd ed. Montreal: Ministère de la Justice du Québec 1981.

Duchesne, Pierre. *Jacques Parizeau*, vol. 1, *Le croisé, 1930–1970*. Montreal: Québec Amérique 2001.

– *Jacques Parizeau*, vol. 2, *Le baron, 1970–1985*. Montreal: Québec Amérique 2002.

Dumont, Fernard. *The Vigil of Quebec*. Translated by Sheila Fischman and Richard Howard. Toronto: University of Toronto Press 1974.

Ferretti, Andrée, and Gaston Miron. *Les grands textes indépendantistes: Écrits, discourse et manifestes québécois, 1774–1992*. Montreal: Éditions de l'Hexagone 1992.

Foisy, Fernand. *Michel Chartrand: La colère du juste*. Outremont, QC: Lanctôt Éditeur, 2003.

Fournier, Louis. *F.L.Q.: The Anatomy of an Underground Movement*, trans. Edward Baxter. Toronto: NC Press 1984.

– *FLQ: Histoire d'un mouvement clandestin*. Montreal: Lanctôt Éditeur 1998.

Gellner, John. *Bayonets in the Streets: Urban Guerrillas at Home and Abroad*. Don Mills, Ont.: Collier-Macmillan 1994.

Gwyn, Richard. *The Northern Magus: Pierre Trudeau and Canadians*. Toronto: McClelland and Stewart 1980.

Haggart, Ron, and Aubrey E. Golden. *Rumours of War*. Toronto: New Press 1971.

Hansard. *Debates*. House of Commons, 1971.

Hudon, Gabriel. *Ce n'était qu'un début, ou la petite histoire des premiers pas du FLQ*. Montreal: Les Éditions Parti Pris 1977.

Journal des débats. Assemblée nationale. 1970.

Kierans, Eric. *Remembering* (with Walter Stewart). Toronto: Stoddart 2001.

Lacoursière, Jacques. *Alarme citoyens!* Montreal: Les Éditions La Presse 1972.

Laporte, Pierre. *Le vrai visage de Duplessis.* Montreal: Les Éditions de l'Homme 1960.

– *The True Face of Duplessis.* Translated by Richard Daignault. Montreal: Harvest House 1974.

Laurendeau, André. *Witness for Quebec.* Introduction by Claude Ryan. Translated by Philip Stratford. Toronto: Macmillan 1973.

Laurendeau, Marc. *Les Québécois violents.* 2nd ed. Sillery, Que.: Les Éditions du Boréal Express 1974.

Leroux, Manon. *Les silences d'octobre.* Montreal: VLB Éditeur 2002.

Lévesque, René. *La passion du Québec.* Montreal: Éditions Québec/Amérique 1978.

– *My Quebec.* Toronto: Methuen Publications 1979.

– *Attendez que je me rappelle.* Quebec: Éditions Québec/Amérique 1986.

– *Memoirs*, trans. Philip Stratford. Toronto: McClelland and Stewart 1986.

Loomis, Dan G. *Not Much Glory: Quelling the FLQ.* Toronto: Deneau Publishers 1984.

McDonald Commission. *Certain R.C.M.P. Activities and the Question of Governmental Knowledge: Third Report of the Commission of Inquiry concerning Certain Activities of the Royal Canadian Mounted Police.* Chairman: Mr Justice D.C. McDonald. Ottawa: Canadian Government Publishing Centre 1981.

MacDonald, David, and Hugh Segal, eds. *Strong and Free: A Response to the War Measures Act.* Toronto: New Press 1970.

MacDonald, L. Ian. *From Bourassa to Bourassa.* Montreal: Harvest House 1984.

Martin's Annual Criminal Code 1970. Toronto: Edmund Montgomery Publications.

Marx, Herbert. "Emergency Power and Civil Liberties in Canada." *McGill Law Journal* 16 (1970): 39–91.

McKenna, Brian and Susan Purcell. *Drapeau.* Toronto: Clarke, Irwin and Co. 1980.

Mongeau, Serge. *Kidnappé par la police.* Montreal: Les Éditions du Jour 1970.

Morf, Gustave. *Terror in Quebec: Case Studies of the FLQ.* Toronto: Clarke, Irwin 1970.

Pelletier, Gérard. *La crise d'octobre.* Montreal: Éditions du Jour 1971.

– *The October Crisis*, trans. Joyce Marshall. Toronto: McClelland and Stewart 1971.

Provencher, Jean. *Québec sous la Loi des Mesures de Guerre, 1918.* Preface by Fernand Dumont. Trois-Rivières, Que.: Boréal Express 1971.

– *La grande peur d'octobre '70.* Montreal: L'Aurore 1974.

– *René Lévesque: Portrait of a Québécois*, trans. David Ellis. Toronto: Gage Publishing 1975.

Radwanski, George, and Kendal Windeyer. *No Mandate but Terror*. Richmond Hill, Ont.: Simon and Schuster 1971.

Regush, Nicholas M. *Pierre Vallières: The Revolutionary Process in Quebec*. Toronto: Fitzhenry and Whiteside 1973.

Riel, Louis. *The Collected Writings of Louis Riel/Les écrits complets de Louis Riel*. Edmonton: University of Alberta Press, 1985.

Rioux, Marcel. *Quebec in Question*. Toronto: James Lewis and Samuel 1971.

– *Les Québécois*. Paris: Éditions du Seuil 1974.

– *La question du Québec*. Montreal: Parti Pris 1976.

Robertson, Gordon. *Memoirs of a Very Civil Servant*. Toronto: University of Toronto Press 2000.

Rotstein, Abraham, ed. *Power Corrupted: The October Crisis and the Repression of Quebec*. Toronto: New Press 1971.

Ryan, Claude. *Le Devoir et la crise d'octobre 70*. Montreal: Leméac 1971.

– *Une société stable*. Montreal: Les Éditions Héritage 1978.

Saint-Pierre, Raymond. *Les années Bourassa: L'intégrale des entretiens Bourassa/Saint-Pierre*. Montreal: Les Éditions Héritage 1977.

Sarra-Bournet, Michel. *Manifeste des intellectuels pour la souveraineté*. Montreal: Éditions Fides 1995.

Savoie, Claude. *La véritable histoire du F.L.Q.* 2nd ed. Montreal: Les Éditions du Jour 1963.

Saywell, John. *Quebec 70: A Documentary Narrative*. Toronto: University of Toronto Press 1971.

Schneider, Pierre. *Boum baby boom: La véritable histoire de Bozo-lesculottes*. Montreal: Les Éditions Québec Amérique 2002.

Scott, Charles F. "The War Measures Act, s. 6(5) and the Canadian Bill of Rights" (1970–71) 13 Crim. L.Q. 342.

Scott, Frank R. *A New Endeavour: Selected Political Essays, Letters, and Addresses*. Toronto: University of Toronto Press 1986.

Segal, Hugh. *No Surrender: Reflections of a Happy Warrior in the Tory Crusade*. Toronto: HarperCollins Publishers 1996.

Sharp, Mitchell. *Which Reminds Me ... A Memoir*. Toronto: University of Toronto Press 1994.

Simard, Francis. *Pour en finir avec octobre*. Montreal: Stanké 1982.

Smith, Denis. *Bleeding Hearts ... Bleeding Country: Canada and the Quebec Crisis*. Edmonton: M.G. Hurtig Publishers 1971.

Trait, Jean-Claude. *FLQ 70: Offensive d'automne*. Montreal: Les Éditions de l'Homme 1970.

Trudeau, Pierre Elliott. *The Asbestos Strike*, trans. James Boake. Toronto: James Lewis and Samuel 1974.

– *Federalism and the French Canadians*. Toronto: Macmillan 1968.

Vallières, Pierre. *Nègres blancs d'Amérique: Autobiographie précoce d'un terroriste québécois*. Montreal: Éditions Parti Pris 1968.
- *White Niggers of America*. Toronto: McClelland and Stewart 1971.
- *The Assassination of Pierre Laporte: Behind the October '70 Scenario*. Toronto: James Lorimer 1977.
Westell, Anthony. *Paradox: Trudeau as Prime Minister*. Scarborough, Ont.: Prentice Hall 1972.
- *Trudeau, le paradoxe*. Montreal: Les Édition de l'Homme 1972.
- *The Inside Story: A Life in Journalism*. Toronto: Dundurn Press 2002.

Index